RELIGION, LAW, AND THE CONSTITUTION

DANIEL O. CONKLE
Robert H. McKinney Professor of Law
Indiana University Maurer School of Law

CONCEPTS AND INSIGHTS SERIES®

Concepts and Insights Series is a trademark registered in the U.S. Patent and Trademark Office.

© 2016 LEG, Inc. d/b/a West Academic
    444 Cedar Street, Suite 700
    St. Paul, MN 55101
    1-877-888-1330

Printed in the United States of America

ISBN: 978-1-63459-764-7

In memory of my parents, Louis and Berniece Conkle, who introduced me to the law and to religion.

PREFACE

This book addresses an important, complex, and controversial topic: religion, law, and the Constitution. In so doing, it provides a theoretical framework for understanding and evaluating a diverse array of First Amendment issues as well as related issues arising under the Religious Freedom Restoration Act, other religious liberty statutes, and state constitutional law.

The Supreme Court's decisionmaking in this area has been highly controversial. It also has produced a body of constitutional and legal doctrine that is complicated and confusing. Even so, as the book explains, the Court's decisionmaking can be seen to have a certain coherency, if only as the product of a complex weighing of various and sometimes conflicting constitutional values.

This book is intended primarily for legal scholars, law students, and lawyers. At the same time, it also may be useful to a broader audience, including students in other disciplines and citizens wishing to educate themselves on this important topic of public concern.

This is a successor to a 2009 volume, the Second Edition of *Constitutional Law: The Religion Clauses*. Readers familiar with that volume will find a similar approach here, along with some of the same content. The current book, however, includes considerably broader coverage, and, of course, it has been thoroughly revised and updated.

Daniel O. Conkle

January 2016

TABLE OF CONTENTS

RELIGION, LAW, AND THE CONSTITUTION

Chapter 1

INTRODUCTION

The first words of the First Amendment refer not to speech but to religion: "Congress shall make no law respecting an establishment of religion, or prohibiting the free exercise thereof." Simple enough, or so the framers might have thought. But history tells a different story, a story of complexity, change, and ongoing controversy.

To be sure, the basic principle of religious liberty emerged in the founding period, and, in one form or another, it has prevailed ever since. The precise meaning of religious liberty, however, was contested from the beginning, and the passage of time has only made the issues more difficult. The First Amendment's Religion Clauses include the Free Exercise Clause and the Establishment Clause. But what does it mean to protect the free exercise of religion? Are religious practices protected from general laws, or only from religious discrimination? What if the religious practices cause harm? Are all acts of religious conscience included? And what makes an act "religious" in the first place? What about the Establishment Clause? Disestablishment precludes the formal recognition of a government church, but what else? Does it bar the government from promoting particular religions, or even religion in general? Even through non-coercive, purely symbolic actions? Are public schools precluded not only from leading students in prayer, but also from permitting students to conduct their own prayers at school functions or during after-school meetings? Can legislatures and local governmental bodies open their meetings with prayer? Even if the prayers are explicitly Christian? Can the government extend nondiscriminatory financial support to private religious schools and organizations? May it accommodate the free exercise of religion by exempting religious practices from general laws, or would that amount to a forbidden establishment?

More generally, by what criteria, and by what process of decisionmaking, should these sorts of questions be confronted and resolved? Viewed through the lens of the First Amendment, they are questions of constitutional law and, as a result, questions ultimately for the Supreme Court. On its face, however, the relevant constitutional text is impossibly vague and general. It requires interpretation. The Court might—and does—look behind the text to the original understanding of the Religion Clauses, but, as we will see in Chapter 2, the original understanding itself is

1

indeterminate. The Justices have cited historical developments in Eighteenth Century America, especially in Virginia. And the intellectual origins of American religious liberty can be traced back even further, to the Seventeenth Century arguments of philosopher John Locke. But the original understanding of the Religion Clauses is a different and more specific historical question, as is the original understanding of the Fourteenth Amendment, which has been used to extend the Religion Clauses to the states. And this more specific historical inquiry, focusing on the original understanding of the relevant constitutional text, simply cannot resolve the issues that have confronted the modern Court.

Although the Justices may be loath to admit it, the Religion Clauses in fact have required creative interpretation. This value-laden process of decisionmaking, however, has not been purely subjective. The Court's creative interpretation has been guided in part by the text and original understanding of the Religion Clauses, but in far greater part by the Court's more general identification and protection of constitutional values. Thus, in interpreting the Religion Clauses, the Court has protected a variety of constitutional values—values deeply embedded in our political and cultural history, if not in the original understanding as such, and values emerging and evolving over time. In the jargon of constitutional theory, the Court's interpretive methodology might fairly be described as "nonoriginalist"; that is, the Court has moved beyond the text and original understanding, interpreting the Religion Clauses in a manner that has reflected not only American history, but also contemporary societal conditions and values.

To critics, the Supreme Court has been all too "creative" in its interpretations, producing a body of constitutional doctrine that is widely regarded as confusing, if not chaotic. On close examination, however, the Court's doctrine can be seen to have a certain coherency, if only as the product of a complex evaluation of various and sometimes competing constitutional values. In an attempt to unearth these values, Chapter 3 will trace the historical development of American religious liberty from the founding to the present. With that development in mind, we will identify and discuss six constitutional values or sets of values that influence contemporary decisionmaking under the Religion Clauses: religious voluntarism; respecting religious identity; religious equality; promoting a religiously inclusive political community and protecting government from improper religious involvement; protecting the autonomy and independence of religious institutions and of religion itself; and preserving traditional governmental practices. We also will note an additional constitutional value, the value of religious free speech, which is linked not so much to the Religion Clauses as to the First Amendment's Free Speech Clause. The book will return to these various values time and again as it explains and evaluates the diverse components of the Supreme Court's constitutional doctrine.

Turning to a direct discussion of that doctrine, Chapter 4 will address fundamental issues common to both of the Religion Clauses. We will see that the Religion Clauses, taken together, can be seen to promote a general policy of governmental neutrality or evenhandedness toward religion, with the Free Exercise Clause prohibiting the mistreatment of religion through the imposition of impermissible burdens and the Establishment Clause forbidding the advancement of religion through the conferral of impermissible benefits. We will discuss the general principle of nondiscrimination, which plays an important role in the Court's decisionmaking under both clauses. We also will address the conundrum of defining "religion," as well as the role of courts in addressing the content and sincerity of religious beliefs.

In Chapter 5, we will discuss the First Amendment's protection of religious freedom, not only under the Free Exercise Clause but also under the Free Speech Clause. We will see that the Free Speech Clause offers significant protection for religious speech. As for religiously motivated conduct other than speech, the Supreme Court's doctrine under the Free Exercise Clause has vacillated over time, especially in addressing claims for religion-based exemptions from generally applicable, nondiscriminatory laws. This issue might arise, for example, from a claim by members of the Native American Church that their religious use of peyote should be exempted from otherwise applicable drug laws. At present, under the restrictive rule of *Employment Division v. Smith*,[1] a 1990 Supreme Court decision, such claims for exemptions generally are rejected, with religious claimants being denied relief, even from substantial burdens on the exercise of religion, except when the government has deliberately targeted their religious conduct for discriminatory disadvantage.

As we will see in Chapter 6, the Court's decision in *Smith* triggered a remarkable congressional response, the Religious Freedom Restoration Act of 1993 (RFRA),[2] which was designed to restore the more generous, pre-*Smith* approach to religion-based exemptions, now as a matter of statutory rather than constitutional right. The Supreme Court has interpreted RFRA expansively and

---

[1]   494 U.S. 872 (1990).

[2]   42 U.S.C. §§ 2000bb to 2000bb–4.

sometimes controversially, as, for example, in its 2014 decision in *Burwell v. Hobby Lobby Stores, Inc.*,[3] which found that RFRA extended to certain for-profit corporations and that it trumped a federal requirement that the companies provide their employees with insurance coverage for contraceptives. Chapter 6 will discuss not only RFRA but also its sister statute, the Religious Land Use and Institutionalized Persons Act of 2000 (RLUIPA);[4] state statutes modeled on RFRA; comparable state constitutional doctrine; and other, more specific accommodation provisions as well. These various sources of religious freedom are important because they sometimes afford protection when the Free Exercise Clause does not.

Chapters 7 and 8 will address the Establishment Clause. In Chapter 7, we will consider the general doctrinal tests and concepts that the Supreme Court has employed. Remarkably enough, the Court has simultaneously recognized three general Establishment Clause tests. The test of *Lemon v. Kurtzman*[5] considers the purpose and effect of the challenged governmental action, as well as the potential for excessive entanglement between religion and government.[6] The endorsement test focuses on the symbolic meaning of the government's action, asking whether it conveys an impermissible message by endorsing religion. And the coercion test asks whether the government is in some manner coercing religious conformity. In addition to these three tests, the Court also considers two other general factors or concepts, tradition and accommodation. Our discussion of accommodation will explain that the Establishment Clause permits the government, within limits, to protect the free exercise of religion to a greater degree than the Free Exercise Clause requires. As a result, the Establishment Clause almost certainly does not imperil RFRA or the other legislative and state constitutional developments discussed in Chapter 6.

In Chapter 8, we will explore the operation of the *Lemon* and endorsement tests, as well as the impact of coercion and tradition, in several important Establishment Clause contexts. We will learn that the Supreme Court, in a long line of cases, has broadly disapproved school-sponsored prayer and religious instruction in the public schools. Conversely, we will see a more nuanced approach with respect to religious expression and symbolism in other settings, where tradition sometimes has played a greater role. Among other issues arising in this context, we will discuss

---

[3]   134 S. Ct. 2751 (2014).

[4]   42 U.S.C. §§ 2000cc to 2000cc–5.

[5]   403 U.S. 602 (1971).

[6]   *See id.* at 612–13.

governmental displays of the Ten Commandments and the permissibility of legislative prayer. Finally, we will examine Establishment Clause limits on the inclusion of religious beneficiaries, including religious schools and organizations, in otherwise general programs of public aid. Although some limits remain, we will see that the Court has embraced an increasingly relaxed approach in this setting, an approach that generally permits public aid to flow to religious schools and organizations, both under voucher programs and otherwise.

The final chapter, Chapter 9, will offer concluding observations. Looking back at the Supreme Court's complex body of constitutional decisionmaking, we will see that certain common themes emerge. We also will take a brief look forward, considering the possibility of doctrinal shifts in the near-term future and the potential for broader developments in the years and decades that lie ahead. The Supreme Court's constitutional doctrine has evolved over time, and there is no reason to doubt that this evolution will continue.

Chapter 2

HISTORY, ORIGINALISM, AND CONTEMPORARY CONSTITUTIONAL MEANING

In its interpretations of the Religion Clauses, the Supreme Court routinely claims an "originalist" pedigree for its rulings, contending that its decisions rest on the original understanding of the First Amendment. In so doing, the Justices often cite the experience of Virginia and the views of James Madison and Thomas Jefferson. As we will see, however, there are serious weaknesses in the Court's originalist claims, primarily because the Religion Clauses, as originally understood, were designed in large part to promote a policy of federalism on religious liberty questions. As such, the Religion Clauses were adopted not so much to resolve these questions as to instruct the national government to stand clear, leaving these issues to be decided by the various states as they thought best. Accordingly, the Supreme Court's contemporary interpretations of the Religion Clauses cannot fairly be described as originalist. Instead, they depend upon a considerably more creative—and "nonoriginalist"—interpretive methodology.

Even so, it is important to understand the history of American religious liberty, including the historical episodes and arguments that the Supreme Court has invoked. At a minimum, the Court's historical reasoning helps us identify the values that the Justices find controlling in the contemporary period. Beyond that, the historical arguments for religious liberty, including those of Madison and Jefferson, deserve attention in their own right. These arguments might still be persuasive, even today, or they at least might point in helpful directions. We cannot evaluate or utilize these historical arguments without knowing what they were. In short, we can learn from history, and the lessons of history are not confined to the original understanding of the First Amendment as such.

Indeed, the intellectual origins of American religious liberty can be traced back to the Old World and especially to the influential work of philosopher John Locke. Accordingly, this chapter will begin with a brief account of the regimes of coerced religion that Locke confronted and his arguments for dismantling them. It then will explain the role of Lockean and similar arguments in Virginia, where Madison led a successful campaign against the establishment of religion and Jefferson authored a famous statute promoting religious freedom. With this background in mind, we will turn to the history of the First Amendment's Religion Clauses and the Supreme Court's interpretations of that history, as well as the Court's extension of the Religion Clauses to the states through the doctrine of Fourteenth Amendment "incorporation." This inquiry will expose the fundamental flaws in the Court's originalist reasoning. But even as we dismiss the Court's originalist pretensions, we will emphasize the distinction between originalism on the one hand and history on the other, noting that historical experiences and arguments may be informative even when originalism is not.

I.   The Lockean Origins of American Religious Liberty[1]

The basic issue of religious toleration—and, more broadly, religious liberty—arises from the existence of competing claims of religious truth. Should nation-states tolerate or grant religious freedom to those who reject the dominant religious view, that is, to those who embrace some other religion or no religion at all? In Western history, states initially reasoned that they should not. But then came John Locke and the emergence and growth of religious toleration and religious liberty.

Prior to what Professor W. Cole Durham, Jr., has called "the Lockean revolution,"[2] governments in the Western world tended toward regimes of coerced religion. European states (and American colonies) embraced different views concerning the proper meaning of Christianity. Many maintained formal religious establishments, complete with coerced religious conformity, taxes supporting the established religion, and compelled religious observance. The underlying justification for such an approach was two-fold, resting in part on religious-moral reasoning and in part on political and pragmatic concerns.[3]

From a religious-moral perspective, it was widely understood that there is but one true religion, and the leaders of each nation-state, of course, believed that their own version of Christianity was that one. Individuals who embraced a competing religious perspective were deluded, as were those who rejected religion

---

[1]   This section draws upon Daniel O. Conkle, *Religious Truth, Pluralism, and Secularization: The Shaking Foundations of American Religious Liberty*, 32 CARDOZO L. REV. 1755, 1757–60 (2011).

[2]   W. Cole Durham, Jr., *Perspectives on Religious Liberty: A Comparative Framework, in* RELIGIOUS HUMAN RIGHTS IN GLOBAL PERSPECTIVE: LEGAL PERSPECTIVES 1, 7 (Johan D. van der Vyver & John Witte, Jr. eds., 1996).

[3]   *See id.*

altogether. The state properly demanded that these dissenters cease
their heresy and follow the true commands of God. By insisting
upon religious conformity, the states themselves were honoring God
by using the power of the state to force all citizens—and therefore
the polity as a whole—to honor God's will. In addition, they were
furthering, paternalistically, the individual religious well-being of
their citizens, including dissenters, by leading them down the one
true path to religious salvation. The dissenters undoubtedly
disagreed, but they were deluded in their false beliefs. Coercing
religious truth was in the interest of all.[4]

This religious-moral justification was joined by a more
pragmatic, political justification for maintaining an established
religion to which all citizens were required to adhere. In particular,
it was believed that enforcing a common religion promoted the
state's interest in political stability and social peace, and that it did
so in two related ways. First, the religion served as a type of social
glue, unifying society by giving citizens a uniform sense of meaning
and purpose. Second, the state's promotion of this religion
encouraged a reciprocal, religion-based motivation for supporting
and obeying the governing regime. As a result, the religious
establishment not only brought citizens together but also promoted
their allegiance to the state that governed them.[5]

In the late Seventeenth Century, John Locke proposed a
dramatic change of thinking that furthered the adoption and spread
of religious toleration and religious liberty. In his 1689 *Letter
Concerning Toleration*,[6] Locke challenged both prongs of the
traditional justification for coercive religious establishments even as
he reaffirmed the idea of religious truth.[7] In so doing, Locke offered
his own competing arguments, both religious-moral and political-
pragmatic.

---

[4] As Professor Leslie C. Griffin has explained, this view conformed to the
teaching of Saint Augustine, who argued that "it is good for individuals to be brought
to the truth by any means, including the use of force." Leslie C. Griffin, *Fighting the
New Wars of Religion: The Need for a Tolerant First Amendment*, 62 ME. L. REV. 23,
28 (2010); *see id.* at 28–29.

[5] From the time of the post-Constantinian Roman Empire, "it was a universal
assumption that the stability of the social order and the safety of the state demanded
the religious solidarity of all the people in one church." Winfred E. Garrison,
Characteristics of American Organized Religion, 256 ANNALS AM. ACAD. POL. & SOC.
SCI., Mar. 1948, at 14, 16. This "theory of compulsory solidarity was . . . of Roman
Catholic origin, . . . but it was also taken over by the major divisions of Protestantism
in so far as these secured establishment as state churches." *Id.* at 17.

[6] JOHN LOCKE, A LETTER CONCERNING TOLERATION (William Popple trans.,
1689), *reprinted in* 33 GREAT BOOKS OF THE WESTERN WORLD 1 (Mortimer J. Adler
ed., 2d ed. 1990).

[7] *See id.* at 4 (noting that there is "but one truth, one way to heaven").

In his principal argument, Locke contended that the traditional religious-moral reasoning was flawed because, in reality, a coercive religious establishment does not conform to true religion. True Christianity, Locke argued, teaches that religious salvation requires inward sincerity and personal faith, meaning that "men cannot be forced to be saved."[8] Coerced religion simply has no religious value. Accordingly, a state that compels religious observance engenders hypocrisy but does not honor God, and neither does it serve the religious well-being of individuals. Much to the contrary, a state honors the will of God and best serves individual religious well-being by permitting genuine religious observance as a matter of voluntary choice.[9]

More briefly, Locke also contested the political-pragmatic argument for coercive establishments. In a religiously pluralistic society, he suggested, religious toleration is politically and pragmatically preferable. Forcing dissenters to practice a religion they reject promotes resentment and anger, not social unity and religion-based support for the state. Conversely, tolerance for competing views gives citizens, including religious minorities, a sense of belonging that in turn promotes the state's interest in political stability and social peace. According to Locke, the social-glue argument fails as contrasted with the "greater ... security of government where all good subjects, of whatsoever Church they be, without any distinction upon account of religion, enjoy[ ] the same favour of the prince and the same benefit of the laws, ... [thus] becom[ing] the common support and guard of it."[10]

Locke himself supported only a restricted regime of religious toleration,[11] but his arguments commonly and properly have been understood to support religious liberty more generally. And Locke's arguments played an important role in early American history. In the late 1700s, as we will see, Madison and Jefferson relied on variants of Locke's arguments in promoting disestablishment and religious freedom in Virginia. And long before that—indeed, long before Locke wrote his 1689 letter—Roger Williams colorfully

---

[8]   *Id.* at 10.

[9]   *See id.* at 3–4, 10, 11. Antecedents of Locke's religious-moral argument for religious toleration can be found in Christian writings as far back as the third and fourth centuries. *See* E. Gregory Wallace, *Justifying Religious Freedom: The Western Tradition*, 114 PENN ST. L. REV. 485, 495–530 (2009).

[10]   LOCKE, *supra* note 6, at 19; *see id.* at 18–19; Durham, *supra* note 2, at 8.

[11]   Much like the contemporary constitutional doctrine of *Employment Div. v. Smith*, 494 U.S. 872 (1990), Locke called for the protection of religious belief and profession and for freedom from religious discrimination, but he rejected religion-based exemptions from generally applicable laws. *See* LOCKE, *supra* note 6, at 12–13, 15, 16. And even this limited degree of toleration seemingly did not extend, at least not fully, to Roman Catholics, Muslims, or nonbelievers. *See id.* at 17–18.

foreshadowed Locke's primary, religious-moral justification for religious liberty. Williams, who founded colonial Rhode Island in 1636 as a haven of religious liberty,[12] argued that "forced worship stinks in God's nostrils,"[13] whereas religious freedom—what Williams called "soul liberty"—is a human right precisely because it is a God-given right, no less than the right of a human to breathe.[14] More broadly, Williams promoted the separation of church and state for religious reasons—to protect religion from contamination and corruption. Thus, as Professor Mark DeWolfe Howe explained, Williams maintained that "government must have nothing to do with religion lest in its clumsy desire to favor the churches or its savage effort to injure religion it bring the corruptions of the wilderness into the holiness of the garden."[15]

II. Disestablishment and Religious Freedom in Virginia[16]

Unlike Rhode Island, Virginia maintained an established religion, the Church of England, also known as the Anglican Church, throughout most of its colonial history. By 1776, however, there was waning political support for this arrangement. In fits and starts, the Virginia legislature relaxed its establishment laws, according greater rights to religious dissenters and exempting them from the compulsory taxation that supported Anglican clergy. It also suspended, and later ended, religious taxation even for Anglicans themselves.[17]

In 1783 and especially in 1784 and 1785, the Virginia legislature considered a proposal—a "general assessment"—that would have reinstated tax support for Anglican clergy but that would have extended similar support to other Christian denominations. Entitled "A Bill Establishing a Provision for Teachers of the Christian Religion," the bill would have created a "multiple establishment" of various Christian churches by providing

---

[12] See WILLIAM G. MCLOUGHLIN, RHODE ISLAND: A HISTORY 3–5 (1978).

[13] PATRICIA U. BONOMI, UNDER THE COPE OF HEAVEN: RELIGION, SOCIETY, AND POLITICS IN COLONIAL AMERICA 35 (1986) (quoting Roger Williams).

[14] See EDWIN S. GAUSTAD, ROGER WILLIAMS 95–96 (2005).

[15] MARK DEWOLFE HOWE, THE GARDEN AND THE WILDERNESS: RELIGION AND GOVERNMENT IN AMERICAN CONSTITUTIONAL HISTORY 149 (1965). For an elaboration of Roger Williams' rich and complex views, see TIMOTHY L. HALL, SEPARATING CHURCH AND STATE: ROGER WILLIAMS AND RELIGIOUS LIBERTY (1998).

[16] For a considerably more elaborate account of the history discussed in this section, see Carl H. Esbeck, *Protestant Dissent and the Virginia Disestablishment, 1776–1786*, 7 GEO. J.L. & PUB. POL'Y 51, 65–89 (2009).

[17] See id. at 70–75.

earmarked tax support for their clergy.[18] The bill included an element of taxpayer choice. Although every citizen would be required to pay the assessment, each would be free to designate the church that he wished to receive his portion of the tax. Only Christian churches could be designated. If a taxpayer made no designation, his tax payment would go to Virginia's "public treasury" to support possible future appropriations for schools in the taxpayer's county, although how this alternative might have worked is not clear. Virginia had no public schools at this time, and private schools were affiliated with particular churches.[19]

In response to this legislative proposal, James Madison authored his famous *Memorial and Remonstrance Against Religious Assessments.*[20] He offered reasons not only for opposing the assessment bill but also, more broadly, for supporting religious liberty, including the separation of church and state. In so doing, Madison relied in part on the Virginia Declaration of Rights of 1776, which had recognized religious free exercise and freedom of conscience. But he also went further, advocating the disestablishment of religion as well.

Echoing Locke, Madison argued that "Religion or the duty which we owe to our Creator and the Manner of discharging it, can be directed only by reason and conviction, not by force or violence."[21] Elaborating, Madison contended that individuals have a natural right to determine their own religion and that this right corresponds to a duty to God that precedes the social contract, rendering both the duty and the right "unalienable." Thus, he wrote, "It is the duty of every man to render to the Creator such homage and such only as he believes to be acceptable to him."[22] He further argued that government is not competent to determine religious truth; that religion falls outside the domain of government; that it is wrong—"an unhallowed perversion of the means of salvation"[23]—for government to use religion in pursuit of secular ends; and that true Christianity does not need the support of government, which tends to corrupt religion rather than enhance

---

[18] The tax money could also have been used for church buildings. *See id.* at 79 n.119.

[19] *See id.* at 79–80.

[20] JAMES MADISON, MEMORIAL AND REMONSTRANCE AGAINST RELIGIOUS ASSESSMENTS (June 20, 1785), *reprinted in* 5 THE FOUNDERS' CONSTITUTION 82 (Philip B. Kurland & Ralph Lerner eds., 1987). A "remonstrance" is a protest or complaint. Madison's "memorial" was his statement of reasons, which consisted of fifteen numbered paragraphs. Madison published the *Memorial and Remonstrance* anonymously, acknowledging his authorship only years later.

[21] *Id.* para. 1 (quoting VIRGINIA DECLARATION OF RIGHTS art. 16 (1776)).

[22] *Id.*

[23] *Id.* para. 5.

it. Madison also invoked the principle of religious equality, objecting that the general assessment bill included special provisions for Quakers and Mennonites[24] and did not extend to non-Christians at all.

Madison's arguments, like Locke's, were primarily religious-moral. Natural law and religion, properly understood, required religious liberty, including the separation of church and state. But Madison, like Locke, also addressed political-pragmatic concerns. Thus, he emphasized the importance of religious equality not only as a matter of natural right but also because it promotes peaceful coexistence and voluntary allegiance to the state. According to Madison, a coercive religious establishment tends to "destroy ... moderation and harmony ... amongst its several sects,"[25] generating religion-based resentment and divisiveness and sometimes religion-based violence. This "malignant influence on the health and prosperity of the State" is an "enemy to the public quiet."[26] It invites widespread resistance by objecting citizens, which "tend[s] to enervate the laws in general, and to slacken the bands of Society."[27] By contrast, "[a] just government ... will be best supported by protecting every citizen in the enjoyment of his Religion with the same equal hand which protects his person and property; by neither invading the equal rights of any Sect, nor suffering any Sect to invade those of another."[28]

In addition to Madison's *Memorial and Remonstrance*, the Virginia legislature received numerous other anti-assessment petitions, mainly from Presbyterians, Baptists, and other religious groups. These petitions were infused with Christian and Protestant theology, but their arguments were in many respects similar to Madison's. Thousands of citizens signed Madison's *Memorial and Remonstrance* or one of the other petitions. It soon became apparent that public opposition to the general assessment was overwhelming, and the bill died a quiet death in the fall of 1785.[29]

Shortly thereafter, the legislature instead adopted Thomas Jefferson's celebrated Virginia Act for Religious Freedom of 1786, which barred coerced religion, including compelled financial

---

[24] Because Quakers and Mennonites had no formal clergy to support, taxes designated for these churches would have been directed to the churches' general funds. *See* Esbeck, *supra* note 16, at 79.

[25] MADISON, *supra* note 20, para. 11.

[26] *Id.*

[27] *Id.* para. 13.

[28] *Id.* para. 8.

[29] *See* Esbeck, *supra* note 16, at 85–87, 92–98.

support, and which declared religious freedom a natural right.[30] In support of the legislation, Jefferson offered various arguments, but, like Madison as well as Locke, he relied heavily on a religious-moral justification. According to the Act's preamble, "Almighty God hath created the mind free," and "all attempts to influence it by temporal punishment, or burthens, or by civil incapacitations, tend only to beget habits of hypocrisy and meanness...."[31] They "are a departure from the plan of the Holy Author of our religion, who, being Lord both of body and mind, yet chose not to propagate it by coercions on either, as it was in his Almighty power to do."[32] The state ought not confer privileges and incapacities on the basis of religious opinion, the preamble continued, because it "tends only to corrupt the principles of that religion it is meant to encourage, by bribing with a monopoly of worldly honours and emoluments, those who will externally profess and conform to it."[33]

III. The First Amendment

In 1789, the First Congress convened in New York City. The Constitution had taken effect, but, in the course of ratification, some states and citizens had expressed reservations. Indeed, two states, Rhode Island and North Carolina, had declined to join the union. Those who objected feared that in the absence of a Bill of Rights, the new general government might overstep its authority, intruding on the rights of individuals and the powers of the states. In response to these concerns, James Madison, now a prominent member of the House of Representatives, proposed a series of constitutional amendments, including the following provision on the subject of religion: "The civil rights of none shall be abridged on account of religious belief or worship, nor shall any national religion be established, nor shall the full and equal rights of conscience be in any manner, or on any pretext, infringed."[34]

Over the course of several months, Madison's proposals were considered and revised, first in the House and then in the Senate. The provision concerning religion underwent various changes in phrasing. At one point, for example, the provision was amended to state that "Congress shall make no laws touching religion, or

---

[30] *See* Virginia Act for Religious Freedom (Jan. 16, 1786) (codified at VA. CODE ANN. § 57–1). No longer a member of the Virginia legislature, Jefferson had drafted the bill years before. Madison called up the bill and promoted it in Jefferson's absence.

[31] *Id.* (preamble).

[32] *Id.*

[33] *Id.*

[34] 1 ANNALS OF CONG. 434 (Joseph Gales ed., 1789). Madison also proposed a separate provision, directed to the states as opposed to the national government, that likewise would have protected "the equal rights of conscience." *Id.* at 435.

infringing the rights of conscience."[35] At another, it was revised to read that "Congress shall make no law establishing articles of faith or a mode of worship, or prohibiting the free exercise of religion."[36] The substantive significance of these changes is not entirely clear. More generally, the congressional record is sparse. In the House, the recorded debate on the religion provision was brief and inconclusive, and the Senate debate was not reported at all. Ultimately, after a House-Senate conference, Congress agreed to the religion provision, now in the version that we know as the Religion Clauses of the First Amendment: "Congress shall make no law respecting an establishment of religion, or prohibiting the free exercise thereof."

Congress having approved the First Amendment, and the Bill of Rights generally, the amendments were submitted to the states for their consideration. Under Article V of the Constitution, the congressional action was no more than a proposal. To be enacted, the amendments required ratification. Some two years later, in 1791, three fourths of the states had ratified. Article V was satisfied, and the Bill of Rights—including the Religion Clauses of the First Amendment—became part of the Constitution.

IV. The Supreme Court's "Virginia Understanding" of the Religion Clauses

Remarkably enough, the Supreme Court had no occasion to interpret the Religion Clauses for almost 90 years. Finally, in 1879, the Court decided *Reynolds v. United States*.[37] In *Reynolds*, the Court held that the Free Exercise Clause did not protect Mormons from a federal statute forbidding polygamy. More important for present purposes, the Court purported to describe and give effect to the original understanding of the Religion Clauses. In so doing, however, the Court invoked pre-constitutional history, including especially the experience in Virginia:

> Before the adoption of the Constitution, attempts were made in some of the colonies and States to legislate not only in respect to the establishment of religion, but in respect to its doctrines and precepts as well. The people were taxed, against their will, for the support of religion, and sometimes for the support of particular sects to whose tenets they could not and did not subscribe. Punishments were prescribed for a failure to attend upon public

---

[35] *Id.* at 731.

[36] 1 DOCUMENTARY HISTORY OF THE FIRST FEDERAL CONGRESS OF THE UNITED STATES OF AMERICA 166 (Linda Grant De Pauw ed., 1972) (Senate Journal).

[37] 98 U.S. 145 (1879).

worship, and sometimes for entertaining heretical
opinions. The controversy upon this general subject was
animated in many of the States, but seemed at last to
culminate in Virginia.[38]

The Court briefly recounted the Virginia tax-assessment
controversy, discussing Madison's *Memorial and Remonstrance* and
Jefferson's Act for Religious Freedom. In particular, it cited the
Act's preamble for the proposition that religious freedom, properly
understood, protects "the profession or propagation of [religious]
principles" but not "overt acts against peace and good order."[39] The
Court went on to note Madison's role in the First Congress, and,
although Jefferson had no such involvement, the Court nonetheless
quoted and relied upon a letter that Jefferson wrote some years
later to the Danbury Baptist Association:

> Believing with you that religion is a matter which lies
> solely between man and his God; that he owes account to
> none other for his faith or his worship; that the legislative
> powers of the government reach actions only, and not
> opinions,—I contemplate with sovereign reverence that act
> of the whole American people which declared that their
> Legislature should "make no law respecting an
> establishment of religion or prohibiting the free exercise
> thereof," thus building a wall of separation between
> church and State. Adhering to this expression of the
> supreme will of the nation in behalf of the rights of
> conscience, I shall see with sincere satisfaction the
> progress of those sentiments which tend to restore man to
> all his natural rights, convinced he has no natural right in
> opposition to his social duties.[40]

Calling Jefferson "an acknowledged leader of the advocates of the
measure," the Court concluded that the opinion he expressed in this
letter "may be accepted almost as an authoritative declaration of
the scope and effect of the amendment thus secured."[41] In thereby
equating Jefferson's understanding with the original
understanding, the Court suggested that the Establishment Clause
erected a "wall of separation" between church and state. As for the
Free Exercise Clause, the Court read Jefferson, and therefore the
original understanding, to mean that "Congress was deprived of all

---

[38] *Id.* at 162–63.

[39] *Id.* at 163 (quoting preamble to Virginia Act for Religious Freedom).

[40] *Id.* at 164 (quoting Letter from Thomas Jefferson to Danbury Baptist
Association (Jan. 1, 1802)). Jefferson's letter is reprinted in 5 THE FOUNDERS'
CONSTITUTION, *supra* note 20, at 96.

[41] *Reynolds*, 98 U.S. at 164.

legislative power over mere opinion, but was left free to reach actions which were in violation of social duties or subversive of good order."[42]

After its 1879 decision in *Reynolds*, the Supreme Court's encounters with the Religion Clauses were no more than sporadic for another 60 years, until 1940, when the Court decided *Cantwell v. Connecticut*.[43] In *Cantwell*, the Justices invalidated Connecticut laws that had restricted the right of Jehovah's Witnesses to promote their faith through sidewalk evangelism and soliciting. In so doing, the Supreme Court held that the Free Exercise Clause, applicable by its terms only to federal action, would be applied to the states as well, based on the Court's determination that the Fourteenth Amendment (which explicitly addresses the states) "incorporated" the provisions of the Free Exercise Clause. *Cantwell* suggested that the Establishment Clause was likewise incorporated, and the Court so ruled a few years later, in its 1947 decision in *Everson v. Board of Education*.[44]

The first of many modern cases challenging financial aid programs, *Everson* narrowly approved a New Jersey state and local program of bus-fare reimbursement that extended to children attending Roman Catholic schools. Even so, in an often-quoted and influential passage, the Court announced a broad and strongly separationist interpretation of the Establishment Clause:

> The "establishment of religion" clause of the First Amendment means at least this: Neither a state nor the Federal Government can set up a church. Neither can pass laws which aid one religion, aid all religions, or prefer one religion over another. Neither can force nor influence a person to go to or to remain away from church against his will or force him to profess a belief or disbelief in any religion. No person can be punished for entertaining or professing religious beliefs or disbeliefs, for church attendance or non-attendance. No tax in any amount, large or small, can be levied to support any religious activities or institutions, whatever they may be called, or whatever form they may adopt to teach or practice religion. Neither a state nor the Federal Government can, openly or secretly, participate in the affairs of any religious organizations or groups and vice versa. In the words of Jefferson, the clause against establishment of

---

[42] *Id.*

[43] 310 U.S. 296 (1940).

[44] 330 U.S. 1 (1947).

religion by law was intended to erect "a wall of separation between church and State."[45]

As it had done decades earlier in *Reynolds*, the Court in *Everson* claimed that its interpretation was grounded in the original understanding of the Religion Clauses, and it tied that original understanding to pre-constitutional history, to the Virginia experience, and to the views of James Madison and Thomas Jefferson. According to the Court, the people of Virginia had "reached the conviction that individual religious liberty could be achieved best under a government which was stripped of all power to tax, to support, or otherwise to assist any or all religions, or to interfere with the beliefs of any religious individual or group."[46] And "the provisions of the First Amendment, in the drafting and adoption of which Madison and Jefferson played such leading roles, had the same objective and were intended to provide the same protection against governmental intrusion on religious liberty as the [Virginia Act for Religious Freedom]."[47]

The Court in *Everson* split five-to-four in the case at hand, but the dissenters' historical analysis was similar to the majority's, and they reached a similar general conclusion about the original understanding of the Religion Clauses. Speaking for the four dissenters, Justice Rutledge declared that "[n]o provision of the Constitution is more closely tied to or given content by its generating history ...,"[48] a history that "includes not only Madison's authorship and the proceedings before the First Congress, but also the long and intensive struggle for religious freedom in America, more especially in Virginia, of which the [First] Amendment was the direct culmination."[49] Invoking the writings of Madison and Jefferson, especially Madison's *Memorial and Remonstrance* and Jefferson's Act for Religious Freedom, Rutledge found "irrefutable confirmation"[50] that the original understanding of the Religion Clauses, and of the Establishment Clause in particular, required a strict separation of church and state. Indeed, for the dissenters, the original understanding rendered the New Jersey bus-fare program unconstitutional, this because it breached "the wall raised between church and state by Virginia's great

---

[45] *Id.* at 15–16.

[46] *Id.* at 11.

[47] *Id.* at 13

[48] *Id.* at 33 (Rutledge, J., dissenting).

[49] *Id.* at 33–34 (footnote omitted).

[50] *Id.* at 34.

statute of religious freedom and the First Amendment, now made applicable to all the states by the Fourteenth."[51]

As we will see in later chapters, the Supreme Court, in the years since *Everson*, has struggled mightily as it has formulated doctrinal tests, revised them, and applied them to specific issues. The Court often has been deeply divided, and its decisions have generated tremendous controversy and debate. Through it all, however, the Supreme Court has not departed from the central interpretive claims set forth in *Reynolds* and reaffirmed in *Everson*: that the Court's decisions are properly based on the original understanding of the Religion Clauses and that the original understanding itself is based on pre-constitutional history, especially in Virginia, with the views of Madison and Jefferson leading the way. Let us call this the "Virginia understanding" of the Religion Clauses.

Some modern Justices have challenged the Court's position. Chief Justice Rehnquist, for example, forthrightly rejected the Virginia understanding. In his dissenting opinion in *Wallace v. Jaffree*,[52] Rehnquist noted that Jefferson was not even in the United States when the First Amendment was proposed and ratified and therefore, contrary to the Court's claim in *Everson*, hardly could have played a "leading role" in its adoption. Rehnquist did not deny the influential role of Madison, but he argued that as a member of the First Congress, Madison was "speaking as an advocate of sensible legislative compromise, not as an advocate of incorporating the Virginia Statute of Religious Liberty into the United States Constitution."[53] Focusing especially on the Establishment Clause and referring to the "wall of separation" as a "misleading metaphor,"[54] Rehnquist argued that Madison and the First Congress did not mean to disturb the then-common belief that it was proper for the government to further and support religion. According to Rehnquist, Madison intended the Establishment Clause "to prohibit the establishment of a national religion, and perhaps to prevent discrimination among sects. He did not see it as requiring neutrality on the part of government between religion and irreligion."[55]

---

[51] *Id.* at 29.

[52] 472 U.S. 38 (1985). Rehnquist was an Associate Justice, not the Chief Justice, at the time of this decision.

[53] *Id.* at 98 (Rehnquist, J., dissenting).

[54] *Id.* at 92.

[55] *Id.* at 98. Justices Scalia and Thomas have offered historical arguments concerning the Establishment Clause that are sympathetic to those of Chief Justice Rehnquist. *See, e.g., McCreary County v. ACLU*, 545 U.S. 844, 885–900 (2005) (Scalia, J., dissenting); *Rosenberger v. Rector & Visitors of the Univ. of Va.*, 515 U.S.

Justice Souter, by contrast, defended the Court's reliance on the Virginia understanding. In his concurring opinion in *Lee v. Weisman*,[56] Souter rejected Rehnquist's historical arguments, and he reaffirmed, on historical grounds, the principle that "the Establishment Clause forbids not only state practices that 'aid one religion . . . or prefer one religion over another,' but also those that 'aid all religions.' "[57] Focusing on the proceedings of the First Congress, Souter offered a detailed, step-by-step account of the various revisions in Madison's original proposal. Noting that the final language of the Establishment Clause was broader and more categorical than some of the earlier alternatives, Souter concluded that the sequence of congressional revisions, combined with the ultimate text, confirm that the First Congress intended to prohibit even nonpreferential aid to religion—that is, aid directed to all religions or to religion in general. He argued that the framers were aware of nonpreferential as well as preferential establishments, and that they had intended to condemn them both, just as Madison and Jefferson had done in Virginia.[58]

Even when they have disagreed on particular Establishment Clause issues, the Justices on each side often have relied heavily on Madison, Jefferson, and the Virginia experience, offering competing views concerning the meaning and significance of these points of historical reference. In its 2005 decision in *McCreary County v. ACLU*,[59] for instance, a five-Justice majority declared that displays of the Ten Commandments in Kentucky courthouses violated the Establishment Clause.[60] Writing for the majority, Justice Souter reiterated that government cannot favor religion over irreligion, and he ruled that this prohibition properly extends to public expression or symbolism such as the Ten Commandments. Souter conceded that the original understanding on this point was not entirely clear, but he claimed the support of "figures no less

---

819, 852–63 (1995) (Thomas, J., concurring); *Lee v. Weisman*, 505 U.S. 577, 632–36, 640–42 (1992) (Scalia, J., dissenting).

[56] 505 U.S. 577 (1992).

[57] *Id.* at 609–10 (Souter, J., concurring)(quoting *Everson*).

[58] *See id.* at 612–16. Justice Souter's analysis was derived in part from Douglas Laycock, *"Nonpreferential" Aid to Religion: A False Claim About Original Intent*, 27 WM. & MARY L. REV. 875 (1986). *See also Rosenberger*, 515 U.S. at 868–72 (Souter, J., dissenting)(reiterating that the Religion Clauses, including especially the Establishment Clause, reflect the views of Madison and Jefferson, as expressed in Virginia).

[59] 545 U.S. 844 (2005).

[60] In a companion case, *Van Orden v. Perry*, 545 U.S. 677 (2005), a different five-Justice majority upheld the constitutionality of a Ten Commandments monument on the outdoor grounds of the Texas State Capitol. We will return to these cases later in the book.

influential than Thomas Jefferson and James Madison."[61] Referring to the Virginia tax-assessment controversy, Souter suggested that Madison's opposition, as expressed in his *Memorial and Remonstrance*, depended in part on symbolic considerations: that the assessment proposal was "a signal of persecution" that "degrades from the equal rank of Citizens all those whose opinions in Religion do not bend to those of the Legislative authority."[62] Souter also relied on Jefferson, who, as President, refused to issue Thanksgiving Proclamations because he thought they were inconsistent with the First Amendment. In his dissenting opinion, Justice Scalia contended that in the context of governmental expression and symbolism, the Establishment Clause should not be construed to forbid generalized endorsements of religion, including monotheistic religion.[63] Scalia's argument rested on broader claims about historical tradition, but, responding to Souter, he gave special attention to Madison, Jefferson, and the Virginia experience. In particular, he argued that Madison's *Memorial and Remonstrance* was irrelevant to the issue at hand; that Jefferson's Virginia Act for Religious Freedom itself endorsed religion by invoking "Almighty God"; and that Madison and Jefferson alike, during presidential inaugural addresses, appealed to the Almighty and asked for divine blessings.[64]

With respect to the Free Exercise Clause, the Supreme Court likewise has continued to invoke the original understanding, and it has traced that understanding to pre-constitutional history, to Virginia, and to James Madison and Thomas Jefferson. In the Court's initial encounter with the Free Exercise Clause, as noted earlier, it held in *Reynolds v. United States* that the Clause did not protect the Mormon practice of polygamy from the operation of a general federal prohibition. *Reynolds* relied on Thomas Jefferson for the proposition that the Free Exercise Clause protects religious beliefs and opinions, but not religious conduct that violates general social duties. To read the Clause to exempt religious conduct from a

---

[61] *McCreary*, 545 U.S. at 878.

[62] *Id.* (quoting MADISON, *supra* note 20, para. 9).

[63] *Id.* at 885–900 (Scalia, J., dissenting). This portion of Scalia's opinion was joined by Chief Justice Rehnquist and Justice Thomas, but not by Justice Kennedy, who was the fourth dissenter in the case.

[64] *Id.* at 888, 895–96. In the Establishment Clause context, the Justices have debated the significance of the Virginia experience, including the tax-assessment controversy and Madison's *Memorial and Remonstrance*, even in determining whether challengers have standing to sue. *Compare Arizona Christian Sch. Tuition Org. v. Winn*, 131 S. Ct. 1436, 1446–47 (2011) (majority opinion, distinguishing the Virginia experience in finding that taxpayers lacked standing to challenge a tax credit program benefitting religious schools), *with id.* at 1459, 1461–62 (Kagan, J, dissenting)(arguing that the Virginia experience supported standing to sue and that the majority had "betray[ed] Madison's vision").

general, nondiscriminatory law, the Court suggested, would improperly permit a religious believer "to become a law unto himself."[65] In more recent decades, as we will see in Chapter 5, the Court has wavered on the question of whether the Free Exercise Clause exempts religious conduct from general laws. In 1990, however, the Court issued a broadly negative ruling on this question. In *Employment Division v. Smith*,[66] the Court refused to recognize an exemption for the sacramental use of an otherwise illegal drug, peyote, by members of the Native American Church. In so doing, it declared that it was reverting largely to the position that it had first announced in *Reynolds*, namely, that the Free Exercise Clause does not require such exemptions.

The Court was deeply divided on the exemptions issue in *Smith*, and it remains divided on this question, but Justices on both sides invoke the same central claims: that they wish to honor the original understanding of the Free Exercise Clause and that their own point of view concerning exemptions is supported not only by the constitutional text, but also by pre-constitutional history and by the Virginia experience. Writing for the majority in *Smith*, Justice Scalia relied on his interpretation of the Court's precedents, including *Reynolds*, but he also focused on the text of the First Amendment. In so doing, he conceded that the "exercise of religion" includes religious conduct, but he argued that general regulations of conduct are not laws "prohibiting the free exercise [of religion]" and therefore do not violate the Free Exercise Clause. In his concurring opinion in *City of Boerne v. Flores*,[67] Scalia supplemented his textual claim by arguing that *Smith*'s rejection of constitutionally required exemptions was consistent with pre-constitutional understandings in the various colonies and states, including Virginia, and that it honored the views of Madison and Jefferson alike. In her dissenting opinion in *Boerne*, by contrast, Justice O'Connor contended that *Smith*'s rejection of constitutionally required exemptions not only contradicted prior precedents, but also dishonored the text and original understanding of the Free Exercise Clause. And just what did she cite in support of her position?—pre-constitutional history, of course, including especially that of Virginia, and the views of Madison and Jefferson alike.[68]

---

[65] *Reynolds v. United States*, 98 U.S. 145, 167 (1879).

[66] 494 U.S. 872 (1990).

[67] 521 U.S. 507, 537–44 (1997) (Scalia, J., concurring in part).

[68] *See id.* at 548–65 (O'Connor, J., dissenting); *see also Smith*, 494 U.S. at 892–903 (O'Connor, J., concurring in the judgment). For further exploration of the original understanding of the Free Exercise Clause, especially as it relates to exemptions, compare Michael W. McConnell, *The Origins and Historical Understanding of Free Exercise of Religion*, 103 HARV. L. REV. 1409 (1990), with

More recently, in its 2012 decision in *Hosanna-Tabor Evangelical Lutheran Church and School v. EEOC*,[69] the Supreme Court distinguished *Smith*, ruling unanimously that the First Amendment requires a "ministerial exception" to otherwise applicable employment discrimination laws. Citing not only the Free Exercise Clause but also the Establishment Clause, the Court declared that churches and other religious bodies have complete autonomy in hiring and firing their religious leaders, free from the usual legal prohibitions on illicit discrimination. The Court referred to *Smith* as "involv[ing] government regulation of only outward physical acts," whereas the case at hand "concern[ed] government interference with an internal church decision that affects the faith and mission of the church itself."[70] More important for present purposes, the Justices grounded their ruling on the original understanding of the Religion Clauses, relying heavily on the views of James Madison. The Court recounted two historical episodes, the first when Madison was Secretary of State and the second when he was President. In each instance, citing constitutional concerns, Madison declined to involve the government—directly or indirectly—in the selection of religious leaders. Madison's views were especially significant, the Court wrote, because he was "the leading architect of the religion clauses of the First Amendment."[71]

V. The Original Understanding, Collective Intentions, and Federalism

In evaluating the Justices' invocations of the original understanding,[72] we need to begin with some general observations about the Supreme Court's enforcement of constitutional values, including "originalist" values. The Court's enforcement of constitutional values is controversial because it frustrates the ordinary process of (representative) majoritarian self-government; at bottom, it permits an unelected Supreme Court to override the policy judgments of elected officials. When Justices rely on the original understanding of the Constitution, however, they are

---

Philip A. Hamburger, *A Constitutional Right of Religious Exemption: An Historical Perspective*, 60 GEO. WASH. L. REV. 915 (1992).

[69] 132 S. Ct. 694 (2012).

[70] *Id.* at 707.

[71] *Id.* at 703 (internal quotation marks and citations omitted). Thomas Jefferson made a cameo appearance in *Hosanna-Tabor*. Jefferson was President during the first historical episode, in which Madison, as Jefferson's Secretary of State, wrote a letter to a Catholic bishop, declining to offer an opinion concerning who the bishop should appoint to direct the church's affairs in the Louisiana Territory. As the Court noted, Madison consulted with Jefferson before writing the letter on Jefferson's behalf. *See id.*

[72] Some of the analysis that follows is adapted from Daniel O. Conkle, *Toward a General Theory of the Establishment Clause*, 82 NW. U. L. REV. 1113, 1129–42 (1988).

claiming an "originalist" justification for their decisionmaking. Thus, they contend, they are protecting originalist values—values that may conflict with contemporary majoritarian policies, but values that, at some point in the past, were themselves placed in the Constitution by a majoritarian process, the process of constitutional enactment. The majoritarian foundation of originalism means that appeals to the original understanding must be appeals to the *collective* intentions of the framers and ratifiers of the relevant constitutional provision.[73] Under this analysis, the values originally embodied in the Religion Clauses are those that the framers and ratifiers collectively—and not merely James Madison or any other individual—understood and intended the Clauses to embrace. Conversely, if the inclusion of any value would have caused the provision to fail in the First Congress or in the ratification process, that value cannot be said to be part of the original understanding.

It can be exceedingly difficult, if not impossible, to determine the original understanding of a provision in the Bill of Rights. The evidentiary materials are woefully incomplete, and it is difficult to determine the relevance and relative weight of the various types of evidence that do exist. The Religion Clauses fall prey to these evidentiary and analytical problems and, as a result, it is difficult to tell precisely what the framers and ratifiers had in mind.

---

[73] In recent years, much academic writing and some judicial opinions have shifted the focus of originalism from the intentions of the framers and ratifiers to a more general sense of the "original public meaning" of the text that they enacted. *See, e.g.*, Vasan Kesavan & Michael Stokes Paulsen, *The Interpretive Force of the Constitution's Secret Drafting History*, 91 GEO. L.J. 1113, 1127–48 (2003). This approach "asks not what the Framers or Ratifiers meant or understood subjectively, but what their words would have meant objectively—how they would have been understood by an ordinary, reasonably well-informed user of the language, in context, at the time, within the relevant political community that adopted them." *Id.* at 1144–45 (footnote omitted). The "original public meaning" approach has certain attractions, but, as suggested in the text, the ultimate focus of originalist inquiry should be the "original understanding" of the framers and ratifiers themselves—their collective understanding and intentions in adopting a constitutional provision. The "original understanding," in this sense, is the proper focus because it more directly honors the majoritarian foundation of originalism. In addition, and relatedly, it reduces the range of plausible interpretive outcomes and therefore the role of judicial discretion in the resolution of constitutional claims. *See* Richard S. Kay, *Original Intention and Public Meaning in Constitutional Interpretation*, 103 NW. U. L. REV. 703, 714–25 (2009); *cf.* Thomas B. Colby, *The Sacrifice of the New Originalism*, 99 GEO. L.J. 713, 715 (2011) (arguing that the "New Originalism," complete with its focus on original public meaning, "affords massive discretion to judges in resolving contentious constitutional issues"); *see generally* Symposium, *The New Originalism in Constitutional Law*, 82 FORDHAM L. REV. 371 (2013). In any event, in the context at hand, there is no indication that the original public meaning is any different than the original understanding of the framers and ratifiers, so shifting the focus to original public meaning would not change any of the basic conclusions that follow.

As discussed earlier, the First Congress considered multiple drafts of what eventually became the Religion Clauses. Indeed, ten different proposals concerning religion were considered in the House of Representatives and five others in the Senate. Congress approved none of these, but instead adopted a sixteenth and final version, which emerged from a joint committee composed of three Representatives (including James Madison) and three Senators. Apart from the text of these various drafts and the sequence of their consideration, however, the legislative history of the Religion Clauses is meager. There is a partial account of deliberations in the House concerning the preliminary drafts that it considered. There is no record of any debates concerning the Senate proposals, nor of the deliberations of the joint committee, nor of any debates in either house on the final language that Congress adopted and sent to the states. Notably absent from the congressional materials is any evidence supporting the Supreme Court's "Virginia understanding" of the Religion Clauses. As Professor Carl H. Esbeck has observed, "There is no indication that the Virginia disestablishment of a few years before was even so much as mentioned during [the congressional] debates or was otherwise a factor."[74] More generally, this legislative history, which can be reproduced in fewer than ten pages,[75] offers very little guidance concerning what the framers in Congress intended, much less what the ratifiers understood in the various states.

Similar evidentiary problems and gaps in the historical record cloud the original understanding of other provisions in the Bill of Rights. In this instance, however, the difficulties are compounded by a fundamental problem: focusing, as we must, on the collective intentions of the framers and ratifiers, the evidence suggests that the Religion Clauses simply were not designed to be used—as they are today—as a statement of general principles concerning religious liberty and the relationship between religion and government. Rather, they were designed to address these issues exclusively as to congressional action and, as such, they were inextricably linked to the value of federalism in this context. James Madison himself, for example, believed that even under the original Constitution, there was "not a shadow of right in the general government to intermeddle with religion" and that the "least interference with it would be a most flagrant usurpation."[76] The framers and ratifiers of

---

[74] Esbeck, *supra* note 16, at 63.

[75] Indeed, Professors John Witte, Jr., and Joel A. Nichols have done just that, helpfully reproducing "all of the surviving data" from the congressional record and debates in the space of about eight pages. *See* JOHN WITTE, JR., & JOEL A. NICHOLS, RELIGION AND THE AMERICAN CONSTITUTIONAL EXPERIMENT 81–89 (3d ed. 2011).

[76] 3 THE DEBATES IN THE SEVERAL STATE CONVENTIONS ON THE ADOPTION OF THE FEDERAL CONSTITUTION 330 (Jonathan Elliot ed., 2d ed. 1836) (quoting Madison

the Religion Clauses agreed with Madison concerning the impropriety of national involvement in this area, but they wished to make the point explicit. Thus, directing themselves explicitly to *Congress*, they acted to limit the scope of national power and to preserve the power of the states to address religion and religious liberty as the states saw fit.

Especially on the issue of disestablishment, the states, as a matter of general principle, in fact reflected divergent views at the time of the First Amendment's adoption. The Virginia understanding was far from universal. Seven states, including Virginia, had adopted a policy of disestablishment. The remaining six states, however, continued to maintain or authorize established religions.[77] Given this widespread and deep division, Congress and the ratifying state legislatures plainly could not have agreed on a statement of general principles concerning religious liberty and the proper relationship between religion and government. Had the First Amendment been thought to adopt such a statement, it would not have been enacted. The framers and ratifiers could and did agree, however, that there should be no *national* church or other *national* establishment of religion, and, more generally, they agreed that *Congress* was not to legislate on the subject of religion. This purpose honored the disestablishment policies of states like Virginia, but it also preserved the establishments that existed elsewhere as a matter of state law. The appropriate breadth—or at least the appropriate phrasing—of the Religion Clauses was a matter that received considerable attention in the First Congress, but the debate was not about general principles divorced from the context at hand. Rather, the overriding objective was to effectuate a policy of federalism on questions of church and state. Indeed, the final language of the Establishment Clause—"Congress shall make no law *respecting* an establishment of religion"—seems well-suited not only to preclude congressional establishments, but also to protect the existing state establishments from congressional interference.

Apart from the protection of state establishments, the framers and ratifiers, without specifying exactly what they meant, clearly intended to prevent Congress from itself establishing religion or prohibiting free exercise. To that extent (whatever it might be), the framers and ratifiers acted to promote religious liberty by protecting citizens from the adverse effects of the prohibited

---

during the Virginia ratification debates, June 12, 1788), *reprinted in* 5 THE FOUNDERS' CONSTITUTION, *supra* note 20, at 88.

[77] For a detailed account of the policies that prevailed in the various states, see LEONARD W. LEVY, THE ESTABLISHMENT CLAUSE: RELIGION AND THE FIRST AMENDMENT 25–62 (1986).

congressional action.[78] But the level of government was hardly an incidental consideration; it was part and parcel of the project at hand. Viewed through the lens of federalism, originalist debates about the meaning of the Religion Clauses take on a different light. From this perspective, a proper reading of the Clauses depends largely on federalistic concerns. Thus, the stronger the framers' and ratifiers' embrace of federalism in this area—that is, the more comprehensive their aversion to federal involvement with religion— the broader their intended prohibition on Congress. As to the Establishment Clause, if the framers and ratifiers intended only a limited prohibition on discriminatory favoritism, as Chief Justice Rehnquist and others have contended, it was because they were satisfied that this would resolve their federalism concerns. If they intended a broader prohibition on generalized support for religion, as the Supreme Court has declared, it was because they supported an even stronger policy of federalism, one that would remove from Congress and preserve to the states an even broader segment of legislative power. As to the Free Exercise Clause, the original understanding might or might not include exemptions from federal regulations of conduct. This question obviously implicates religious liberty, but it cannot be divorced from the congressional context and the fundamental policy of federalism. Thus, in resolving the exemptions question, the search is for the original understanding of a federalistic prohibition on congressional "intermeddling" or "interference" with religion.[79]

VI. The Original Understanding and Fourteenth Amendment "Incorporation"

Despite the Justices' protestations, their debates about the original understanding of the Religion Clauses are of limited help and of limited importance. Even as to congressional action and even

---

[78] *See* Frederick Mark Gedicks, *Incorporation of the Establishment Clause Against the States: A Logical, Textual, and Historical Account*, 88 IND. L.J. 669, 696– 702 (2013)(explaining that the Religion Clauses, including the Establishment Clause, did not merely reserve power to the states but also disabled congressional action in a manner that accorded protections—constitutional "immunities"—to the people as well as the states).

[79] This federalistic interpretation of the original understanding of the Religion Clauses is not undisputed, but it remains the most coherent explanation of why the Clauses were adopted. As to the Establishment Clause in particular, compare, for example, Noah Feldman, *The Intellectual Origins of the Establishment Clause*, 77 N.Y.U. L. REV. 346 (2002) (rejecting the federalistic interpretation and arguing that the Establishment Clause was designed to promote a substantive value, liberty of conscience) with Steven D. Smith, *The Jurisdictional Establishment Clause: A Reappraisal*, 81 NOTRE DAME L. REV. 1843 (2006) (systematically rebutting the criticisms and competing arguments of Feldman and others and concluding that the federalistic or "jurisdictional" interpretation is the best and most persuasive account of the original understanding).

when informed by the appropriate federalistic perspective, the debates are inconclusive. More important, the bulk of the Court's cases address state, not federal, governmental policies, and the framers and ratifiers of the First Amendment certainly did not intend to impose any limitations on the states. As noted above, the Supreme Court has cited the Fourteenth Amendment as authority for applying the Religion Clauses to the states. To evaluate this claim of "incorporation" as a matter of originalist inquiry, of course, we must consider the original understanding not of the First Amendment, but of the Fourteenth. Ratified in 1868 during the aftermath of the Civil War, the Fourteenth Amendment includes general language barring the states from "abridg[ing] the privileges or immunities of citizens of the United States" and from "depriv[ing] any person of life, liberty, or property, without due process of law."[80]

The Supreme Court's incorporation doctrine, which has extended most of the Bill of Rights to the states, is as well-settled as constitutional doctrine can be. In terms of the original understanding, however, the issue is considerably more controversial, at least with respect to the Religion Clauses. In 1875 and 1876, less than ten years after the adoption of the Fourteenth Amendment, Congress carefully considered, but eventually rejected, a proposed constitutional amendment that was specifically designed to make the Religion Clauses applicable to the states. The proposed "Blaine Amendment" (so labeled because it was introduced by Representative James G. Blaine) would have provided, in part, that "[n]o *State* shall make any law respecting an establishment of religion or prohibiting the free exercise thereof."[81] The Blaine Amendment generated considerable attention and debate in Congress, but there was little if any suggestion that the amendment's establishment and free exercise provisions were constitutionally superfluous—as they would have been, of course, if the Fourteenth Amendment had *already* incorporated the Religion Clauses. Post-ratification congressional action or inaction can be a hazardous basis for determining the original understanding of a constitutional amendment, and it would be a mistake to rely too heavily on this episode.[82] Even so, the post-ratification evidence concerning the Blaine Amendment at least suggests that the

---

[80] "No State shall make or enforce any law which shall abridge the privileges or immunities of citizens of the United States; nor shall any State deprive any person of life, liberty, or property, without due process of law. . . ." U.S. CONST. amend. XIV, § 1.

[81] H.R.J. Res. 1, 44th Cong., 1st Sess., 4 CONG. REC. 205 (1875) (emphasis added).

[82] *See* Gedicks, *supra* note 78, at 685–86, 708–09.

Fourteenth Amendment, as originally understood, did not
incorporate the Religion Clauses for application to the states.

More generally, an originalist incorporation of the Religion
Clauses, at least on first consideration, seems logically problematic.
As to incorporation generally, the originalist contention is that the
framers and ratifiers of the Fourteenth Amendment intended to
incorporate the Bill of Rights by reference, making its principles—
as originally understood for application to the federal government—
henceforth apply to the states in the same way. To the extent that a
Bill of Rights provision, as originally understood, reflected a general
principle concerning the proper role of government and the rights of
individuals, the framers and ratifiers of the Fourteenth Amendment
might logically have concluded that the Constitution should be
extended to protect that principle against state as well as federal
infringement. As we have seen, however, the Religion Clauses, as
originally understood, were not intended to adopt general
principles. Instead, they were linked directly to the policy of
federalism, and, accordingly, they were specifically designed to limit
congressional power and congressional power alone. Indeed, to the
extent that the Religion Clauses reflect a policy of states' rights, to
incorporate the Clauses for application *against* the states would be
logical non-sense, akin to applying the Tenth Amendment against
the states.

Justice Thomas recently has embraced this view in part,
contending that the Establishment Clause—but not the Free
Exercise Clause—should be understood as "a federalism provision,
which, for this reason, resists incorporation."[83] As Justice Thomas
has suggested, the originalist argument for incorporating the
Establishment Clause is especially difficult. In addition to the
logical problem, there is a textual problem. The text of the
Fourteenth Amendment refers to the protection of "privileges" and
"immunities" of "citizens," as well as the rights of "persons" to be
free from unlawful "deprivations" of "life, liberty, or property." This
language seems ill-suited for incorporating the Establishment
Clause, which, at least in part, is a structural provision that is not
directly linked to the rights or liberties of specific individuals.
According to Justice Thomas, therefore, the Establishment Clause
should be incorporated, if at all, only to the extent that it protects
individual religious liberty.[84]

---

[83] *Elk Grove Unified Sch. Dist. v. Newdow*, 542 U.S. 1, 45 (2004) (Thomas, J.,
concurring in the judgment); *see id.* at 49–51. No other Justice has adopted this
position.

[84] *See Zelman v. Simmons-Harris*, 536 U.S. 639, 677–80 (2002) (Thomas, J.,
concurring).

Scholars have attempted to overcome these apparent difficulties, defending the incorporation of the Religion Clauses in originalist terms. Professor Frederick Mark Gedicks, for instance, has argued that even as a structural, federalistic provision, the Establishment Clause, as originally understood, disabled Congress in a manner that protected not only the states but also the people, providing constitutional "immunities" to each. And there is nothing illogical or counter-textual, he concludes, about reading the Fourteenth Amendment to extinguish the states' immunities and to extend the Clause's protection of the people to include state as well as federal establishments.[85] Gedicks' reasoning surely would extend to the Free Exercise Clause as well.

To a certain extent, Gedicks' points are well-taken. One can read the text of the Fourteenth Amendment broadly enough to support the incorporation of the Establishment and Free Exercise Clauses. And it would not have been strictly illogical for the framers and ratifiers of the Fourteenth Amendment to have incorporated the Religion Clauses by extending their restrictions to the states. Thus, even though the Religion Clauses were originally designed primarily to advance the policy of federalism, their prohibitions against federal action could have been extended to the states for other, non-federalistic reasons. In particular, the framers and ratifiers of the Fourteenth Amendment might have intended to impose on the states, as a matter of general principle, prohibitions that had been formulated for a quite different and more limited purpose—that of restricting federal power and, at the same time, preserving the power of the states. This is not impossible as a matter of logic. Even so, it would have been a rather odd decision for the framers and ratifiers to make, an unusual and circuitous way to fashion constitutional norms.

Professor Kurt T. Lash has advanced a different argument. Unlike Gedicks, he does not contend that the Fourteenth Amendment incorporated the original understanding of the Religion Clauses. Instead, Lash contends that the framers and ratifiers of the Fourteenth Amendment, by the time that amendment was adopted, had their own understandings of religious free exercise and disestablishment, and that they meant to include them in the Fourteenth Amendment—without regard to the original understanding or original purpose of the First Amendment as such.[86] This claim is more plausible than incorporation pure and

---

[85] *See* Gedicks, *supra* note 78.

[86] *See* Kurt T. Lash, *The Second Adoption of the Free Exercise Clause: Religious Exemptions Under the Fourteenth Amendment*, 88 NW. U. L. REV. 1106 (1994); Kurt T. Lash, *The Second Adoption of the Establishment Clause: The Rise of the Nonestablishment Principle*, 27 ARIZ. ST. L.J. 1085 (1995). *Cf. School Dist. of*

simple, but much of the historical evidence supporting this argument is linked to the framers' and ratifiers' special concerns about slave religion and its suppression in the South. Professor Gedicks relies on similar evidence in making his claim of incorporation pure and simple.[87] Perhaps the historical evidence surrounding the adoption of the Fourteenth Amendment is sufficient to support a collective intention to protect general free exercise and disestablishment values, beyond the particular context of slavery, race, and the Civil War, but this is not at all clear, especially in light of the Blaine Amendment.

Contrary to the Supreme Court's position, it is difficult to maintain that the Fourteenth Amendment, as originally understood, incorporated the Religion Clauses for application to the states. Professor Lash's argument is more plausible than the Court's, but his historical evidence is far from conclusive. In any event, the Supreme Court has not embraced Lash's argument, relying instead on incorporation pure and simple, which leads the Court back to the First Amendment and to arguments invoking Madison and Jefferson. At the very least, the federalistic purpose of the Religion Clauses makes the case for Fourteenth Amendment incorporation contentious at best, especially with respect to the Establishment Clause. All of this makes it difficult to claim that the Supreme Court, in considering the constitutionality of state laws and practices, is truly engaged in originalist reasoning.

VII.   Originalism, History, and the Religion Clauses

In summary, the Supreme Court's decisionmaking under the Religion Clauses, as applied to congressional action, can reasonably be debated in originalist terms, although these debates too often ignore the important role of federalism. In any event, the debates are inconclusive. More important, the vast majority of the Court's decisionmaking addresses state, not federal, governmental policies. This decisionmaking rests on a theory of Fourteenth Amendment incorporation that, in originalist terms, is dubious at best. To put it mildly, the original understanding is an overrated source of

---

Abington Township v. Schempp, 374 U.S. 203, 253–58 (1963) (Brennan, J., concurring)(defending the incorporation of both Religion Clauses on the ground that, at least by 1868, when the Fourteenth Amendment was ratified, the Establishment Clause could be understood, along with the Free Exercise Clause, as a "co-guarantor" of religious liberty).

[87] *See* Gedicks, *supra* note 78, at 710–20.

constitutional values in this area. Although the Justices frequently invoke it, their arguments are misleading and unhelpful.[88]

As we conclude this chapter, however, one point bears emphasis: to say that the original understanding is largely unimportant in this context is not to say that *history* is unimportant. The original understanding depends on the collective intentions of the framers and ratifiers of the First and Fourteenth Amendments, that is, on the values that they placed in the Constitution through the formal process of constitutional amendment. History, as a source of constitutional values, is not so limited. And as we will see in the next chapter, American history, from the founding to the present, reveals a set of embedded and evolving constitutional values that inform the Religion Clauses in helpful and important ways.

---

[88] No discussion of the Supreme Court's originalist maneuvering is complete without mention of *Marsh v. Chambers*, 463 U.S. 783 (1983). In *Marsh*, the Court upheld the constitutionality of state-sponsored legislative prayer, even though this practice would appear to violate the Court's general Establishment Clause doctrine. In support of its ruling, the Court suggested that the practice of legislative prayer was exceptional. This practice had been specifically approved by the First Congress, the Court reasoned, rendering it immune from constitutional invalidation because such a result could not be defended in originalist terms. As we have seen, however, the Supreme Court's *general doctrine* under the Religion Clauses—especially as applied to the states—cannot be defended in originalist terms. As a result, the Court's reliance on the original understanding in *Marsh*, as the basis for creating an exception to its general doctrine, does nothing but exacerbate the Court's cut-and-paste use of the historical record. Even so, as we will discuss later, the Court recently has reaffirmed and extended *Marsh*, holding that *Marsh* permits prayer in local legislative bodies and that such prayer can be specifically Christian or otherwise sectarian, even if Christian prayer predominates. *See Town of Greece v. Galloway*, 134 S. Ct. 1811 (2014).

Chapter 3

EMBEDDED AND EVOLVING
CONSTITUTIONAL VALUES

As Chapter 2 revealed, originalism cannot explain or justify the Supreme Court's decisionmaking under the Religion Clauses. Despite the Court's claims to the contrary, it has been engaged in a more creative, nonoriginalist process of constitutional interpretation, a process through which the Court has given constitutional effect to values not enacted by the framers and ratifiers of the First Amendment, the Fourteenth Amendment, or any other constitutional provision. And in so doing, the Court has overridden the policy judgments of elected officials, thereby frustrating the ordinary process of majoritarian self-government.

Nonoriginalist constitutional interpretation is controversial, and it exposes the Supreme Court to the charge of judicial activism. Yet the Court's interpretation of the Religion Clauses has not been purely subjective. Although the Court's decisionmaking cannot be defended in originalist terms, it has been informed by history in important ways. Thus, the constitutional law of the Religion Clauses can be seen as "a thoroughly historical phenomenon" that, over time, reveals a significant measure of "continuity and intellectual coherence."[1] But along with continuity there has been change. The influence of history has not been static. And this is as it should be. Indeed, as Professor Harold J. Berman observed, "the strength of a historical argument, in the American legal tradition, depends on the concept of history as an ongoing process rather than as something that stopped at some particular date in the past."[2]

The Court's decisionmaking under the Religion Clauses has been influenced not only by early American history, especially from the founding period, but also by later developments and, indeed, by contemporary considerations. Properly understood, it reflects an evolving tradition of American religious liberty, a tradition that grows and adapts in response to changing circumstances and changing values. Accordingly, Justice Harlan's description of the

---

[1] H. JEFFERSON POWELL, A COMMUNITY BUILT ON WORDS: THE CONSTITUTION IN HISTORY AND POLITICS 3, 5 (2002). Speaking of constitutional law in general, Professor Powell offers a "historicist" understanding, contending that interpretations of the Constitution are dependent "on the contingencies of time and political circumstances" but that constitutional law, over the course of American history, is nonetheless "a coherent tradition of argument." *Id.* at 7.

[2] Harold J. Berman, *Religion and Law: The First Amendment in Historical Perspective*, 35 EMORY L.J. 777, 779 (1986).

Court's function under the Due Process Clause seems equally fitting here: the Court's constitutional decisionmaking is guided, and properly so, by "what history teaches are the traditions from which [the country] developed as well as the traditions from which it broke. That tradition is a living thing."[3]

Resting as it does on historical and evolving understandings of American religious liberty, the Supreme Court's decisionmaking reflects broadly shared values—sometimes complementary, sometimes in tension—that have emerged, grown, and developed over the course of American history. This has not meant unanimity in the Court's rulings; far from it. Sometimes the Justices have disagreed concerning the basic content of the general values that are in play. More often, they have disagreed only about their significance or about their implementation in specific contexts. In any event, the Justices' frequent disagreements are not surprising, because the Court's nonoriginalist decisionmaking is value-laden, complex, and multifaceted.

More art than science, the Court's decisionmaking mediates past and present. It taps values that are deeply embedded in our political and cultural history, tracks their development over time, and determines their significance for contemporary societal issues. For better or for worse, the Court is not merely a passive interpreter. It is an active and creative interpreter, and its decisions themselves contribute to the evolving content of constitutional values, laying the groundwork for future decisions and continuing constitutional change.

The Supreme Court's nonoriginalist decisionmaking, therefore, is anything but ahistorical. To the contrary, it proceeds from and contributes to the continuing history of American religious liberty. We turn next to that history and to the values that it reflects.

I. A Brief History of American Religious Liberty[4]

As Chapter 2 explained, the original understanding of the Religion Clauses is much more a statement about federalism than it is a statement about the substance of religious liberty. Even so, the

---

[3] *Poe v. Ullman*, 367 U.S. 497, 542 (1961) (Harlan, J., dissenting); *see* Steven D. Smith, *Separation as a Tradition*, 18 J. LAW & POLITICS 215 (2002) (arguing that tradition, understood as dynamic rather than static, can offer a persuasive descriptive and normative account of the American experience of religious freedom and church-state separation); *see id.* at 256 (suggesting that constitutional law in this area should respect and honor "the living practices of the American people") (quoting MARK DEWOLFE HOWE, THE GARDEN AND THE WILDERNESS: RELIGION AND GOVERNMENT IN AMERICAN CONSTITUTIONAL HISTORY 174 (1965)).

[4] Portions of this section draw upon Daniel O. Conkle, *The Path of American Religious Liberty: From the Original Theology to Formal Neutrality and an Uncertain Future*, 75 IND. L.J. 1 (2000).

substantive idea of religious liberty was firmly planted in the
founding period—in Virginia and elsewhere. There was deep
disagreement on basic issues, including especially the issue of
disestablishment. As noted earlier, this precluded an agreement on
substance when the Religion Clauses were enacted. Despite the
differences among the various states, however, all of them, to one
degree or another, embraced the general idea of religious liberty.

For the Founders,[5] the substantive idea of religious liberty—
whatever its precise boundaries—was rooted not in secular
philosophy, but in theology. As discussed in Chapter 2, the
Founders were influenced by John Locke's *Letter Concerning
Toleration*,[6] which relied mainly on religious-moral reasoning. More
broadly, as Professor Steven D. Smith has explained, the central
justification for religious liberty in the founding period was
distinctly religious, resting on the combination of two theological
principles: first, that religious duties are more important than
secular duties; and second, that individuals must undertake their
religious duties voluntarily, not under legal compulsion.[7] This
religious justification for religious liberty was prominent in the
arguments "not only of ministers and religious leaders, but also of
political leaders such as Madison and Jefferson."[8] Thus, James
Madison declared in his *Memorial and Remonstrance Against
Religious Assessments* that "[i]t is the duty of every man to render
to the Creator such homage and such only as he believes to be
acceptable to him. This duty is precedent, both in order of time and
in degree of obligation, to the claims of Civil Society."[9] To the same
effect, Thomas Jefferson's Virginia Act for Religious Freedom
asserted that "Almighty God hath created the mind free" and that
compelled religion is "a departure from the plan of the Holy Author
of our religion, who, being Lord both of body and mind, yet chose not
to propagate it by coercions on either, as was in his Almighty power
to do."[10]

---

[5] Freed from the constraints of originalist inquiry, the discussion here is not
about the framers and ratifiers of the First Amendment, but about the Founders
generally, describing their dominant arguments and understandings.

[6] JOHN LOCKE, A LETTER CONCERNING TOLERATION (William Popple trans.,
1689), *reprinted in* 33 GREAT BOOKS OF THE WESTERN WORLD 1 (Mortimer J. Adler
ed., 2d ed. 1990).

[7] *See* Steven D. Smith, *The Rise and Fall of Religious Freedom in
Constitutional Discourse*, 140 U. PA. L. REV. 149, 153–66 (1991).

[8] *Id.* at 162.

[9] JAMES MADISON, MEMORIAL AND REMONSTRANCE AGAINST RELIGIOUS
ASSESSMENTS (June 20, 1785), para. 1, *reprinted in* 5 THE FOUNDERS' CONSTITUTION
82 (Philip B. Kurland & Ralph Lerner eds., 1987).

[10] Virginia Act for Religious Freedom (Jan. 16, 1786) (preamble) (codified at VA.
CODE ANN. § 57–1).

The Founders' religious justification for religious liberty, complete with its emphasis on religious voluntarism, was grounded in Protestant Christian thought. More generally, Christian values and insights were intrinsically connected to the political culture of the new nation. As Professors Richard Vetterli and Gary C. Bryner have explained, "There was a general consensus that Christian values provided the basis for civil society. Religious leaders had contributed to the political discourse of the Revolution, and the Bible was the most widely read and cited text."[11] The Founders believed that religion "fostered republicanism and was therefore central to the life of the new nation."[12]

There was rhetoric of religious equality during this period, but it was designed largely to protect the equality of competing Christian—mainly Protestant—denominations. As between Christian and non-Christian religions, the Founders clearly presupposed the primacy of Christianity. They understood that at least at the state level, Christianity was entitled to political and legal support as the favored, if not established, religion. Indeed, even the new federal government, despite the Religion Clauses, offered certain forms of support for Christianity. Federal facilities in all three branches, including the hall of the House of Representatives, were routinely used for Sunday worship services. As president, Thomas Jefferson regularly attended Sunday services in the House, where, with Jefferson's tacit approval, the Marine Band provided accompaniment for the hymns. Notably, President Jefferson began his attendance the first Sunday after he sent his famous letter to the Danbury Baptists, lauding the Religion Clauses and declaring that they had created a "wall of separation" between church and state![13]

In his *Commentaries on the Constitution*, Justice Joseph Story captured the general sentiment of the Founders: "that Christianity ought to receive encouragement from the state, so far as was not incompatible with the private rights of conscience, and the freedom of religious worship."[14] "An attempt to level all religions," he

---

[11] Richard Vetterli & Gary C. Bryner, *Religion, Public Virtue, and the Founding of the American Republic, in* TOWARD A MORE PERFECT UNION: SIX ESSAYS ON THE CONSTITUTION 91, 92 (Neil L. York ed., 1988).

[12] *Id.; see id.* at 91–117; *see also* RICHARD VETTERLI & GARY C. BRYNER, IN SEARCH OF THE REPUBLIC: PUBLIC VIRTUE AND THE ROOTS OF AMERICAN GOVERNMENT (1987).

[13] *See* JAMES H. HUTSON, RELIGION AND THE FOUNDING OF THE AMERICAN REPUBLIC 84–94 (1998).

[14] 3 JOSEPH STORY, COMMENTARIES ON THE CONSTITUTION § 1868 (1833), *reprinted in* 5 THE FOUNDERS' CONSTITUTION, *supra* note 9, at 108, 109.

continued, "would have created universal disapprobation, if not universal indignation."[15]

Justice Story was describing the founding period, but similar understandings prevailed throughout the Nineteenth Century and well into the Twentieth. To be sure, the states with formal religious establishments dissolved them in the early decades of the new nation, thereby moving, in that respect, to adopt the Virginia understanding for themselves. The last formal establishment was dissolved by Massachusetts in 1833.[16] Formal disestablishment achieved an important measure of institutional separation between church and state, protecting the jurisdictional domain of each from improper intrusion by the other. Formal disestablishment, however, certainly did not mean the end of primacy and legal favoritism for Christianity.

In the Nineteenth Century, states promoted and protected Christianity through the enforcement of Sunday Sabbath laws, laws prohibiting blasphemy, and religious oath requirements. Courts defended such laws in explicitly Christian terms, often declaring that Christianity was part of the common law.[17] In a leading case from New York, for example, the state's highest court ruled that uttering blasphemous insults against Jesus Christ was a common law criminal offense. "[T]o scandalize the author of [Christian] doctrines," the court wrote, is both "extremely impious" and "a gross violation of decency and good order." Other religions, which the court called "impostors," did not warrant similar protection.[18] States also promoted Christianity during this period by teaching its tenets in various institutional settings. Thus, "states did not hesitate to require the teaching of the Christian religion in prisons, reformatories, orphanages, homes for soldiers, and asylums. State colleges and universities as well as elementary and secondary schools required the reading of the Bible and singing of hymns and saying of prayers."[19]

These common practices, especially in elementary and secondary schools, gave rise to serious controversy as the country experienced massive waves of Roman Catholic immigration. Catholics objected to Protestant religious practices in the public

---

[15] *Id.*

[16] *See* LEONARD W. LEVY, THE ESTABLISHMENT CLAUSE: RELIGION AND THE FIRST AMENDMENT 38 (1986).

[17] *See* STEVEN K. GREEN, THE SECOND DISESTABLISHMENT: CHURCH AND STATE IN NINETEENTH-CENTURY AMERICA 160–90 (2010).

[18] *People v. Ruggles*, 8 Johns. 290 (N.Y. 1811), *quoted in* GREEN, *supra* note 17, at 162–63.

[19] Berman, *supra* note 2, at 782; *see id.* at 782–83.

schools even as they were denied public funding for their own, private Catholic schools. With strong support from the politically dominant Protestants, most states adopted state constitutional amendments—still in place and relevant today—to bar the funding of such "sectarian" schools.[20] At the same time, Protestants insisted, and courts generally agreed, that religious instruction and religious exercises in the public schools were "nonsectarian" and therefore permissible because, although plainly Christian and rather clearly Protestant, they did not reflect the teachings of any particular sect or denomination.

As these tensions continued, there were other developments in the law, including new and more secular jurisprudential theories, which gradually weakened the legal dominance of Protestant Christianity.[21] Even so, as late as 1892, based on its survey of American law and culture, the Supreme Court declared that "this is a Christian nation."[22] As Professor Harold J. Berman concluded, similar understandings prevailed well into the Twentieth Century. "Prior to World War I," wrote Berman, "the United States thought of itself as a Christian country, and more particularly as a Protestant Christian country."[23] Indeed, a decade after the war, in 1931, the Supreme Court officially reaffirmed that "[w]e are a Christian people."[24]

This sort of language soon disappeared from judicial opinions, but even as the Twentieth Century moved forward, the legal favoritism of Christianity continued for some time. In the public schools, for example, Christian prayers and religious exercises remained common for another thirty years—until the Supreme Court's historic school prayer decisions of 1962 and 1963.[25] As the decades passed, however, the American understanding of religious liberty was evolving. Especially in the middle and latter parts of the Twentieth Century, there was increasing religious diversity in the

---

[20] These state constitutional amendments are sometimes called "Blaine Amendments" because of their similarity to provisions in the proposed federal Blaine Amendment, which Congress considered in 1875 and 1876. As discussed in Chapter 2, the proposed—but unadopted—federal amendment would have explicitly extended the Religion Clauses to the states. But it also contained additional provisions that would have restricted state funding of "religious sects." H.R.J. Res. 1, 44th Cong., 1st Sess., 4 CONG. REC. 205 (1875).

[21] See GREEN, supra note 17, at 205–47. There were shifting understandings in the public school context as well, with movement toward secularization, but only to a limited degree. See id. at 251–325.

[22] Church of the Holy Trinity v. United States, 143 U.S. 457, 471 (1892).

[23] Berman, supra note 2, at 779.

[24] United States v. MacIntosh, 283 U.S. 605, 625 (1931).

[25] Engel v. Vitale, 370 U.S. 421 (1962); School Dist. of Abington Township v. Schempp, 374 U.S. 203 (1963).

United States, and societal values were changing, especially on issues of equality. As a result, it was increasingly difficult to defend the idea of legally sanctioned Christian dominance, much less Protestant dominance.

The 1960s marked an important turn. Although the Supreme Court had foreshadowed this shift in earlier decisions,[26] it was only in the 1960s that the American understanding of religious liberty firmly rejected the idea of legally sanctioned Christian dominance and firmly embraced a vigorous requirement of religious equality. The Court's school prayer decisions were momentous steps in this direction. Also important was the Court's 1968 invalidation of a law that banned the teaching of human evolution in the public schools— a law that had been grounded in a prominent form of Christian thinking concerning the origins of the human race.[27] Although the school prayer and evolution decisions were (and remain) unpopular in many quarters, the Court's underlying principle of religious equality was championed in the 1960s not only by the Court but also by Congress. Thus, in the Civil Rights Acts of 1964 and 1968, Congress broadly prohibited religious discrimination in various arenas, including public accommodations, employment, and housing.[28] Under the Supreme Court's decisions, the law could no longer provide overt favoritism for Christianity, and under the legislation enacted by Congress, even nongovernmental favoritism was forbidden in the quasi-public arenas addressed by the Civil Rights Acts. Clearly, the legal culture, and with it the public culture, was shifting decidedly from Christian dominance to religious equality.

This trend has continued, and today religious equality is a central and uncontested constitutional value. The Supreme Court has renounced the Christian dominance that prevailed in the past, and it has interpreted the Religion Clauses to reflect a strong constitutional commitment to equal treatment for all religions, Christian and non-Christian alike. Even the Court's critics have applauded this "no preference" requirement. Chief Justice Rehnquist, for example, despite his fundamental disagreement with other aspects of the Court's doctrine, agreed that the government was precluded "from asserting a preference for one religious denomination or sect over others."[29] As we will see in later chapters,

---

[26] *See, e.g., Everson v. Board of Educ.*, 330 U.S. 1, 15 (1947) (declaring that government cannot "prefer one religion over another").

[27] *See Epperson v. Arkansas*, 393 U.S. 97 (1968).

[28] *See* Title II of the Civil Rights Act of 1964, 42 U.S.C. § 2000a (public accommodations); Title VII of the Civil Rights Act of 1964, 42 U.S.C. § 2000e–2 (employment); Fair Housing Act of 1968, 42 U.S.C. § 3604.

[29] *Wallace v. Jaffree*, 472 U.S. 38, 113 (1985) (Rehnquist, J., dissenting).

the value of religious equality plays a powerful role in contemporary constitutional interpretation, strongly influencing the Court's decisionmaking under both the Free Exercise Clause and the Establishment Clause.

More controversially, the law has increasingly extended the idea of religious equality to mean equality not only among religions, but also between religion and irreligion. According to this view, the government cannot disfavor religion in general, but neither can the government favor or support it, for example, by sponsoring a nondenominational prayer in the public schools or by promoting religion with a general religious message or symbolic display. A far cry from the Founders' preferential treatment of religion in general and Christianity in particular, the idea of equal treatment for religion and irreligion is largely a product of the modern era. It reflects the ever-increasing importance of equality as a basic value in the United States. It also reflects the secularization of public life, the growth of new and unusual forms of religion, and a diminished ability to distinguish what is "religious" from what is not. Although some Justices have strongly objected, the Supreme Court generally has embraced the idea of equal treatment between religion and irreligion, and, along with the requirement of equal treatment among religions, it has become a dominant theme in contemporary doctrine. Although not invariably controlling, this theme disfavors special or discriminatory treatment of religion, whether for its benefit or to its disadvantage. Thus, under the Free Exercise Clause, the Court generally has rejected claims that religious conduct should be granted special exemptions from nondiscriminatory laws, and, under the Establishment Clause, the Court has been inclined to permit the nondiscriminatory inclusion of religious beneficiaries in general funding programs.

At the founding, America was almost exclusively Christian and was overwhelmingly Protestant. Today, by contrast, as Professor Diana L. Eck has argued, the United States may be "the most religiously diverse nation on earth."[30] Christianity still predominates, but with Catholics as the single largest Christian group, a wide range of competing Protestant denominations, and a substantial Mormon population. We have significant numbers of Jews and Muslims, also with competing subgroups; a complex array of Buddhists and Hindus; and a wide variety of other religious believers. At the same time, growing numbers of Americans do not subscribe to any religion at all.

---

[30] DIANA L. ECK, A NEW RELIGIOUS AMERICA: HOW A "CHRISTIAN COUNTRY" HAS NOW BECOME THE WORLD'S MOST RELIGIOUSLY DIVERSE NATION 4 (2001).

In response to the religious diversity of contemporary America, the Supreme Court's recent emphasis on religious equality sometimes has included special sensitivity to the interests of religious minorities and nonbelievers. For example, the Court has broadly expanded an individual's "freedom to choose his own creed" and "his right to refrain from accepting the creed established by the majority":

> At one time it was thought that this right merely proscribed the preference of one Christian sect over another, but would not require equal respect for the conscience of the infidel, the atheist, or the adherent of a non-Christian faith such as Islam or Judaism. But when the underlying principle has been examined in the crucible of litigation, the Court has unambiguously concluded that the individual freedom of conscience protected by the First Amendment embraces the right to select any religious faith or none at all.[31]

In its interpretations of the Establishment Clause, the Supreme Court sometimes has gone even further, stating that the government cannot endorse a majority faith, or religion in general, because of the affront and offense that the government's message might inflict upon religious minorities and nonbelievers. The Court's concern about endorsement and affront is designed to protect not only the consciences of dissenting citizens, but also their religious identities and personal self-understandings. In addition, it is intended to promote the maintenance of a religiously inclusive political community. According to an influential opinion by Justice O'Connor, governmental endorsement of religion "sends a message to nonadherents that they are outsiders, not full members of the political community, and an accompanying message to adherents that they are insiders, favored members of the political community."[32] The Establishment Clause forbids such messages, she wrote, because it "prohibits government from making adherence to a religion relevant in any way to a person's standing in the political community."[33] This reasoning supports the view that governmental endorsement of religion, however generic, is constitutionally unacceptable in the contemporary United States.

As this brief historical survey suggests, the Founders started America on the path of religious liberty, but they did not chart our ultimate destination. Over more than two centuries of history, old values have been sometimes reaffirmed and sometimes transformed

---

[31] *Wallace v. Jaffree*, 472 U.S. 38, 52–53 (1985) (footnotes omitted).

[32] *Lynch v. Donnelly*, 465 U.S. 668, 688 (1984) (O'Connor, J., concurring).

[33] *Id.* at 687.

as more modern values and new circumstances have risen to prominence. The contemporary Supreme Court claims an originalist pedigree for its decisionmaking under the Religion Clauses. In reality, the Court has played a far more creative role, drawing upon a complex and interrelated set of evolving constitutional values.

II. Contemporary Constitutional Values

In the contemporary period, the Religion Clauses can be understood to protect at least six values or groups of values. The first three attend primarily to the rights and interests of individuals: protecting religious voluntarism, religious identity, and religious equality. The next three focus on broader institutional or structural values, including political values, religious values, and historical tradition. An additional and final First Amendment value, linked in part to the Free Exercise Clause but mainly to the Free Speech Clause, protects religious liberty in the context of speech. These various values sometimes work in harmony, but they are sometimes in conflict.[34]

A. Rights and Interests of Individuals

With respect to individual rights and interests, the Religion Clauses can be seen to protect the religious voluntarism of individual citizens, to require the government to respect their religious identity, and to promote religious equality.

1. Religious Voluntarism

In its most basic and fundamental sense, religious "liberty" means religious voluntarism, that is, the freedom to make religious choices for oneself, free from governmental compulsion or improper influence. The value of religious voluntarism emerged in the founding period, supported by the Founders' religious justification for religious liberty. The contours of this value have evolved over time, influenced by the growing importance of religious equality and by an increased sensitivity to the interests of religious minorities and nonbelievers. Today, the value of religious voluntarism promotes the right to choose any religion or none at all, and it guards not only against governmental compulsion or coercion, but also against more subtle forms of governmental influence. Standing alone and given vigorous protection, this value, in the words of Professor Douglas Laycock, would require that government

---

[34] For other attempts to catalog religious liberty values or principles, see JOHN WITTE, JR., & JOEL A. NICHOLS, RELIGION AND THE AMERICAN CONSTITUTIONAL EXPERIMENT 41–70 (3d ed. 2011) (discussing "the 'essential rights and liberties' of religion"); Steven H. Shiffrin, *The Pluralistic Foundations of the Religion Clauses*, 90 CORNELL L. REV. 9 (2004).

"minimize the extent to which it either encourages or discourages religious belief or disbelief, practice or nonpractice, observance or nonobservance," leaving religion "as wholly to private choice as anything can be."[35]

2.   *Respecting Religious Identity*

An individual's religious identity—whether it affirms a particular religion or rejects religion altogether—often is central to his or her self-understanding. It can "define a person's very being—his sense of who he is, why he exists, and how he should relate to the world around him."[36] Religious voluntarism protects religious choices, including the choice of rejecting religion. Yet the government might cause religion-related injuries, albeit intangible, even when its actions do not affect religious choices and therefore do not impair the value of religious voluntarism. If the government fails to respect the religious identity of one of its citizens, the government's action, even if purely symbolic, may assault the person's sense of self, causing offense, affront, and alienation.[37] The contemporary Supreme Court has been attentive to this concern, and it has afforded constitutional protection to the value that it implicates—respecting the religious identity of citizens. This value has played an important role, for example, in Establishment Clause decisions prohibiting the government from endorsing religion even when there is little risk that the government's endorsement will meaningfully influence religious choices. As suggested earlier, this prohibition can be linked to the protection of dissenters—typically, religious minorities and nonbelievers—whose religious identity and sense of self can be threatened when the government endorses religious beliefs the dissenters do not share, sending a message that the dissenters are "outsiders, not full members of the political community."[38]

3.   *Religious Equality: "Substantive Equality" and "Formal Equality"*

As we have seen, the value of religious equality has evolved dramatically over the course of American history, especially since the middle of the Twentieth Century. In recent decades, it has grown to become a critical value under the Religion Clauses. Indeed, it may now be the most important value of all, at least in

---

[35] Douglas Laycock, *Formal, Substantive, and Disaggregated Neutrality Toward Religion*, 39 DEPAUL L. REV. 993, 1001–02 (1990).

[36] Daniel O. Conkle, *Toward a General Theory of the Establishment Clause*, 82 NW. U. L. REV. 1113, 1164 (1988).

[37] *See id.* at 1164–66, 1172–74.

[38] *Lynch v. Donnelly*, 465 U.S. 668, 688 (1984) (O'Connor, J., concurring).

the eyes of the contemporary Supreme Court. Religious equality today includes not only equality between and among religions, Christian and non-Christian alike, but also between religion and irreligion.[39] Thus, according to this value, the government should not take action that prefers or disfavors Christianity or Christians, as opposed to other religions or religious believers, nor should it act to advantage or disadvantage religion or religious individuals in general, as opposed to nonbelief or nonbelievers.

This general description of religious equality, sometimes called religious neutrality, leaves open the question of precisely how this value should be understood and implemented.[40] "Substantive equality" or "substantive neutrality," as discussed by Professor Laycock, promotes governmental action that has an equal impact on citizens of all religions or of no religion, even if this requires the government to take religion into account in certain contexts.[41] The equal-impact model would work hand in hand with the value of religious voluntarism by seeking to minimize the government's promotion or discouragement of religious choices and conduct. More precisely, it would strive to minimize governmental incentives to either embrace or reject religious beliefs or practices, even if this means that governmental action sometimes is not religion-blind.[42] For example, as Professor Laycock has argued, this approach would support a religion-based exemption from a law that otherwise forbids children from consuming alcoholic beverages, with the exemption permitting children to take communion wine. The exemption would accommodate certain religious beliefs and practices, but it is quite unlikely that it would incentivize them; that is, the exemption probably would not induce anyone to believe or act in a manner they otherwise would not. Conversely, extending the alcohol prohibition without an exemption would strongly discourage an act of worship.[43] Thus, the exemption would promote substantive equality or neutrality with respect to religion.

---

[39] *See* William P. Marshall, *What Is the Matter with Equality?: An Assessment of the Equal Treatment of Religion and Nonreligion in First Amendment Jurisprudence*, 75 IND. L.J. 193, 196 (2000) (arguing that the Supreme Court's Religion Clause decisionmaking has been strongly influenced, and properly so, "by a general notion of equality—both equality between religions and between religion and nonreligion").

[40] *See* Robin Charlow, *The Elusive Meaning of Religious Equality*, 83 WASH. U. L.Q. 1529 (2005).

[41] *See* Laycock, *supra* note 35, at 997, 1003 (analogizing the issue to that of affirmative action).

[42] *See* Douglas Laycock, *Substantive Neutrality Revisited*, 110 W. VA. L. REV. 51, 54–56 (2007).

[43] *See id.* at 55.

"Formal equality" or "formal neutrality," by contrast, looks not to impact or incentives but to the form or purpose of the government's action. It precludes formal or deliberate discrimination either between or among religions or between religion and irreligion. As such, it would forbid a religion-specific exemption for communion wine. More broadly, it would support a principle that mirrors the Fourteenth Amendment's Equal Protection Clause prohibition on purposeful discrimination based on race.[44] Thus, in the context of religion, formal equality would prohibit the government from taking religion into account by forbidding "classification in terms of religion either to confer a benefit or to impose a burden."[45] As later chapters will show, the contemporary Supreme Court has increasingly utilized the formal model of equality, a model that sometimes complements other constitutional values, including religious voluntarism, but that sometimes conflicts with them.

B. Institutional and Structural Values

The Religion Clauses can be seen to serve institutional or structural values in addition to values linked more directly to the rights and interests of individuals. These values reflect political interests, the interests of religion and religious institutions, and the societal interest in preserving traditional governmental practices.

1. Political Values: Promoting a Religiously Inclusive Political Community and Protecting Government from Improper Religious Involvement

The Religion Clauses—and the Establishment Clause in particular—can be understood to serve political values, protecting the government and the political community from certain forms of religious involvement. Concerns along these lines date back to the founding era. For example, as discussed in Chapter 2, James Madison's arguments for religious liberty, including disestablishment, were in part political-pragmatic. In his *Memorial and Remonstrance*, Madison contended that coercive establishments of religion had generated deep resentment and resistance on the

---

[44] *See, e.g., Washington v. Davis*, 426 U.S. 229 (1976); *Village of Arlington Heights v. Metropolitan Housing Corp.*, 429 U.S. 252 (1977); *Hunter v. Underwood*, 471 U.S. 222 (1985). The Supreme Court itself has invoked this analogy in interpreting the Free Exercise Clause, citing *Washington v. Davis* as a relevant precedent. *See Employment Div. v. Smith*, 494 U.S. 872, 886 n.3 (1990).

[45] Philip B. Kurland, *Of Church and State and the Supreme Court*, 29 U. CHI. L. REV. 1, 96 (1961); *see* Laycock, *supra* note 35, at 999. The distinction between "substantive" and "formal" equality or neutrality is drawn from Professor Laycock, although Laycock would further distinguish "equality" from "neutrality." *See* Laycock, *supra* note 35, at 997, 1011; *cf. id.* at 995 (noting that equality and neutrality are "near cousins").

part of dissenting citizens, tending "to enervate the laws in general, and to slacken the bands of Society."[46] In the contemporary period, the Supreme Court has accepted Madison's concern and has extended it beyond the context of formal religious establishments, suggesting that religious issues should not be decided by governmental mechanisms, including majoritarian voting, in part because "[s]uch a system encourages divisiveness along religious lines."[47] Furthermore, under the reasoning of Justice O'Connor, even the mere governmental endorsement of religion is understood to affront and alienate dissenting citizens, relegating them to "outsider" status and thereby weakening the political community itself.[48] In these respects, the contemporary Establishment Clause is promoting a political value, the maintenance of a religiously inclusive political community.

In its decisions promoting a religiously inclusive political community, the Supreme Court typically has focused on governmental action addressing matters that are inherently and indisputably religious, such as the government's promotion of prayer or its endorsement of particular understandings of God. Some have contended that the Court's concern should also extend to governmental policymaking on other, more worldly issues—issues such as abortion, the death penalty, welfare, or environmental protection—when the policymaking rests on moral values that are religious in derivation. They argue that even in the context of worldly issues, religious politics can be divisive and can be "undemocratic" to the extent that the religious viewpoints are closed-minded or are "inaccessible" to other citizens. Professor Kathleen M. Sullivan, for instance, has contended that although the Establishment Clause does not forbid religious arguments in public debate, it does demand that "public moral disputes"—even on worldly issues—ultimately "be resolved only on grounds articulable in secular terms."[49] Under such an approach, laws forbidding assisted suicide, for example, might be ruled invalid under the Establishment Clause if they were found to rest on religious understandings.[50]

Others reject this position, noting that religiously informed moral values have played an important political role throughout American history—"[f]rom the War for Independence to the

---

[46] MADISON, *supra* note 9, para. 13.

[47] *Santa Fe Indep. Sch. Dist. v. Doe,* 530 U.S. 290, 317 (2000).

[48] *See Lynch v. Donnelly,* 465 U.S. 668, 688 (1984) (O'Connor, J., concurring).

[49] Kathleen M. Sullivan, *Religion and Liberal Democracy,* 59 U. CHI. L. REV. 195, 197 (1992).

[50] *See* Edward Rubin, *Assisted Suicide, Morality, and Law: Why Prohibiting Assisted Suicide Violates the Establishment Clause,* 63 VAND. L. REV. 763 (2010).

abolition movement, women's suffrage, labor reform, civil rights, nuclear disarmament, and opposition to pornography."[51] They contend that to restrict this role would impair the political equality of religious citizens, and they claim that religiously informed moral arguments are not invariably more closed-minded or inaccessible than secular ones. Professor Michael W. McConnell, for instance, has argued that the Establishment Clause "leave[s] the choice of public philosophy to the people" and that they and their elected representatives are "free to seek guidance about contentious questions from whatever sources they might find persuasive, religious as well as secular."[52] To say that the Establishment Clause "forbid[s] the legislature from making religiously-informed judgments, or basing legislation on the religiously-informed judgments of their constituents," writes McConnell, "would be bizarre, for religion remains the single most important influence on the values of ordinary Americans."[53]

The Supreme Court's stance is not entirely clear. Although the Court has declared that lawmaking must be supported by a "secular legislative purpose,"[54] it has never used this requirement to invalidate a law addressing a matter that is not inherently religious. Even so, there are continuing suggestions that the contemporary Establishment Clause may or should protect the government from the influence of religion, not only on specifically religious matters but even in the context of worldly issues. If and to the extent that this view prevails, it would reflect a new and evolved understanding, moving well beyond the understandings of prior historical periods and reading the Establishment Clause to promote a political community that is not merely religiously inclusive, but also decidedly secular.

---

[51] Michael W. McConnell, *Religious Freedom at a Crossroads*, 59 U. CHI. L. REV. 115, 144 (1992).

[52] *Id.* at 191; *see also* Steven D. Smith, *The Constitution and the Goods of Religion, in* DIMENSIONS OF GOODNESS 319, 333 (Vittorio Hösle ed., 2013) (concluding that the Establishment Clause does not forbid religious believers from "speaking, acting, and voting on the basis of religiously-informed valuations of the good life and the good society—interests that are squarely within the legitimate purview of government").

[53] McConnell, *supra* note 51, at 144. This debate about the meaning of the Establishment Clause overlaps with broader questions concerning whether and how religious values should inform governmental policymaking in a liberal, morally pluralistic democracy. For sophisticated discussions, see KENT GREENAWALT, RELIGIOUS CONVICTIONS AND POLITICAL CHOICE (1988); KENT GREENAWALT, PRIVATE CONSCIENCES AND PUBLIC REASONS (1995); MICHAEL J. PERRY, LOVE AND POWER: THE ROLE OF RELIGION AND MORALITY IN AMERICAN POLITICS (1991); MICHAEL J. PERRY, RELIGION IN POLITICS: CONSTITUTIONAL AND MORAL PERSPECTIVES (1997).

[54] *Lemon v. Kurtzman*, 403 U.S. 602, 612 (1971).

> 2. *Religious Values: Protecting the Autonomy and Independence of Religious Institutions and of Religion Itself*

In addition to political values, the Religion Clauses also serve religious values that likewise are institutional or structural in nature: protecting the autonomy of religious institutions and, more broadly, protecting religion as an independent force in American society.

The Supreme Court recently reaffirmed that the First Amendment "gives special solicitude to the rights of religious organizations,"[55] granting them a degree of institutional autonomy that does not extend to nonreligious groups. As the Court explained, our legal system has long reflected "a spirit of freedom for religious organizations, an independence from secular control or manipulation—in short, power to decide for themselves, free from state interference, matters of church government as well as those of faith and doctrine."[56] As suggested in Chapter 2, this respect for the institutional autonomy of religious organizations can be traced back to the Founders. James Madison, for example, citing constitutional concerns, declined to involve the government—directly or indirectly—in the selection of religious leaders.[57] And this value continues to command support. Religious bodies are voluntary associations that facilitate, support, and nourish the exercise of religious freedom by individuals. At the same time, they permit fellow believers to join together as a normative community. Religious organizations thus serve an important role as mediating institutions, mediating between individuals, on the one hand, and the state or society, on the other. Nonreligious organizations also can perform this mediating function, but religious bodies, from the founding to the present, "have been the preeminent example of private associations that have 'act[ed] as critical buffers between the individual and the power of the State.' "[58]

In the founding period, support for the institutional autonomy of religious organizations was accompanied by a related but distinctive belief: that religion, as such, warrants special respect and special protection. Thus, the Founders believed that religion was valuable and important, both intrinsically and for the

---

[55] *Hosanna-Tabor Evangelical Lutheran Church & Sch. v. EEOC*, 132 S. Ct. 694, 706 (2012).

[56] *Id.* at 704 (quoting *Kedroff v. Saint Nicholas Cathedral of Russian Orthodox Church in North America*, 344 U.S. 94, 116 (1952) (discussing the Supreme Court's opinion in *Watson v. Jones*, 80 U.S. (13 Wall.) 679 (1872)).

[57] *See id.* at 703–04.

[58] *Id.* at 712 (Alito, J., concurring) (quoting *Roberts v. United States Jaycees*, 468 U.S. 609, 619 (1984)).

maintenance of the American society and political system. As discussed earlier, they believed that government should encourage religion to a degree, but they also believed that government should neither coerce religion nor tarnish or corrupt it for secular purposes, allowing religion to thrive in the private domain and in the hands of religious institutions. Often associated with Roger Williams, the leader of colonial Rhode Island, this view supported not only the free exercise of religion but also the historical trend toward disestablishment. As noted in Chapter 2, Williams urged the separation of church and state to protect "the holiness of the garden" from "the corruptions of the wilderness."[59] Echoing this sentiment in his *Memorial and Remonstrance*, James Madison argued that the establishment of religion actually harmed religion and that for the government to "employ Religion as an engine of Civil policy" was "an unhallowed perversion of the means of salvation."[60]

These sorts of arguments, supporting a separation of church and state to promote religious values, are somewhat less common today, but they have continuing force in contemporary law[61] and in contemporary societal understandings. Most Americans continue to believe that religion is valuable and important, and they believe that religious institutions play an important role in our society. At the same time, many would contend that in today's cultural climate, governmental "support" for religion, even short of formal establishment, runs the risk of degrading and weakening religion and of compromising the independence and integrity of religious institutions. The government might attempt to promote religion symbolically, perhaps through the sponsorship of prayer or religious displays. But if the government is to respect the religious diversity of contemporary America, it might be inclined to invoke a broadly inclusive or generic religion—in effect, a "lowest common denominator" religion—that itself might tend to undermine, not support, the special and sacred character of genuine religion. In the alternative, the government might attempt to provide more tangible support for religion, directly or indirectly, perhaps by including religious schools or other religious institutions in more general funding programs. But governmental funding programs typically include conditions that participants must honor, conditions that

---

[59] MARK DEWOLFE HOWE, THE GARDEN AND THE WILDERNESS: RELIGION AND GOVERNMENT IN AMERICAN CONSTITUTIONAL HISTORY 149 (1965).

[60] MADISON, *supra* note 9, para. 5.

[61] *See* Andrew Koppelman, *Corruption of Religion and the Establishment Clause*, 50 WM. & MARY L. REV. 1831 (2009) (elaborating and defending a religion-protective argument for understanding contemporary Establishment Clause doctrine).

may expand over time even as the participants become more and more dependent on the government's financial support. These sorts of conditions can threaten the autonomy of religious institutions, inducing them to modify and weaken their religious practices and requirements in response to the government's demands.

These arguments suggest that religious values—protecting religion and its maintenance and nurture by autonomous religious institutions—may support both the free exercise of religion and at least some degree of separation between church and state. If so, these religious values may often work in tandem with other constitutional values, including religious voluntarism as well as the political values of promoting an inclusive political community and protecting government from improper religious involvement. They may sometimes be in conflict with other values, however, including the value of religious equality, at least when religious equality is understood in terms of formal equality, which disfavors special protection or special treatment for religion or religious institutions.

3.   Preserving Traditional Governmental Practices

Some Justices, including especially Justice Scalia, have argued that tradition—understood as a strictly historical (rather than evolutionary) concept—should be a basic touchstone of constitutional interpretation. In its interpretations of the Religion Clauses, the contemporary Supreme Court has not followed this approach. Indeed, some of the Court's Establishment Clause doctrine, requiring a secular purpose for lawmaking and precluding the government from endorsing religion, is inconsistent with the traditional understanding—dating back to the founding—that the government should (to some degree) promote and encourage religion. Even so, the Supreme Court does not ignore historical tradition, which can be seen as a structural value that acts as something of a wild card in the Court's Establishment Clause decisionmaking.

As the Supreme Court has noted, "We are a religious people whose institutions presuppose a Supreme Being."[62] More specifically, our religious heritage and character are embodied in various traditional practices that might be unconstitutional except for the weight of tradition. The practice of legislative prayer by a paid legislative chaplain, for example, might seem a quintessential violation of the Establishment Clause, but the Court has upheld it in a decision emphasizing that legislative prayer is such a longstanding American tradition that it is "part of the fabric of our

---

[62]   *Zorach v. Clauson,* 343 U.S. 306, 313 (1952).

society."[63] Tradition might also explain the constitutionality of certain other governmental practices that endorse religion, including our national motto, "In God We Trust." In cases such as these, the value of preserving traditional governmental practices acts as a counterweight to other constitutional values that might suggest a constitutional violation. The precise weight of historical tradition, relative to other values, is not entirely clear, but it tends to support the constitutionality of governmental endorsements of religion that are deeply traditional, nonsectarian, symbolic (as opposed to financially substantial), and non-coercive.[64]

C. Freedom of Speech

A final First Amendment value is freedom of religious speech as a form of expressive and religious liberty. This value is not an institutional or structural value. Rather, it protects an interest in individual liberty, much like the first and most basic value of the Religion Clauses, religious voluntarism. Indeed, freedom of religious speech protects and promotes religious voluntarism in the context of speech, a context that generates distinctive considerations linked to general free speech principles. Accordingly, this value is derived in part from the Free Exercise Clause, but it is grounded mainly in the Free Speech Clause.

At least in the absence of governmental sponsorship, religious speech, including prayer and worship, is high-value speech under the Free Speech Clause, no less than core political speech.[65] This is hardly surprising, because religious speech reflects and manifests fundamental personal beliefs[66] even as it addresses matters of broad societal interest. As the Supreme Court has explained, "private religious speech, far from being a First Amendment orphan, is as fully protected under the Free Speech Clause as secular private expression."[67] Indeed, according to the Court,

---

[63] *Marsh v. Chambers*, 463 U.S. 783, 792 (1983). As discussed in the final footnote of Chapter 2, the Court also observed that the practice of legislative prayer had been specifically approved by the First Congress and therefore could not be said to violate the original understanding of the First Amendment.

[64] Relying on tradition and other factors, including freedom-of-speech considerations, the Supreme Court has extended its approval of legislative prayer even to prayers that are specifically Christian or otherwise sectarian. *See Town of Greece v. Galloway*, 134 S. Ct. 1811 (2014). We will discuss legislative prayer in Chapters 7 and 8.

[65] *See, e.g., Widmar v. Vincent*, 454 U.S. 263, 269 (1981); *Capitol Square Review & Advisory Bd. v. Pinette*, 515 U.S. 753, 760 (1995).

[66] *See* Steven D. Smith, *Believing Persons, Personal Believings: The Neglected Center of the First Amendment*, 2002 U. ILL. L. REV. 1233, 1311 (arguing that the First Amendment protects the manifestation of belief, especially "ultimate or constitutive belief," and that religious speech therefore "is bound up with the First Amendment's central purpose in a distinctively vital way").

[67] *Capitol Square*, 515 U.S. at 760.

"government suppression of speech has so commonly been directed *precisely* at religious speech that a free-speech clause without religion would be Hamlet without the prince."[68]

Like political speech, religious speech—if privately sponsored—is strongly protected from censorship or discriminatory treatment at the hands of government, including the judiciary, even when the speech occurs in the public schools or in other governmental settings. The Free Speech Clause thereby protects not only the constitutional value of expressive liberty in general, but also, and more specifically, the value of religious liberty in the realm of privately sponsored religious expression. When religious expression takes place in governmental settings, however, the expression may be the combined product of private and governmental action, complicating the issue of sponsorship and potentially putting the value of religious free speech in tension with competing values under the Religion Clauses, including especially the Establishment Clause.

III. Constitutional Values and Constitutional Interpretation

This chapter has outlined the history of American religious liberty and has explained how, over the course of that history, the Supreme Court has drawn upon and contributed to an evolving set of constitutional values.[69] These values are the primary source for the Court's interpretations of the Religion Clauses (and of the Free Speech Clause as it relates to religious speech). But the guidance that they provide is insufficient to dictate particular decisions or particular formulations of constitutional doctrine. Taken individually, the various values are sufficiently vague and general that their implications are not always clear. Taken together, they may point in different directions. The Court's interpretations therefore depend not only on these values, but also on the Court's evaluation of these values and their implications, both individually and collectively. This evaluation is reflected in the Court's doctrinal formulations as well as its particular decisions. We turn next to a systematic examination of the Court's decisionmaking, beginning with doctrinal fundamentals under the Religion Clauses.

---

[68] *Id.* (emphasis in original).

[69] The various constitutional values we have identified, taken together, often work to preserve and promote religious pluralism, which might be regarded as a constitutional value in and of itself. *See* WITTE & NICHOLS, *supra* note 34, at 46–49; Derek H. Davis, *Introduction: Religious Pluralism as the Essential Foundation of America's Quest for Unity and Order, in* THE OXFORD HANDBOOK OF CHURCH AND STATE IN THE UNITED STATES 3 (Derek H. Davis ed., 2010).

Chapter 4

THE RELIGION CLAUSES: DOCTRINAL FUNDAMENTALS

The Supreme Court's First Amendment doctrine concerning religion is complex and multifaceted. As noted in Chapter 3, the Free Speech Clause sometimes raises distinctive issues, but we will put those issues aside in this chapter and focus instead on the Religion Clauses. As we will see in later chapters, the Court's doctrine under the Religion Clauses is complicated in and of itself, without regard to the Free Speech Clause. Thus, the Court has separate doctrinal tests and approaches for the Free Exercise and Establishment Clauses, and its decisions, especially under the Establishment Clause, can be further divided into a number of doctrinal categories.

In due course, we will examine the Supreme Court's decisionmaking in all its fullness. But it is helpful to begin with doctrinal fundamentals, that is, with general concepts and principles that are basic to the Religion Clauses generally. Accordingly, in this chapter we will examine the concepts of impermissible burdens and impermissible benefits, the general principle of nondiscrimination, the definition of "religion," and judicial inquiries into the content and sincerity of religious beliefs. These fundamentals will serve as building blocks for understanding the Court's more specific doctrine and decisions under the Religion Clauses, which will occupy much of the remainder of the book. They also will assist our understanding when we address related issues under the Free Speech Clause and when we discuss the protection of religious liberty under statutory and state constitutional provisions.

I. Impermissible Burdens and Impermissible Benefits

At the broadest level, the Supreme Court reads the Religion Clauses, taken together, to promote a general policy of governmental neutrality or evenhandedness toward religion. In so doing, however, the Court treats the Free Exercise and Establishment Clauses as distinct, albeit related, provisions. The Free Exercise Clause prohibits the government from mistreating religion through the imposition of impermissible burdens. Conversely, the Establishment Clause forbids the government from

53

advantaging religion through the conferral of impermissible benefits.[1]

What counts as "impermissible" under either clause is a critical and often difficult question. But even the question of what counts as a "burden" or a "benefit" can be troublesome, and, given the differing implications of the two clauses, this question also can be quite important. Suppose, for example, that a law makes it a crime to use peyote, an hallucinogenic drug, but that the law includes an exception for the religious use of peyote, which is commonly consumed for sacramental purposes by members of the Native American Church.[2] The religious exemption removes what would otherwise be a legal burden on religion—a criminal penalty—and it therefore could be seen to conform to the Free Exercise Clause. Conversely, this exemption from an otherwise general law arguably confers a special benefit on religion, or perhaps on the particular religion of the Native American Church, thereby raising an issue under the Establishment Clause. As this example suggests, the burden-versus-benefit issue creates a potential tension between the two clauses, a tension to which we will return later.

A.   Impermissible Burdens: Basic Free Exercise Doctrine

For now, however, let us put aside the burden-versus-benefit issue and assume the presence of what is properly regarded as a burden on religion, potentially implicating the Free Exercise Clause. What sorts of burdens are constitutionally impermissible? We will explore the Supreme Court's doctrine under the Free Exercise Clause in the next chapter, but it is helpful at this point to highlight the Court's general stance on two basic issues.

---

[1]   In rare circumstances, the Establishment Clause may play a different role, working alongside the Free Exercise Clause to prevent the government from mistreating religion through the imposition of impermissible burdens. In *Hosanna-Tabor Evangelical Lutheran Church & Sch. v. EEOC*, 132 S. Ct. 694 (2012), for example, the Supreme Court cited the Establishment Clause as well as the Free Exercise Clause in granting churches and other religious bodies a "ministerial exception" to otherwise applicable employment discrimination laws, thereby permitting them to select their religious leaders free from the impermissible burden of those laws. But the Court's invocation of the Establishment Clause to protect religion from impermissible burdens is decidedly atypical, and, as discussed in Chapter 5, *Hosanna-Tabor* probably is best understood as a free exercise case.

[2]   A description of the Native American Church and its use of peyote can be found in *People v. Woody*, 394 P.2d 813 (Cal. 1964). As the court explained, "the theology of the church combines certain Christian teachings with the belief that peyote embodies the Holy Spirit and that those who partake of peyote enter into direct contact with God." *Id.* at 817. Consumed in a special ceremony, "peyote serves as a sacramental symbol similar to bread and wine in certain Christian churches," but "it is more than a sacrament" in that it "constitutes in itself an object of worship" and is regarded as both a "teacher" and a "protector." *Id.* at 817–18.

First, there is a broad consensus on the Court that, at a minimum, the Free Exercise Clause prohibits discriminatory burdens. More precisely, the Clause forbids the government from imposing a substantial legal burden in a manner that discriminates either against religion in general or against any particular religion—at least if the discrimination amounts to formal or deliberate discrimination. Thus, the government cannot target religion for substantial burdens that are not imposed more generally. For example, it clearly would violate the Free Exercise Clause for the government to forbid the use of peyote only when the use is religious or only when the use occurs as part of a Native American Church religious ritual. This constitutional prohibition on discriminatory burdens is presumptive, not absolute, but such burdens trigger an extremely demanding test of strict judicial scrutiny, a test that the government can rarely if ever satisfy.

Second, there is considerably more debate, and there are changing judicial perspectives over time, concerning the question of whether the Free Exercise Clause prohibits substantial burdens on religion that are not discriminatory, or at least not discriminatory in the obvious sense of formal or deliberate discrimination. For example, if a general and nondiscriminatory prohibition on the use of peyote is applied to its sacramental use, is the religious use protected by the Free Exercise Clause? The Court sometimes has suggested that the Free Exercise Clause is implicated in this context and that it might provide protection under a case-by-case evaluation, effectively requiring religion-based exemptions from some nondiscriminatory laws. More recently, however, the Court has broadly rejected this idea. But as we will see in the next chapter, Chapter 5, the Court's rejection of constitutionally required exemptions is contested, and its constitutional doctrine includes qualifications and exceptions. Furthermore, as discussed in Chapters 6 and 7, the Court's doctrine does not preclude the recognition of religion-based exemptions—even exemptions that are not required by the Free Exercise Clause—under the authority of religious liberty statutes or state constitutional law. As a result, there is still some room for religion-based exemptions and therefore some protection from nondiscriminatory burdens, in part under the Free Exercise Clause but mainly under statutory and state constitutional provisions that offer protection beyond that available under the First Amendment itself.

B. Impermissible Benefits: Basic Establishment Clause Doctrine

The Supreme Court's doctrine of impermissible benefits under the Establishment Clause, the topic of Chapters 7 and 8, is quite complex. But it, too, reflects a distinction between discriminatory and nondiscriminatory laws, albeit with various complications. Three broad points are worth noting.

First, the Establishment Clause, as interpreted by the Supreme Court, strongly disfavors discriminatory benefits. Thus, the Clause generally forbids the government from conferring benefits in a manner that discriminates either in favor of religion in general or in favor of any particular religion—again, at least if the discrimination amounts to formal or deliberate discrimination. For example, it violates the Establishment Clause for a public school to sponsor or promote classroom prayer, whether nonsectarian or Christian. A school that engages in this practice is targeting religion or Christianity for a special benefit. The selective favoritism amounts to deliberate discrimination, preferring religion over irreligion or Christianity over other faiths. Likewise, it clearly would violate the Establishment Clause for the government to fund private religious schools but not secular ones, or to fund only those private schools that are Roman Catholic.

Second, the Court's Establishment Clause doctrine is especially averse to sectarian discrimination, that is, governmental action that discriminates in favor of one or more particular religions, such as Christianity, as opposed to others.[3] There is a broad consensus that it is presumptively unconstitutional for the government to engage in such discrimination. By contrast, some Justices have protested the general Establishment Clause prohibition on nonsectarian discrimination, that is, discrimination that favors religion over irreligion but that does not favor any particular religion over others. Likewise, the Court itself has suggested that there are exceptions to the prohibition on nonsectarian discrimination, for example, to permit the validation of certain traditional governmental practices, including our national motto, "In God We Trust."

Third, there is debate and uncertainty, and there are changing judicial perspectives over time, concerning the question of whether the Establishment Clause forbids the conferral of benefits on religion that are not discriminatory, or at least not discriminatory in the sense of formal or deliberate discrimination. For example, if a legislature adopts a general and nondiscriminatory funding program that includes all private schools, does the Establishment Clause nonetheless prevent the extension of this funding to private

---

[3] This understanding of "sectarian" discrimination includes governmental favoritism for Christianity over other religions, even if the favoritism is not more narrowly focused on particular Christian denominations or groups. It thus departs from the Nineteenth Century view, as discussed in Chapter 3, that treated the promotion of generic Christianity and even the promotion of generic Protestantism (for example, in the public schools) as "nonsectarian" and therefore unobjectionable.

religious schools? The Court has determined that the Establishment Clause does impose some limits even on nondiscriminatory benefits. Recent cases have suggested that these limits are few, or at least fewer than previously believed, but the Court is deeply divided in this area, and its doctrine remains unsettled.

II. The General Principle of Nondiscrimination

As our discussion of impermissible burdens and benefits suggests, a general principle of nondiscrimination, disfavoring formal or deliberate discrimination on the basis of religion, is common ground under the Free Exercise and Establishment Clauses. Thus, the Supreme Court's doctrine recognizes—not as an absolute rule but as a general proposition—that the Religion Clauses mean "that government [usually] cannot utilize religion as a standard for action or inaction because these clauses, read together as they should be, [usually] prohibit classification in terms of religion either to confer a benefit or to impose a burden."[4] The principle of nondiscrimination thus encompasses the Court's general disfavoring of discriminatory burdens and discriminatory benefits. Indeed, the Court's reliance on this principle sometimes collapses the distinction between burdens and benefits and gives the Religion Clauses a single and unitary meaning.

The merger of doctrine under the Free Exercise and Establishment Clauses is especially evident in the context of sectarian discrimination. For example, in *Church of the Lukumi Babalu Aye, Inc. v. City of Hialeah*,[5] a case to which we will return in the next chapter, the Court relied on the Free Exercise Clause to invalidate a set of city ordinances that selectively outlawed the Santería practice of animal sacrifice.[6] The ordinances were carefully crafted to leave other animal killings unaffected—including not only secular killings, but also the Orthodox Jewish practice of Kosher slaughter. According to the Court, the city had deliberately discriminated not so much against religion in general as against the particular religion of Santería, thereby effecting a type of sectarian discrimination. In *Larson v. Valente*,[7] by contrast, the Court invoked the Establishment Clause as the basis for invalidating a

---

[4]   Philip B. Kurland, *Of Church and State and the Supreme Court*, 29 U. CHI. L. REV. 1, 96 (1961). Professor Kurland urged this principle—without the softening of the bracketed qualifiers inserted here—as something much closer to an absolute rule.

[5]   508 U.S. 520 (1993).

[6]   Santería is a religion that developed in Cuba in the Nineteenth Century. It combines elements of Yoruba religion, brought to Cuba by African slaves, with elements of Roman Catholicism. Santería calls for animal sacrifice as a principal form of devotion.

[7]   456 U.S. 228 (1982).

Minnesota law that exempted religious organizations from certain reporting requirements only if they received no more than half of their contributions from nonmembers. The Court found that the selective exemption was designed to prefer mainstream and longstanding religions, which generally rely on member contributions, over the unorthodox and unfamiliar religions that do not, including the sometimes controversial Unification Church.[8] In *Larson* no less than in *Lukumi*, the government had engaged in sectarian discrimination, discrimination between or among religions amounting to an impermissible "religious gerrymander."[9]

Although the Court in *Larson* emphasized that the challenged law selectively benefitted mainstream religions, it also noted that the law selectively burdened the disadvantaged religions that were required to report. Likewise, if the Court in *Lukumi* had followed the reasoning of *Larson*, it perhaps could have found not only an impermissible burden on Santería, but also an impermissible benefit for other religions, or at least for Orthodox Judaism. And yet *Lukumi* rested exclusively on the Free Exercise Clause, and *Larson* entirely on the Establishment Clause. Perhaps this makes sense and perhaps not, but in the end it does not particularly matter. When sectarian discrimination is present, the two clauses have virtually the same meaning, rendering the benefit-versus-burden question—and therefore the question of which clause to apply—of little if any doctrinal consequence.

Under each clause, a finding of sectarian discrimination triggers an extremely rigorous test of strict judicial scrutiny,[10] a test that is virtually impossible to satisfy. As the Court declared in *Larson*, sectarian discrimination violates "[t]he clearest command of the Establishment Clause."[11] The contemporary Court apparently is unanimous on this point, which is accepted even by Justices who do not join the Court's disapproval of more generalized, nonsectarian discrimination favoring religion in general.[12] By all indications,

---

[8] Founded in the 1950s by Rev. Sun Myung Moon of Korea, the Unification Church claims to be Christian but espouses unorthodox views. Its followers have sometimes been derided as "Moonies."

[9] *See Lukumi*, 508 U.S. at 535.

[10] With respect to the Free Exercise Clause, the Supreme Court has said that such discrimination "will survive strict scrutiny only in rare cases." *Id.* at 546. Likewise, with respect to the Establishment Clause, the Court has emphasized that a law "granting a denominational preference . . . [is] suspect and . . . must be invalidated unless it is justified by a compelling governmental interest and unless it is closely fitted to further that interest." *Larson*, 456 U.S. at 246–47 (citation omitted).

[11] *Larson*, 456 U.S. at 244.

[12] *See, e.g., Wallace v. Jaffree*, 472 U.S. 38, 113 (1985) (Rehnquist, J., dissenting) (agreeing that the government is precluded "from asserting a preference for one religious denomination or sect over others"); *Lee v. Weisman*, 505 U.S. 577,

moreover, the clearest command of the Establishment Clause is also the clearest command of the Free Exercise Clause. To the extent that sectarian discrimination is at work, the general principle of nondiscrimination is very close to an absolute rule.

With respect to nonsectarian discrimination, by contrast, the Court's doctrine under the Free Exercise and Establishment Clauses is neither unitary nor categorical. As we will see in later chapters, the government sometimes is permitted—and, indeed, it sometimes is required—to discriminate between religion and irreligion. In certain contexts, this discrimination might be said to favor religion. For example, the Supreme Court has ruled that the First Amendment demands a "ministerial exception" to otherwise applicable employment discrimination laws, an exception that permits churches and other religious bodies—but not nonreligious organizations—to select their leaders as they see fit.[13] Morever, as long as it avoids sectarian discrimination of the sort at issue in *Larson*, the government has considerable discretion to go beyond the ministerial exception, granting religious organizations special, religion-based exemptions from employment regulations and other regulatory requirements. In addition, as noted earlier, it appears that the government can deliberately favor religion through certain traditional practices, such as our national motto. In other contexts, the discrimination runs in the opposite direction, a direction that might be seen to disadvantage religion. For instance, there are Establishment Clause limitations on the flow of governmental financial support to religion and to religious organizations. These limitations effectively require religion-based exclusions from otherwise general programs of funding, exclusions that discriminate on the basis of religion. And the government has some discretion to impose additional religion-based funding exclusions, even beyond those that the Establishment Clause demands.

Although not a categorical rule in every context, the general principle of nondiscrimination is extremely important. This principle gives particular meaning and doctrinal effect to the constitutional value of religious equality. In dramatic contrast with earlier periods of American history, the Supreme Court today understands this value to include equality not only between and among religions, but also, at least in general, between religion and irreligion. At the same time, the Court understands the value

---

641 (1992) (Scalia, J., dissenting) (agreeing that the Establishment Clause "rule[s] out of order government-sponsored endorsement of religion ... where the endorsement is sectarian").

[13] *See Hosanna-Tabor Evangelical Lutheran Church & Sch. v. EEOC*, 132 S. Ct. 694 (2012). We will discuss *Hosanna-Tabor* in Chapter 5.

primarily in terms of formal as opposed to substantive equality,[14] and, accordingly, its doctrine implements the value primarily by disfavoring formal or deliberate discrimination on the basis of religion. Thus, although sometimes permitted or even required, the Court tends to view religion-based discrimination as presumptively problematic under both the Free Exercise and the Establishment Clauses, honoring the value of religious equality in the formal sense by reading the principle of nondiscrimination as a general prohibition on formal or deliberate discrimination.

To the extent that the Court's doctrine diverges from the general principle of nondiscrimination, it is serving other constitutional values. Depending on the context, it might be honoring the value of religious equality in the sense of substantive equality, or it might be furthering one or more of the other constitutional values—outlined in Chapter 3—that the First Amendment can be read to protect: religious voluntarism; respecting religious identity; promoting a religiously inclusive political community and protecting government from improper religious involvement; protecting the autonomy and independence of religious institutions and of religion itself; preserving traditional governmental practices; and protecting religious free speech. As noted above and as discussed in later chapters, the Court's contemporary doctrine in fact includes some departures from the principle of nondiscrimination. These departures are notable and important, but they are departures. As we will see, in most settings the Court honors the principle of nondiscrimination and thus gives priority to the value of religious equality in a formal sense, an emphasis that diminishes the significance of other values.

III. Defining "Religion"

The definition of religion is a critical issue under the Religion Clauses. The need for a constitutional definition is present even when the doctrinal test is nondiscrimination. The problem of definition, moreover, takes on added importance and complexity to the extent that the Free Exercise and Establishment Clauses are construed to deviate from the principle of nondiscrimination, permitting or requiring special treatment for religion either in the imposition of burdens or in the conferral of benefits. Remarkably, however, the Supreme Court has never adopted a constitutional definition as such, and, indeed, it has offered no more than partial and sometimes conflicting suggestions. Generally speaking, the Court's decisions under the Religion Clauses have involved religion

---

[14] On the distinction between substantive and formal equality, see the discussion of religious equality in Chapter 3.

in a conventional and indisputable sense, obviating the need for definitional discussions. But the Court's avoidance of this subject may also reflect, in part, its desire to evade what has become a contentious if not intractable problem.[15]

For most of our nation's history, the constitutional definition of religion was not an issue. Thus, for the Founders and for generations that followed, the defining characteristic of religion was easily stated and utterly uncontroversial: it was the performance of duties owed to God. James Madison, for example, equated "religion" with "the duty which we owe to our Creator and the Manner of discharging it."[16] This understanding encompassed not only the various strands of Protestant Christianity, but also other traditional religions, including Catholic Christianity and Judaism. As religious diversity grew in America, religious liberty did not always follow,[17] but the definition of religion was not the obstacle. In fact, the definition of religion did not become a serious question until the latter half of the Twentieth Century. By then, however, increasing pluralism and changing values had placed the Founders' understanding in question.

In its 1965 decision in *United States v. Seeger*,[18] the Supreme Court confronted this new set of circumstances in its most notable attempt to give a modern definition to religion. The Court's effort occurred in the context of statutory interpretation, but it has potential implications for a constitutional definition. In *Seeger*, the Court addressed a statutory religious liberty provision through which Congress provided an exemption from compulsory military service for individuals who were conscientiously opposed to participation in war by reason of their "religious training and belief."[19] In its definition of religion, the statute referred to "an individual's belief in a relation to a Supreme Being involving duties superior to those arising from any human relation, but [not including] essentially political, sociological, or philosophical views or a merely personal moral code."[20] To earlier generations, this

---

[15] Some of the discussion that follows draws upon Daniel O. Conkle, *The Path of American Religious Liberty: From the Original Theology to Formal Neutrality and an Uncertain Future*, 75 IND. L.J. 1, 28–32 (2000).

[16] JAMES MADISON, MEMORIAL AND REMONSTRANCE AGAINST RELIGIOUS ASSESSMENTS, para. 1 (June 20, 1785) (quoting VIRGINIA DECLARATION OF RIGHTS art. 16 (1776)), *reprinted in* 5 THE FOUNDERS' CONSTITUTION 82 (Philip B. Kurland & Ralph Lerner eds., 1987).

[17] *See, e.g., Reynolds v. United States*, 98 U.S. 145 (1878) (refusing to protect Mormons from a federal ban on polygamy).

[18] 380 U.S. 163 (1965).

[19] *Id.* at 165 (quoting 50 U.S.C. APP. § 456(j) (1958)).

[20] *Id.*

definition would have seemed entirely unexceptional.[21] But by 1965, it seemed problematic—so much so that the Court saw fit to rewrite the definition, through creative statutory interpretation, to include any "sincere and meaningful" belief that "occupies a place in the life of its possessor parallel to that filled by the orthodox belief in God of one who clearly qualifies for the exemption."[22] So understood, the definition included the beliefs of Daniel Seeger, a conscientious objector who acknowledged his skepticism concerning the existence of God but who claimed a "belief in and devotion to goodness and virtue for their own sakes, and a religious faith in a purely ethical creed."[23]

Seeger's expansive, "parallel position" understanding of religion—an understanding that included deeply held moral beliefs that were not theistic—reflected the rapidly changing character of religion in the United States. As the Court observed, American religion was remarkably diverse by the 1960s, and it extended well beyond the traditional confines of Christianity and Judaism. Perhaps more important, modern theology was transforming certain strands of the traditional faiths themselves. The Court noted, for example, that Protestant theologian Paul Tillich had concluded that God should no longer be understood "as a projection 'out there' or beyond the skies but as the ground of our very being."[24] And "if that word [God] has not much meaning for you," Tillich explained, "translate it, and speak of the depths of your life, and the source of your being, of your ultimate concern, of what you take seriously without any reservation."[25]

The Court's decision in *Seeger* rested on statutory interpretation, but it appeared to be influenced by constitutional considerations. A longstanding principle of statutory interpretation, known as the canon of constitutional avoidance, cautions against interpreting a statute in a manner that might render the statute unconstitutional.[26] In a concurring opinion in *Seeger*, Justice

---

[21] Indeed, in the specific context of military conscientious objection, the statute, having no requirement of formal religious affiliation or membership, was considerably broader than its predecessors, which generally had confined objector status to those who were members of pacifist religious sects or denominations. *See id.* at 170–72.

[22] *Id.* at 166.

[23] *Id.*

[24] *Id.* at 180.

[25] *Id.* at 187 (quoting PAUL TILLICH, THE SHAKING OF THE FOUNDATIONS 57 (1948)). The source of "meaning within meaningless," wrote Tillich, "is not the God of traditional theism but the 'God above God,' the power of being, which works through those who have no name for it, not even the name God." *Id.* at 180 (quoting 2 PAUL TILLICH, SYSTEMATIC THEOLOGY 12 (1957)).

[26] Thus, "where an otherwise acceptable construction of a statute would raise serious constitutional problems, the Court will construe the statute to avoid such

Douglas expressly referred to this principle, and, indeed, it appears that the principle informed the Court's decision.

As the Court noted, Daniel Seeger argued that if the conscientious objector statute did not extend to him, it violated the Religion Clauses. As discussed in Chapter 7, however, Congress generally is free to provide religion-based exemptions from laws that otherwise would impose substantial burdens on the exercise of religion. Thus, the statute's preference for religious objectors, as opposed to other objectors, probably did not raise a serious constitutional problem. But religion-based exemptions cannot be sectarian. As a result, Seeger's constitutional argument was potentially quite strong, but only if Seeger's beliefs were "religious" *for purposes of the First Amendment*. If they were, but if they were nonetheless excluded from the statute, the statutory provision would amount to sectarian discrimination, which, as we have seen, is a core violation of the Religion Clauses. On this view, as Justice Douglas explained in his concurring opinion, if the statute did not include beliefs such as Seeger's, "then those who embraced one religious faith rather than another would be subject to penalties" and the statute would unconstitutionally "prefer[ ] some religions over others."[27]

The Court avoided this potential constitutional problem by construing the statute as it did. Seeger prevailed under the statute. This result required an expansive and creative interpretation of the statute, but, as Douglas noted, "the words of a statute may be strained 'in the candid service of avoiding a serious constitutional doubt.' "[28] So strain the Court did, because it evidently shared Douglas's concern about sectarian discrimination, leading it to adopt its broadly inclusive construction of the statute.[29] But the constitutional concern about sectarian discrimination was present only if there was at least a strong argument that religion *under the First Amendment* extends to beliefs such as Seeger's, that is, to non-theistic moral beliefs that satisfy the Court's "parallel position" test.

---

problems unless such construction is plainly contrary to the intent of Congress." *Edward J. DeBartolo Corp. v. Fla. Gulf Coast Bldg. & Constr. Trades Council*, 485 U.S. 568, 575 (1988).

[27] *Seeger*, 380 U.S. at 188 (Douglas, J., concurring). Douglas cited the Free Exercise Clause as well as the equal protection component of the Fifth Amendment's Due Process Clause. *See id.*

[28] *Id.* (quoting *United States v. Rumely*, 345 U. S. 41, 47 (1953)).

[29] *Cf. id.* at 176 (opinion of the Court) ("This construction avoids imputing to Congress an intent to classify different religious beliefs, exempting some and excluding others, and is in accord with the well-established congressional policy of equal treatment for those whose opposition to service is grounded in their religious tenets.").

As a result, the Court's decision provides some support, albeit indirectly, for a broad *constitutional* definition of religion.[30]

The trends in American religion that the Court identified in *Seeger* have only accelerated since the 1960s. Thus, the diversity of the American religious experience is ever more extraordinary, and the diversity of thought within the traditional faiths is ever more pronounced. As a result, the Court's expansive definition of religion, if appropriate for the 1960s, arguably is even more compelling today. But however reflective of contemporary understandings, the *Seeger* definition inevitably blurs the distinction between religion and nonreligion.[31] Indeed, if religion includes "the source of your being, of your ultimate concern, of what you take seriously without any reservation," then religious liberty itself becomes potentially problematic, because a broad range of human thought and activity might very well qualify as religious. For example, the Free Exercise Clause could be read to protect a wide range of morally-based objections to legal burdens, and the Establishment Clause might broadly preclude the government from conferring legal benefits or favor on various moral perspectives or ideas. Especially in an era of pervasive government, religious liberty could potentially become unmanageable.

In light of these difficulties, it is perhaps not surprising that the Supreme Court—despite the arguable underpinnings and implications of *Seeger*—has never adopted the *Seeger* approach as a *constitutional* definition of religion.[32] In its 1972 decision in

---

[30] In a later case, *Gillette v. United States*, 401 U.S. 437 (1971), the Supreme Court confronted a claim that the conscientious objector statute, even as extended in *Seeger*, still preferred some religions over others and therefore entailed sectarian discrimination. The challengers argued that the statute was unconstitutional because, while it protected pacifists who objected to participating in any and all wars, it did not protect individuals who were opposed to participating only in wars that they regarded as unjust. The Court rejected the constitutional challenge, finding that the statute's distinction rested on religiously neutral, secular considerations, including concerns about the fair and evenhanded adjudication of objector claims. As a result, the statute did not reflect an unconstitutional preference for some religions over others. *See id.* at 448–60.

[31] *Cf. Welsh v. United States*, 398 U.S. 333 (1970) (extending the *Seeger* definition to include a conscientious objector who had stricken the word "religious" from his application and who had declared that his beliefs were not religious in any conventional sense); *id.* at 344 (plurality opinion) (concluding that the conscientious objector statute "exempts from military service all those whose consciences, spurred by deeply held moral, ethical, or religious beliefs, would give them no rest or peace if they allowed themselves to become a part of an instrument of war").

[32] Prior to *Seeger*, the Court had hinted that it might offer a broad constitutional definition, suggesting that the Religion Clauses would extend to "religions . . . which do not teach what would generally be considered a belief in the existence of God" and offering as examples not only Buddhism and Taoism, but also Ethical Culture and Secular Humanism. *Torcaso v. Watkins*, 367 U.S. 488, 495 n.11 (1961).

Wisconsin v. Yoder,[33] for example, the Court ruled that the religious beliefs and practices of the Amish, including their objection to compulsory high school education, were entitled to constitutional protection under the Free Exercise Clause, but it also declared that such protection would not extend to other "way[s] of life, however virtuous and admirable," if they were "based on purely secular considerations."[34] The Court emphasized that "the traditional way of life of the Amish" was "not merely a matter of personal preference, but one of deep religious conviction, shared by an organized group, . . . in response to their literal interpretation of the Biblical injunction from the Epistle of Paul to the Romans, 'be not conformed to this world . . . .' "[35] Conversely, the Court stated, the Free Exercise Clause would not apply to practices that were merely "philosophical and personal," based on a "subjective evaluation and rejection of the contemporary secular values accepted by the majority."[36] As an example, the Court contrasted the separatist beliefs of the Amish with the decision of Henry David Thoreau to isolate himself at Walden Pond: "Thoreau's choice was philosophical and personal rather than religious, and such belief does not rise to the demands of the Religion Clauses."[37] In his separate opinion, Justice Douglas noted and protested the Court's apparent departure from the *Seeger* approach.[38]

In a later Free Exercise Clause case, the Supreme Court clarified its discussion in *Yoder* by rejecting any implication that beliefs or practices can never qualify as religious in the absence of communal or institutional support. Thus, in its 1989 ruling in *Frazee v. Illinois Department of Employment Security*,[39] the Court protected an individual's strict observance of the Sunday Sabbath

---

[33]   406 U.S. 205 (1972).

[34]   *Id.* at 215.

[35]   *Id.* at 216.

[36]   *Id.*

[37]   *Id.; see also id.* at 215–19. For a recent decision invoking the distinction that the Supreme Court discussed in *Yoder*, see *Moore-King v. County of Chesterfield*, 708 F.3d 560 (4th Cir. 2013). In *Moore-King*, a "spiritual counselor," known as "Psychic Sophie" and describing herself as "very spiritual," objected on "religious" grounds to various regulations of fortune tellers. *Id.* at 564, 570–72. Relying on *Yoder*, however, the U.S. Court of Appeals for the Fourth Circuit denied her claims. According to the court, the challenger's beliefs, which rejected organized religion and instead called for "pretty much go[ing] with [her] inner flow" in response to "an eclectic range of sources," albeit including the teachings of Jesus, "more closely resemble personal and philosophical choices consistent with a way of life, not deep religious convictions shared by an organized group deserving of constitutional solicitude." *Id.* at 571–72. As a result, she could not "avail herself of the protections afforded those engaged in the practice of religion," including the protections of the Free Exercise Clause. *Id.* at 572.

[38]   *See Yoder*, 406 U.S. at 247–49 (Douglas, J., dissenting in part).

[39]   489 U.S. 829 (1989).

even though the individual's belief was not based upon the tenet or teaching of a church or any other religious body. Even so, the individual in *Frazee* was a Christian, and he derived the belief from his own interpretation of the Bible. *Frazee* involved a personal belief, but a belief that was nonetheless religious in a very conventional sense. As a result, *Frazee* provides little support for the much broader approach of *Seeger*.

Taken together, *Yoder* and *Frazee* could be read to suggest that for purposes of the Religion Clauses, religion can be individual, but it must be theistic (or otherwise "religious" in a conventional sense, such as Buddhism).[40] More recently, however, the Court has hinted—albeit in defining constitutional "liberty" outside the specific setting of the Religion Clauses—that it might yet embrace a more capacious, *Seeger*-like understanding. Thus, in its 1992 decision reaffirming the right to choose abortion, the Court spoke of a constitutionally protected "zone of conscience and belief," "choices central to personal dignity and autonomy," "spiritual imperatives," and "the right to define one's own concept of existence, of meaning, of the universe, and of the mystery of human life."[41] And in 2003, the Court spoke in similar terms in recognizing the right of adults, including homosexuals, to engage in consensual sexual conduct.[42] Although written outside the context of the Religion Clauses, the language used in these cases strongly suggests that the contemporary Court finds constitutional value in decisions of conscience, that is, decisions of moral self-definition and self-determination that might or might not be religious in a conventional sense.

In reality, the problem of definition is even more complex than this discussion might suggest, because the exercise of conscience, whether traditionally religious or otherwise, plainly does not exhaust the scope of "religion." Rather, even under a conventional understanding, the concept of religion is commonly associated not only with conscience but also with a wider range of beliefs and practices. As Professor Kent Greenawalt has explained, these various beliefs and practices include

> a belief in God; a comprehensive view of the world and human purposes; a belief in some form of afterlife; communication with God through ritual acts of worship

---

[40] Buddhism is essentially non-theistic. Even under a conventional definition of religion, however, Buddhism presumably would qualify on the basis of its traditional stature as a religion.

[41] *Planned Parenthood v. Casey*, 505 U.S. 833, 851–52 (1992).

[42] *See Lawrence v. Texas*, 539 U.S. 558, 574 (2003) (citing and quoting *Planned Parenthood v. Casey*, 505 U.S. at 851).

and through corporate and individual prayer; a particular perspective on moral obligations derived from a moral code or from a conception of God's nature; practices involving repentence and forgiveness of sins; "religious" feelings of awe, guilt, and adoration; the use of sacred texts; and organization to facilitate the corporate aspects of religious practice and to promote and perpetuate beliefs and practices.[43]

According to Greenawalt, no one feature is essential to make something religious, but the typical characteristics of religion create a pattern of "family resemblances."[44] Greenawalt further contends that in considering whether beliefs or practices should count as "religious" in doubtful cases, courts should reject "dictionary" approaches in favor of a process of analogical reasoning, "decid[ing] whether something is religious by comparison with the indisputably religious, in light of the particular legal problem involved."[45] As examples of analogical reasoning along these lines, Greenawalt highlights two notable opinions by Judge Arlin Adams of the U.S. Court of Appeals for the Third Circuit. In one, Judge Adams concluded that a public school course on Creative Intelligence and Transcendental Meditation was religious and therefore violated the Establishment Clause.[46] In the other, he rejected—as insufficiently religious—a claim under the Free Exercise Clause by a prisoner who was seeking a diet of raw food based on his membership in MOVE, a loosely structured "revolutionary" organization that espoused various ideas and principles.[47]

The issue of defining religion presents the Supreme Court with a dilemma. A narrow and conventional definition—generally confining religion to theistic beliefs and practices—might be more readily formulated and certainly would permit a more manageable

---

[43] Kent Greenawalt, *Religion as a Concept in Constitutional Law*, 72 CAL. L. REV. 753, 767–68 (1984).

[44] Greenawalt cites the example of philosopher Ludwig Wittgenstein, who advanced a "family resemblances" approach for determining what counts as a "game." *See id.* at 763 & n.47 (citing LUDWIG WITTGENSTEIN, PHILOSOPHICAL INVESTIGATIONS ¶¶ 66–67 (3d ed. 1958)); *cf.* NINIAN SMART, THE WORLD'S RELIGIONS 11, 13 (2d ed. 1998) (rejecting the search for an "essence which is common to all religions" in favor of an identification of various "aspects or dimensions of religion").

[45] Greenawalt, *supra* note 43, at 753; *cf.* George C. Freeman, III, *The Misguided Search for the Constitutional Definition of "Religion"*, 71 GEO. L.J. 1519 (1983) (proposing a similar but distinctive analogical approach).

[46] *Malnak v. Yogi*, 592 F.2d 197, 200–15 (3d Cir. 1979) (Adams, J., concurring in the result); *see* Greenawalt, *supra* note 43, at 774–75.

[47] *Africa v. Commonwealth of Pennsylvania*, 662 F.2d 1025 (3d Cir. 1981) (Adams, J.); *see* Greenawalt, *supra* note 43, at 775–76.

constitutional doctrine.[48] But a much broader definition, along the lines of *Seeger*, or perhaps reflecting an open-ended and generous version of analogical reasoning, might better reflect the evolving values and changing "religious" understandings of the contemporary United States. A partial response to this dilemma is the Court's frequent emphasis on the value of formal equality and on a doctrinal test of nondiscrimination, a test that reduces the significance of the definitional issue. More generally, the Court has managed largely to evade the problem, leaving the issue of definition unsettled and unresolved.

Some scholars have proposed a dual approach that would define religion broadly for the Free Exercise Clause but more narrowly for the Establishment Clause.[49] A unitary conventional definition might work for both clauses, but if one departs from a conventional definition, some type of dual or variable approach might indeed be appropriate. For example, relying on changing values and understandings of the sort described in *Seeger*, one can argue that the contemporary Free Exercise Clause should protect claims of conscience that are not conventionally religious as well as those that are. But the changes discussed in *Seeger* are not necessarily relevant to the Establishment Clause, which serves different functions. Thus, even if religion is defined broadly for the purpose of evaluating legal burdens under the Free Exercise Clause, perhaps the Establishment Clause should limit the award of legal benefits only when the benefitted organizations or practices are conventionally religious. A dual approach along these lines, however, is not without problems. Notably, it stretches the language of the First Amendment, which uses the word "religion" a single time, with reference to both clauses: "Congress shall make no law respecting an establishment of religion, or prohibiting the free exercise thereof."[50] In addition, a dual approach might create an

---

[48] For a proposed definition that would be even more narrow—and that would exclude many conventionally religious beliefs and practices, see Jesse H. Choper, *Defining "Religion" in the First Amendment*, 1982 U. ILL. L. REV. 579 (proposing a definition that would confine religion to concerns about "extemporal consequences," such as life after death).

[49] *See, e.g.,* LAURENCE H. TRIBE, AMERICAN CONSTITUTIONAL LAW § 14–6 (1978) (urging "variable definitions of religion" under the two Religion Clauses, with anything "arguably religious" qualifying under the Free Exercise Clause but anything "arguably non-religious" being excluded from the Establishment Clause); Note, *Toward a Constitutional Definition of Religion*, 91 HARV. L. REV. 1056 (1978) (urging a *Seeger*-like approach for purposes of the Free Exercise Clause but a more narrow definition under the Establishment Clause).

[50] U.S. CONST. amend. I; *see Everson v. Board of Educ.*, 330 U.S. 1, 32 (1947) (Rutledge, J., dissenting) (" 'Thereof' brings down 'religion' with its entire and exact content, no more and no less, from the first into the second guaranty. . . ."); LAURENCE H. TRIBE, AMERICAN CONSTITUTIONAL LAW § 14–6, at 1186 & n.53 (2d ed. 1988) (criticizing the dual-definition approach that Tribe himself had advocated in

unbalanced doctrine that would actually favor unconventional over conventional religion by granting it free exercise protection, but not the offsetting disadvantages that spring from Establishment Clause limitations. The Supreme Court perhaps could finesse these issues by adopting a unitary but flexible *approach* to the concept of religion even as it recognizes, as Professor Greenawalt contends, that "what amounts to religion in one context may not amount to religion in another."[51]

For now, all we can say is that the constitutional definition of religion remains unsettled. It certainly includes conventional religion, as the Founders had assumed it would. It might—or might not—also include a broader set of beliefs and practices that are not conventionally religious, but, if so, this more expansive understanding of religion might be limited to the Free Exercise Clause. In the chapters that follow, we will focus on cases involving conventional, theistic religion, because that is the nature of the cases the Supreme Court has decided. Even so, it is important to remember that the definitional issue lingers, and its lurking presence may influence the content and direction of the Court's doctrine.

IV. The Content and Sincerity of Religious Beliefs: Prohibited and Permissible Judicial Inquiries

The Supreme Court's reluctance to define religion is paired with, and perhaps related to, its longstanding rejection of any judicial power to examine the content of religious beliefs or doctrines in order to determine their truth or reasonableness. The leading case, from 1944, is *United States v. Ballard*.[52] In *Ballard*, members of the "I Am" movement had been charged with mail fraud, based in part on their claims that they were divine messengers of a "Saint Germain" and that they possessed supernatural healing powers. The Court reasoned that the Religion Clauses forbid the government, including the judiciary, from adopting or rejecting any particular religious creed, suggesting that such a governmental declaration would amount to a form of forbidden sectarian discrimination. " 'The law knows no heresy,' " the Court declared, " 'and is committed to the support of no dogma,

---

the first edition of his treatise, noting that "such an approach presents a number of problems, most importantly the first amendment's text").

    51 Greenawalt, *supra* note 43, at 758; *see id.* at 769 (calling for "a unitary method for ascertaining religion" but one that recognizes that the Free Exercise and Establishment Clauses raise distinctive concerns); *cf.* TRIBE, *supra* note 50, § 14–6, at 1186 (noting that even if the word "religion" has a single meaning under the First Amendment, the words "free exercise" and "establishment" do not).

    52 322 U.S. 78 (1944).

the establishment of no sect.' "[53] Thus, the Court ruled that in deciding the issue of fraud, the jury could not be instructed to decide the truth or falsity of the defendants' religious assertions, however "incredible" or "preposterous" they might seem. Citing more common religious beliefs, including beliefs about Biblical miracles, the divinity of Christ, life after death, and the power of prayer, the Court noted that "[m]en may believe what they cannot prove" and "may not be put to the proof of their religious doctrines or beliefs."[54]

The Supreme Court reaffirmed and extended this principle in its 1981 decision in *Thomas v. Review Board*,[55] a case arising under the Free Exercise Clause, stating that "religious beliefs need not be acceptable, logical, consistent, or comprehensible to others in order to merit First Amendment protection."[56] In *Thomas*, a Jehovah's Witness named Eddie Thomas accepted employment in a foundry, fabricating sheet steel for various uses. But Thomas objected when he was transferred to a department that made turrets for military tanks. The Court ruled that Thomas was free to decide for himself, without judicial second-guessing, that his religion precluded this direct involvement in the manufacture of weapons even though it permitted more indirect involvement, including the making of sheet steel that might in turn be used to make weapons. It did not matter that others, including other Jehovah's Witnesses, might think Thomas's religious understanding incorrect or difficult to justify.[57] "Thomas drew a line," the Court stated, "and it is not for us to say that the line he drew was an unreasonable one."[58]

The Supreme Court has stated that the judiciary should avoid inquiries not only into the truth or reasonableness of religious beliefs, but also into their importance or "centrality" for the religious believer or religious group. In the context of property disputes within or between religious groups or denominations, for

---

[53] *Id.* at 86 (quoting *Watson v. Jones*, 80 U.S. (13 Wall.) 679, 728 (1872)).

[54] *Id.* at 86–87.

[55] 450 U.S. 707 (1981).

[56] *Id.* at 714.

[57] The Court reiterated this principle in *Holt v. Hobbs*, 135 S. Ct. 853 (2015), a case decided under a religious liberty statute, the Religious Land Use and Institutionalized Persons Act of 2000 (RLUIPA), 42 U.S.C. §§ 2000cc to 2000cc–5. In *Holt*, the Court ruled that RLUIPA protected the right of a Muslim prisoner to wear a beard, even if other Muslims might not share his view of what Islam requires, because "the protection of RLUIPA, no less than the guarantee of the Free Exercise Clause, is 'not limited to beliefs which are shared by all of the members of a religious sect.' " *Id.* at 862–63 (quoting *Thomas*, 450 U.S. at 715–16). We will discuss RLUIPA in Chapter 6.

[58] *Thomas*, 450 U.S. at 715. Thomas quit his job rather than work in the direct production of weapons. Relying on the Free Exercise Clause and citing Thomas's religious reasoning, the Court ruled that he could not be denied unemployment compensation.

example, courts can utilize "neutral principles of law, developed for use in all property disputes," but cannot interpret "particular church doctrines and the importance of those doctrines to the religion."[59] More generally, the Court has declared that "[i]t is not within the judicial ken to question the centrality of particular beliefs or practices to a faith, or the validity of particular litigants' interpretations of those creeds."[60]

In its 2014 decision in *Burwell v. Hobby Lobby Stores, Inc.*,[61] the Court relied upon these principles in extending religious liberty protection—in this instance, under the Religious Freedom Restoration Act of 1993 (RFRA)[62]—to Hobby Lobby and other employers who objected on religious grounds to provisions of the Affordable Care Act of 2010 (ACA) and related regulations. The ACA, as implemented by the Department of Health and Human Services (HHS), required the employers to provide their employees with insurance coverage for various contraceptives. The employers objected to providing coverage for four particular forms of contraception—two types of intrauterine devices (IUDs) and two types of "morning-after pills"—that the employers found morally objectionable because they could operate after fertilization, thus resulting in the destruction of human embryos. *Hobby Lobby* is an important interpretation of RFRA, which we will consider in Chapter 6. But the case deserves attention here because it strongly reaffirms, and arguably extends, the Court's refusal to evaluate religious claims.

RFRA provides protection from federal laws such as the ACA, but only if they "substantially burden" the exercise of religion.[63] Focusing on this provision of RFRA, the government argued that the ACA's contraceptive coverage requirement did not impose a "substantial burden," thus precluding the employers' RFRA claims. It argued—and Justice Ginsburg agreed in her dissenting opinion—that the connection between the ACA's insurance coverage requirement and the potential destruction of an embryo was simply too attenuated to give rise to a "substantial burden" on the

---

[59] *Presbyterian Church in the United States v. Mary Elizabeth Blue Hull Memorial Presbyterian Church*, 393 U.S. 440, 449–50 (1969); *see also Jones v. Wolf*, 443 U.S. 595 (1979). We will discuss church property disputes in Chapter 5.

[60] *Hernandez v. Commissioner*, 490 U.S. 680, 699 (1989); *see also Employment Div. v. Smith*, 494 U.S. 872, 887 (1990) ("Judging the centrality of different religious practices is akin to the unacceptable 'business of evaluating the relative merits of differing religious claims.'") (quoting *United States v. Lee*, 455 U.S. 252, 263 n.2 (1982) (Stevens, J., concurring in the judgment)).

[61] 134 S. Ct. 2751 (2014).

[62] 42 U.S.C. §§ 2000bb to 2000bb–4.

[63] *Id.* § 2000bb–1(a).

employers' religious freedom. Relying on *Thomas* and other precedents, the Supreme Court rejected the government's position.

Although the government had couched its argument in the language of "substantial burden," the Court stated that the argument in fact addressed "a very different question that the federal courts have no business addressing," that is, "whether the religious belief asserted in a RFRA case is reasonable."[64] The Court elaborated, explaining the employers' religious understanding of impermissible complicity:

> The [employers] believe that providing the coverage demanded by the HHS regulations is connected to the destruction of an embryo in a way that is sufficient to make it immoral for them to provide the coverage. This belief implicates a difficult and important question of religion and moral philosophy, namely, the circumstances under which it is wrong for a person to perform an act that is innocent in itself but that has the effect of enabling or facilitating the commission of an immoral act by another. Arrogating the authority to provide a binding national answer to this religious and philosophical question, HHS and the principal dissent in effect tell the plaintiffs that their beliefs are flawed. For good reason, we have repeatedly refused to take such a step.[65]

As in *Thomas*, the Court stated, the religious objectors in *Hobby Lobby* drew a line. They "believe that providing the insurance coverage demanded by the HHS regulations lies on the forbidden side of the line, and it is not for us to say that their religious beliefs are mistaken or insubstantial."[66]

Under *Ballard, Thomas, Hobby Lobby*, and similar precedents, the judiciary cannot second-guess the truth, reasonableness, or centrality of religious beliefs, not even if the beliefs in question relate to claims of impermissible complicity. By contrast, the Supreme Court has indicated that courts are free to evaluate the *sincerity* of religious assertions. In *Ballard*, for instance, the Court ruled that in determining the question of fraud, the jury could not address the truth of the defendants' religious claims, but it could consider whether the defendants *sincerely believed* their own statements to be true. Likewise, in *Thomas,* the Court noted that the Free Exercise Clause is properly limited to "honest

---

[64]   134 S. Ct. at 2778.

[65]   *Id.* (footnote omitted).

[66]   *Id.* at 2779.

conviction[s]."[67] The same limitation applies to RFRA claims, but this was not an issue in *Hobby Lobby*, because the employers' religious objections to the ACA were concededly sincere.

The risk of insincere religious claims is significant, especially when there are nonreligious incentives for making a "religious" assertion. Consider, for example, a prisoner who claims that his religion requires a diet of sirloin steak and lobster. Without a requirement of judicially tested sincerity, dishonest religious claims, including fraudulent claims for protection under the Free Exercise Clause or RFRA, potentially could be asserted at will.

In lower court decisions, failure to satisfy the requirement of sincerity sometimes has been the basis for denying religious liberty claims. In the early 1990s, for example, a colorful case arose from the prosecution of a husband and wife for pimping and prostitution. The couple asserted a free exercise defense, claiming to be the "high priest" and "high priestess" of the "Church of the Most High Goddess," which worshiped Isis, the ancient Egyptian goddess of fertility. The church's religious practice, they claimed, called for the wife and other "priestesses" to have sex with multiple partners in exchange for "sacrifices" in the form of monetary payments. But a federal district court ruled that the couple's asserted religious beliefs were not sincere, and the U.S. Court of Appeals for the Ninth Circuit affirmed.[68] Likewise, in a more recent decision, the U.S. Court of Appeals for the Tenth Circuit upheld a district court finding of insincerity in rejecting a RFRA defense to drug charges.[69] The defendants claimed that the "Church of Cognizance," which one of them had founded, regarded marijuana as a deity and sacrament. But the Tenth Circuit cited "overwhelming ... evidence that the [defendants] were running a commercial marijuana business with a religious front."[70]

Although the requirement of sincerity serves the important purpose of precluding fraudulent claims, the inquiry into sincerity is problematic, because it is difficult to cabin: how is a court or jury to evaluate sincerity without considering the underlying content of the religious claim and whether the claim seems true, or at least reasonable enough to be sincerely believed? As Justice Jackson wrote in his dissenting opinion in *Ballard*, "I do not see how we can separate an issue as to what is believed from considerations as to

---

[67] *Thomas v. Review Bd.*, 450 U.S. 707, 716 (1981).
[68] *See Tracy v. Hahn*, 1991 U.S. App. LEXIS 18437 (9th Cir. 1991); *Judge Weighing Claims of a Religion Based on Sex*, N.Y. TIMES, May 2, 1990, at A11.
[69] *United States v. Quaintance*, 608 F.3d 717 (10th Cir. 2010).
[70] *Id.* at 724.

what is believable."[71] As Jackson's observation suggests, a test of sincerity almost inevitably favors the familiar beliefs of traditional and mainstream religions over the unorthodox views of new and unusual ones.

This risk of improper favoritism is substantial, but courts have been sensitive to the problem. Courts generally are reluctant to dispute the sincerity of religious claims, and, as a result, findings of insincerity are not common. The risk of favoritism also is mitigated by the contemporary Supreme Court's emphasis, in many settings, on the value of formal equality implemented through a doctrinal test of nondiscrimination. That approach limits the significance of the sincerity issue by minimizing special treatment for religion, whether sincere or otherwise. Even so, the question of sincerity continues to arise when religion is accorded special protection, for example, under RFRA and other religious liberty statutes.

V. Doctrinal Fundamentals and Doctrinal Elaborations

This chapter has highlighted general concepts and principles under the Religion Clauses. Even at this general level, we have seen a doctrine that is unsettled and problematic. But despite the uncertainties and problems, our discussion of doctrinal fundamentals provides a framework that will help inform our more specific doctrinal inquiries. In the following chapters, we will build upon this framework as we examine, in turn, the Supreme Court's decisionmaking under the Free Exercise Clause and the Establishment Clause.

---

[71] *United States v. Ballard*, 322 U.S. 78, 92 (1944) (Jackson, J., dissenting).

Chapter 5

FREE EXERCISE AND FREE SPEECH: FIRST AMENDMENT PROTECTION

The Free Exercise Clause, originally directed to Congress and later extended to the states, precludes the government from "prohibiting the free exercise" of religion. We have already discussed, in Chapter 4, the conundrum of defining religion. But even assuming a conventional or other agreed definition of religion, what constitutes "the free exercise" of religion, and what constitutes a law that unconstitutionally "prohibits" it?

As discussed in Chapter 3, the Religion Clauses can be understood to protect a variety of constitutional values. First and foremost is the value of religious voluntarism, the freedom of individuals to make religious choices for themselves, free from governmental compulsion or inappropriate influence. A robust interpretation of the Free Exercise Clause surely would honor and build upon this value. Extended to organizational behavior, a strong interpretation also would protect a related but distinct constitutional value, the autonomy of religious institutions. In addition, a vigorous free exercise doctrine would respect the religious identity of individuals and would permit religion to flourish in the private domain, free from the contaminating effects of governmental authority. It also would serve the value of religious equality, but not necessarily in the sense of formal equality and not to the exclusion of other values.

As we will see, however, the Supreme Court in recent years has rejected a robust interpretation of the Free Exercise Clause, favoring instead a far more minimal view. In so doing, the Court has emphasized the value of formal equality and has given only limited weight to religious voluntarism and other constitutional values. But the picture in reality is more complex, because in certain contexts the free exercise of religion continues to garner protection, and, indeed, this protection sometimes is quite vigorous.

The free exercise of religion derives some protection from the First Amendment, and it derives additional protection from religious liberty statutes and state constitutional law. Under the First Amendment, the Supreme Court, relying mainly on the Free Speech Clause, has afforded considerable constitutional protection to religious *speech*, thus protecting the value of religious free speech, a form of expressive and religious liberty. In addition, the

Court's interpretation of the Free Exercise Clause, although generally restrictive, has not always precluded free exercise claims. For example, the Justices have continued to protect the internal decisionmaking and governance of religious organizations, thus honoring the value of institutional autonomy. In general, however, religious claimants under the Free Exercise Clause have been denied protection except in rare circumstances, when the government actually targets religion for discriminatory disadvantage. But this restrictive approach to constitutional claims has given rise to notable developments both legislatively and in state constitutional law. These important developments offer free exercise protection that can be seen to serve First Amendment values but that does not flow from the First Amendment as such. We will discuss these alternative sources of free exercise protection in Chapter 6; in the current chapter, we will focus on the First Amendment itself.

In our discussion of the Court's First Amendment doctrine, we will first examine the protection of religious beliefs and the freedom to express them through religious speech. We will then consider what sorts of conduct, beyond speech, might also warrant protection as the "exercise" of religion, and we will discuss the types of laws or governmental action affecting religion that might constitute "prohibiting the free exercise thereof." We will address governmental burdens on religious conduct, including burdens that discriminate against religion and those that do not. Discriminatory burdens, although rare, generally are unconstitutional. By contrast, under current constitutional doctrine, nondiscriminatory burdens generally are not impermissible and, indeed, they normally do not even raise a free exercise issue. These general principles are subject to exceptions, caveats, and complications, which we will explore.

I.   Freedom of Belief

The Supreme Court has held that freedom of religious *belief* is absolutely protected by the Free Exercise Clause and that this absolute protection extends to disbelief as well, meaning that the Clause to this extent shelters religion and irreligion alike. Here, the value of religious voluntarism is paramount and controlling, and it is implemented through a doctrinal principle that precludes the government from mandating, prohibiting, or regulating religious or irreligious beliefs as such.

The Supreme Court articulated and relied upon this principle in its 1961 decision in *Torcaso v. Watkins.*[1] The State of Maryland had precluded Roy Torcaso from taking office as a notary public

---

[1]   367 U.S. 488 (1961).

because he would not declare his belief in God, as required by the Maryland Constitution. The Court ruled that the Maryland constitutional provision violated the First Amendment and, more broadly, that the First Amendment categorically precludes religious oath requirements for state office holders. Notably, Article VI of the original Constitution explicitly bans such religious tests, but only for *federal* offices.[2] According to *Torcaso*, however, the Free Exercise Clause, incorporated through the Fourteenth Amendment, extends the same prohibition to the states and, more generally, forbids mandatory religious oaths of any sort. "[N]either a State nor the Federal Government," wrote the Court, "can constitutionally force a person 'to profess a belief or disbelief in any religion.' "[3]

As *Torcaso* suggests, the Free Exercise Clause protects not only the right to hold religious or irreligious beliefs, but also the right to declare them or to refuse to do so. These rights are basic and important. Needless to say, religious liberty would be impoverished if we did not protect religious belief, religious disbelief, and the profession or denial of either. Yet freedom of belief, however fundamental, is rarely an issue. As a practical matter, it is virtually impossible—in the absence of incredibly coercive and intrusive means—to control the inner thoughts that people hold, and, thankfully, our contemporary government is not inclined to make the effort. To be sure, as the oath requirement in *Torcaso* attests, the open expression of religious or irreligious beliefs is more readily subject to governmental regulation or control. But because the First Amendment independently protects freedom of speech, it is not clear that the Free Exercise Clause is needed to prevent the government from mandating or precluding religious or irreligious speech. For that matter, the Clause is not necessarily essential, even in theory, for the protection of internal belief. Without regard to the Free Exercise Clause, freedom of speech protects the right to hold and express beliefs and to refuse to express contrary views, whether religious or otherwise. Free speech doctrine in fact provides important protection for religious speech, as the following discussion will explain. Because free speech does most of the work, however, the Free Exercise Clause has limited significance in this context.

---

[2]   Article VI provides that "no religious Test shall ever be required as a Qualification to any Office or public Trust under the United States." U.S. CONST. art. VI, cl. 3.

[3]   *Torcaso*, 367 U.S. at 495 (quoting *Everson v. Board of Educ.*, 330 U.S. 1, 15 (1947)). As support for its ruling, the Court cited not merely the Free Exercise Clause but the First Amendment generally, including the Establishment Clause.

II. Freedom of Religious Speech

Freedom of religious speech is a fundamental component of religious liberty in the United States. This constitutional protection springs mainly from the First Amendment's Free Speech Clause,[4] but the Free Exercise Clause may play an indirect role. As *Torcaso* implies, religious speech is not just speech, but also the exercise of religion. Its dual constitutional status may support the favored position of religious speech under free speech doctrine, as well as the Supreme Court's strong protection of such speech from discriminatory treatment.

Free speech doctrine protects not only religiously motivated speech on political and social issues but religious speech pure and simple, including prayer and religious worship. Thus, private religious speech of any sort is regarded as fully protected, high-value speech under the First Amendment, subject only to the same free speech tests and analyses that apply to core political speech.[5] As noted in Chapter 3, this doctrine honors the value of religious free speech, not only as an aspect of religious liberty but also as a component of freedom of expression more broadly understood. Like other important speech, religious speech reflects and manifests fundamental personal beliefs[6] even as it addresses, directly or indirectly, matters of broad societal interest. Accordingly, it is not surprising that the Supreme Court has said that "private religious speech, far from being a First Amendment orphan, is as fully protected under the Free Speech Clause as secular private expression" and that "a free-speech clause without religion would be Hamlet without the prince."[7]

A. Compelled Speech

Recognizing that freedom of belief lies at the core of the First Amendment, the Supreme Court has ruled that freedom of speech

---

[4] The Free Speech Clause provides that "Congress shall make no law . . . abridging the freedom of speech." U.S. CONST. amend. I. This clause is joined by related provisions protecting freedom of the press, the right of assembly, and the right "to petition the Government for a redress of grievances." *Id.* Like the Free Speech Clause, these related provisions extend to expressive activities that are religious as well as secular. The Free Speech Clause and these other provisions, moreover, have been "incorporated" through the Fourteenth Amendment, so they apply not only to the federal government but also to the states. *See, e.g., Edwards v. South Carolina,* 372 U.S. 229, 235 (1963); *Near v. Minnesota,* 283 U.S. 697, 707 (1931).

[5] *See, e.g., Widmar v. Vincent,* 454 U.S. 263, 269 (1981); *Capitol Square Review & Advisory Bd. v. Pinette,* 515 U.S. 753, 760 (1995).

[6] *See* Steven D. Smith, *Believing Persons, Personal Believings: The Neglected Center of the First Amendment,* 2002 U. ILL. L. REV. 1233, 1311.

[7] *Capitol Square Review & Advisory Bd.,* 515 U.S. at 760.

protects not only the right to speak, but also the right to refrain from speaking. Accordingly, the First Amendment generally forbids the government from forcing citizens to express messages or opinions with which they disagree. This protection against compelled speech extends to religious objectors, among others, thus protecting their religious beliefs and values. In its landmark 1943 decision in *West Virginia State Board of Education v. Barnette*,[8] for example, the Supreme Court—overruling a contrary decision of just three years before[9]—held that public schools could not require school children to salute the American flag and to recite the Pledge of Allegiance.[10] Notably, the successful challengers were Jehovah's Witnesses, who, resisting fervent wartime patriotism and persecution,[11] insisted that participation in the pledge would violate the Biblical prohibition on worshiping "graven images."[12] In often-quoted language, Justice Jackson's eloquent opinion for the Court declared that "no official, high or petty, can prescribe what shall be orthodox in politics, nationalism, religion, or other matters of opinion or force citizens to confess by word or act their faith therein."[13] Decades later, the Court reaffirmed this principle in *Wooley v. Maynard*,[14] ruling that the State of New Hampshire could not require objecting citizens to display the state's motto, "Live Free or Die," on their automobile license plates. The successful challengers once again were Jehovah's Witnesses, who objected to the motto on religious and political grounds.

The First Amendment's prohibition on compelled speech is important, offering protection to religious as well as nonreligious objectors. But this prohibition has a limited reach and is not often

---

[8]   319 U.S. 624 (1943).

[9]   *Minersville Sch. Dist. v. Gobitis*, 310 U.S. 586 (1940).

[10]   At that time, the Pledge of Allegiance did not refer to God. Instead, it read as follows: "I pledge allegiance to the Flag of the United States of America and to the Republic for which it stands; one Nation, indivisible, with liberty and justice for all." *Barnette*, 319 U.S. at 628–29.

[11]   Across the country, Jehovah's Witnesses had been subjected to hostility and violence for refusing to participate in the pledge, a stance that critics had reviled as disloyal. *See* Vincent Blasi & Seana V. Shriffin, *The Story of* West Virginia State Board of Education v. Barnette: *The Pledge of Allegiance and the Freedom of Thought, in* FIRST AMENDMENT STORIES 99, 109–12 (Richard W. Garnett & Andrew Koppelman eds., 2012).

[12]   The Court explained: "Their religious beliefs include a literal version of Exodus, Chapter 20, verses 4 and 5, which says: 'Thou shalt not make unto thee any graven image, or any likeness of anything that is in heaven above, or that is in the earth beneath, or that is in the water under the earth; thou shalt not bow down thyself to them nor serve them.' They consider that the flag is an 'image' within this command." *Id.* at 629.

[13]   *Id.* at 642.

[14]   430 U.S. 705 (1977).

implicated.[15] Far more frequently, governmental action is challenged not for compelling speech but for restricting it, sometimes because of its content and sometimes for other reasons.

B. Content-Neutral Regulation; Enhanced Protection in "Traditional Public Forums"

The Free Speech Clause provides only limited protection against the content-neutral regulation of speech, regardless of whether the speech is religious. Under prevailing Supreme Court doctrine, content-neutral laws—laws that restrict speech without regard to its particular message or subject matter—are subject to First Amendment review, but they typically are evaluated under a relatively lenient balancing test. Under this test, the government is free to engage in content-neutral regulation if the regulation is "narrowly tailored to serve a significant governmental interest,"[16] a test that is satisfied as long as the government's interest is "sufficiently substantial" and the restriction on expression is not "substantially broader than necessary" to protect that governmental interest.[17] Thus, the government is permitted to restrict speech, within limits, in order to further content-neutral interests such as traffic safety, esthetics, or the prevention of unreasonable noise. In *Members of City Council v. Taxpayers for Vincent*, for example, the Court upheld a content-neutral Los Angeles code provision that prohibited the posting of signs on public property, including utility poles, even as applied to political campaign signs. The Court found that the prohibition was justified by the city's esthetic interest in avoiding visual clutter.[18]

Under this constitutional test, the government has considerable room to regulate the time, place, or manner of expression, for instance, by imposing content-neutral restrictions on the size or location of billboards[19] or by prohibiting excessive

---

[15] In a well-publicized recent case, the Christian owners of a photography business, who had declined on religious grounds to photograph a same-sex wedding ceremony, unsuccessfully invoked the First Amendment's prohibition on compelled speech in resisting a discrimination claim under New Mexico's public accommodations law. According to the New Mexico Supreme Court, the First Amendment in this setting required only that the company remain free to express its opposition to same-sex marriage in other ways. *See Elane Photography, LLC v. Willock*, 309 P.3d 53, 63–72 (N.M. 2013).

[16] *Clark v. Community for Creative Non-Violence*, 468 U.S. 288, 293 (1984).

[17] *Members of City Council v. Taxpayers for Vincent*, 466 U.S. 789, 805, 808 (1984); *see also Ward v. Rock Against Racism*, 491 U.S. 781, 798 (1989) ("a regulation of the time, place, or manner of protected speech must be narrowly tailored to serve the government's legitimate, content-neutral interests but . . . it need not be the least restrictive or least intrusive means of doing so").

[18] *See Taxpayers for Vincent*, 466 U.S. at 805–17.

[19] *See id.* at 806–07 (suggesting that the First Amendment would permit even a complete prohibition on billboards, as long as the prohibition was content-neutral).

noise.[20] As long as such laws are not unduly restrictive, they are likely to be upheld. And if they indeed are constitutionally valid under this relatively undemanding inquiry, they properly can be applied not only to secular political speech, as in *Taxpayers for Vincent*, but also to political or other speech that is religiously motivated or to religious speech pure and simple. For example, content-neutral billboard restrictions could be applied to religious billboards, and noise regulations could be applied to religiously motivated demonstrations addressing political or social issues.

In certain contexts, however, the Supreme Court has applied a more vigorous version of the balancing test, leading to the invalidation of content-neutral laws. In particular, the Court sometimes has afforded special protection to speech that takes place in a "traditional public forum," a category of governmental property that generally includes public streets, sidewalks, and parks. This special protection is justified in part on the basis of history and tradition. As Justice Roberts noted in a much-cited 1939 opinion, "streets and parks . . . have immemorially been held in trust for the use of the public and, time out of mind, have been used for purposes of assembly, communicating thoughts between citizens, and discussing public questions," thus making freedom of expression in these places "a part of the privileges, immunities, rights, and liberties of citizens."[21] Accordingly, as the Court has stated more recently, "Traditional public forum property occupies a special position in terms of First Amendment protection."[22]

Speech in a traditional public forum is not immune from content-neutral regulation, as long as the government can satisfy the Supreme Court's balancing test. In this setting, however, the Court often gives enhanced protection to freedom of speech, essentially placing a "thumb" on the First Amendment side of the scale.[23] As a result, content-neutral restrictions on speech in a traditional public forum are more likely to be invalidated.[24] The Supreme Court has extended a similar approach to regulations of door-to-door canvassing, which, like speech in a traditional public

---

[20] *See Kovacs v. Cooper*, 336 U.S. 77 (1949) (upholding a Trenton, New Jersey, ordinance that prohibited "loud and raucous" sound trucks); *Ward*, 491 U.S. 781 (upholding a New York City regulation mandating the use of city-provided sound systems and technicians to control the volume of Central Park concerts).

[21] *Hague v. CIO*, 307 U.S. 496, 515 (1939) (opinion of Roberts, J.).

[22] *United States v. Grace*, 461 U.S. 171, 180 (1983); *see also id.* at 177 (suggesting that the government's power to restrict expression in a traditional public forum is "very limited").

[23] *See* Harry Kalven, Jr., *The Concept of the Public Forum: Cox v. Louisiana*, 1965 SUP. CT. REV. 1, 28.

[24] *See, e.g., Grace*, 461 U.S. 171 (invalidating a prohibition on picketing and leafleting on the public sidewalks surrounding the United States Supreme Court).

forum, the Court also regards as a time-honored and valuable method of communication.

On occasion, this sort of reasoning has been used to protect religious and religiously motivated speech even from content-neutral laws. In *Watchtower Bible & Tract Society of New York, Inc. v. Village of Stratton*,[25] for example, Jehovah's Witnesses—who believe that the Bible commands them to proselytize from house to house[26]—successfully challenged a content-neutral permit requirement for door-to-door canvassing. Noting "the historical importance of door-to-door canvassing and pamphleteering as vehicles for the dissemination of ideas,"[27] the Supreme Court followed earlier precedents, many of them also involving Jehovah's Witnesses, that had invalidated various restrictions on this sort of door-to-door expressive activity.

Likewise, in a series of recent cases, the Court has relied in part on its traditional public forum doctrine in addressing anti-abortion protests, which often include religious and religiously motivated speech. These cases have considered statutes and judicially imposed injunctions that restrict speech on public streets and sidewalks, for example, by barring protesters from designated buffer zones around abortion clinics. Over the objection of some Justices, the Court typically has treated the challenged statutes and injunctions as content-neutral, and it has upheld some restrictions on the ground that they properly serve substantial interests, such as protecting access to the clinics and preventing excessive noise.[28] Even so, the Court has applied its content-neutral balancing test with greater-than-usual vigor in this setting, leading it to invalidate other restrictions. For instance, in the most recent case in this series, *McCullen v. Coakley*,[29] the Court struck down a Massachusetts statute that had created a 35-foot buffer zone around the entrances and driveways of abortion-providing facilities.

---

[25] 536 U.S. 150 (2002).

[26] As the Supreme Court explained, "the Jehovah's Witnesses 'claim to follow the example of Paul, teaching "publickly, and from house to house." Acts 20:20. They take literally the mandate of the Scriptures, "Go ye into all the world, and preach the gospel to every creature." Mark 16:15.' " *Id.* at 161 (quoting *Murdock v. Pennsylvania*, 319 U.S. 105, 108 (1943)).

[27] *Id.* at 162.

[28] *See, e.g., Madsen v. Women's Health Center, Inc.*, 512 U.S. 753 (1994) (selectively upholding certain portions of a state-court injunction, including a 36-foot buffer zone around an abortion clinic's entrances and driveway as well as a noise restriction, based in part on the particular facts of the case under review); *Hill v. Colorado*, 530 U.S. 703 (2000) (upholding a statute, applicable in the vicinity of health care facilities, that barred protestors from knowingly approaching within eight feet of another person, including a woman entering an abortion clinic, unless the person consented to be approached).

[29] 134 S. Ct. 2518 (2014).

Emphasizing the important role of expression in a traditional public forum, the Court found that the law, although content-neutral, unduly restricted speech, especially one-on-one communication between pro-life "sidewalk counselors" and women who might be seeking abortions. In so ruling, the Court emphasized that this was speech "about an important subject on the public streets and sidewalks—sites that have hosted discussions about the issues of the day throughout history."[30]

C. Content-Based Regulation and the Equal Access Doctrine

Within or outside the setting of a traditional public forum, free speech doctrine strongly disfavors content-based regulation and especially viewpoint-based discrimination. In most contexts, it is unconstitutional for the government to engage in content-based regulation, that is, regulation that targets speech because of its message or subject matter.[31] Such regulation typically can be justified only if it is "necessary" to serve a "compelling" governmental interest, a test of "strict scrutiny" that is extremely difficult for the government to satisfy.[32] This general prohibition on content-based regulation extends to the regulation of religious and religiously motivated speech. And the prohibition applies no matter how offensive or distasteful the expression might seem.[33]

Notably, moreover, governmental action that formally or deliberately discriminates against religious speech generally is treated as not only content-based, but also viewpoint-based. As a matter of free speech doctrine, a finding of viewpoint discrimination triggers strict scrutiny of not only regulatory penalties, but also governmental attempts to selectively deny religious speakers access to public property that serves as a forum for private expression— whether or not the forum is a traditional public forum. Thus, the presumptive prohibition on viewpoint discrimination extends to so-

---

[30] *Id.* at 2541. The Justices were unanimous in finding the statute unconstitutional, but they were divided in their reasoning. The majority opinion, by Chief Justice Roberts, was joined by five Justices. The other four Justices argued that the law was content-based, not content-neutral, and that the law plainly could not survive the strict judicial scrutiny that such laws demand. *See id.* at 2541–49 (Scalia, J., joined by Kennedy and Thomas, JJ., concurring in the judgment); *id.* at 2549–50 (Alito, J., concurring in the judgment).

[31] *See Reed v. Town of Gilbert,* 135 S. Ct. 2218, 2226–27 (2015).

[32] *See Brown v. Entertainment Merchants Ass'n,* 131 S. Ct. 2729, 2738 (2011).

[33] *See, e.g., Cantwell v. Connecticut,* 310 U.S. 296 (1940) (protecting evangelism by Jehovah's Witnesses in a heavily Roman Catholic neighborhood even though their appeals included strongly worded attacks on the Catholic religion); *Snyder v. Phelps,* 131 S. Ct. 1207 (2011) (protecting viciously anti-gay, anti-Catholic, and other vitriolic speech by members of the Westboro Baptist Church during a protest they staged near the funeral of a fallen Marine).

called "nonpublic forums" or "limited public forums," such as governmental meeting rooms that are made available to private speakers. In this particular corner of free speech doctrine, the government is free to impose reasonable content-based restrictions if they depend on the subject matter of the speech. For example, a school board is free to restrict its public comment period to school-board business and accordingly can exclude speakers who wish to discuss other topics, such as income tax reform or international terrorism. But the general prohibition on viewpoint discrimination remains in place; the school board could not welcome speakers who support the board's current curriculum but exclude those who oppose it.[34]

One could argue that rules or policies excluding religious speech from nonpublic or limited public forums depend on the subject matter of the speech, not its particular viewpoint. If this argument were accepted, then such exclusions would not require strict scrutiny under the Free Speech Clause. In a series of cases, however, the Supreme Court instead has treated such exclusions as viewpoint-based, finding that they disfavor religious as opposed to secular perspectives. As a result, the Court has invoked strict scrutiny, and it has concluded that the exclusions cannot survive that review.

In these "equal access" cases, the religious claimants have challenged policies permitting the after-hours use of public buildings by secular groups or for secular purposes, but expressly precluding such use by religious groups or for religious purposes. The claimants rely on free speech, typically asserting viewpoint discrimination. The government denies it, but goes on to argue that even if there were a presumptive violation of free speech, the Establishment Clause would preclude the requested access to the public property. Honoring the Establishment Clause by excluding the religious speakers, the government contends, serves a compelling interest that satisfies free speech doctrine even if strict scrutiny is required.

---

[34] This basic free speech framework for analyzing claims of access to public property was formulated in *Perry Education Ass'n v. Perry Local Educators' Ass'n*, 460 U.S. 37 (1983). *See id.* at 45–46 & n.7. In *Perry*, the Supreme Court suggested that there is a distinction between "nonpublic forums" and "limited public forums," but the Court increasingly has used this terminology interchangeably. In any event, in either a nonpublic forum or a limited public forum, the government is free to make reasonable distinctions on the basis of subject matter, but not on the basis of viewpoint. (In either setting, as long as it avoids viewpoint discrimination, the government also is free to make reasonable distinctions based on speaker identification. For example, a public university could limit the after-hours use of its classrooms to faculty and student groups, as opposed to community groups not connected to the university.)

Ruling in favor of the religious claimants, the Supreme Court has accepted the claimants' free speech argument and rejected the government's Establishment Clause defense, essentially by finding that the government's fear of breaching the Establishment Clause is misplaced because equal access for religious and secular speech would not be a violation. The Court's Establishment Clause reasoning in these cases is important and controversial, and it is a topic to which we will return in Chapter 8. For now, it is sufficient to highlight some of the Court's free speech rulings, which have broadly protected private religious speech from discriminatory exclusions from governmental property.

In *Widmar v. Vincent*,[35] the first case in this series, the Court ruled that a state university, which generally permitted student groups to use its facilities for meetings, could not exclude religious student groups under a policy banning the use of university property "for purposes of religious worship or religious teaching."[36] As Justice Stevens explained in his separate opinion, the university's policy discriminated on the basis of viewpoint by permitting university facilities to be used to discuss religious skepticism or hostility to religion but not "to express a belief in God."[37] Likewise, in *Lamb's Chapel v. Center Moriches Union Free School District*,[38] the Justices ruled that a public school district, having opened its facilities for after-hours use by a variety of community groups, could not prevent a church and its pastor from using school facilities for a film series promoting Christian family values. The Court found the exclusion viewpoint-based because the school district "permit[ted] school property to be used for the presentation of all views about family issues and child rearing except those dealing with the subject matter from a religious standpoint."[39]

Using similar reasoning, the Court has extended its equal access doctrine to after-school religious meetings at public schools, including meetings for young students. In *Good News Club v. Milford Central School*,[40] the Good News Club, a Christian organization, sought to hold meetings for elementary school

---

[35]   454 U.S. 263 (1981).

[36]   *Id.* at 265.

[37]   *Id.* at 281 (Stevens, J., concurring in the judgment); *see id.* at 280–81. The majority opinion in *Widmar* found a free speech violation without concluding that the university's content-based policy was viewpoint-based, but Justice Stevens' analysis, finding illicit viewpoint discrimination, is more in keeping with the analysis of all of the cases that followed.

[38]   508 U.S. 384 (1993).

[39]   *Id.* at 393.

[40]   533 U.S. 98 (2001).

students immediately after school, meetings at which the students would sing songs, hear Bible lessons, memorize scripture, and pray. The school denied the Club's request, citing a policy that permitted privately sponsored after-school meetings for various purposes, including morals and character education for children, but that prohibited the use of school facilities for religious purposes. According to the Court, the Club was excluded from the school because it sought to teach children morals and character from a religious perspective, in part through the use of prayer and religious instruction. As a result, the school's policy, as applied to the proposed meetings, constituted impermissible viewpoint discrimination and violated freedom of speech.[41]

Moving beyond physical facilities, the Supreme Court also has applied its equal access reasoning to public property in the form of financial support. Thus, in *Rosenberger v. Rector and Visitors of the University of Virginia*,[42] the Justices held that the University of Virginia could not deny "student activities" funding for a student group's religious publication, "Wide Awake: A Christian Perspective at the University of Virginia." The Court found that the university, by funding a variety of student groups and publications, had created a forum for expression, albeit "a forum more in a metaphysical than in a spatial or geographic sense."[43] And the challenged university policy, barring funding for any publication that "primarily promotes or manifests a particular belie[f] in or about a deity or an ultimate reality,"[44] violated the Free Speech Clause by discriminating on the basis of viewpoint. As the Court observed, the policy "select[ed] for disfavored treatment those student journalistic efforts with religious editorial viewpoints."[45] It

---

[41] Following the Supreme Court's 1981 decision in *Widmar*, addressing equal access in the context of public universities, Congress extended the equal access principle to public secondary schools by statute, through the Equal Access Act of 1984, 20 U.S.C. §§ 4071–4074. The Supreme Court later upheld the Act against an Establishment Clause challenge. *See Board of Educ. of Westside Community Schools v. Mergens*, 496 U.S. 226 (1990). At least after *Good News Club*, however, it seems that the Equal Access Act does little or nothing more than the First Amendment itself requires as a matter of freedom of speech.

[42] 515 U.S. 819 (1995).

[43] *Id.* at 830.

[44] *Id.* at 825.

[45] *Id.* at 831. The Supreme Court's findings of viewpoint discrimination in *Rosenberger* and in the other cases in this series do not rule out the possibility of religion-based exclusions from nonpublic or limited public forums that might be regarded as subject-matter rather than viewpoint-based. Despite this series of cases, for example, the U.S. Court of Appeals for the Second Circuit, in a case that did not reach the Supreme Court, ruled that a New York City policy excluding "religious worship services" from otherwise available public school facilities was not viewpoint-based. As a result, the policy did not trigger strict scrutiny under the Free Speech Clause; instead, it warranted only a test of reasonableness. Applying this far more deferential approach, the court found that the exclusion was justified by the school

is important to note that *Rosenberger* does not authorize free speech challenges to discriminatory funding programs in general. But it does support such challenges when the government funds a broad and diverse range of private speech, thereby creating a "metaphysical" free speech forum.[46]

D. Limitations on the Equal Access Doctrine

The Supreme Court's equal access doctrine protects religious speech from discriminatory exclusions from governmental property, but the doctrine applies only when the government is denying access to a forum for private expression. There is no right to equal access when the government itself is speaking, even if the government is expressing a particular viewpoint and excluding expression to the contrary. Moreover, even when the government has created a nonpublic or limited public forum for private expression, the Court's doctrine offers very little protection when religious speakers or groups are adversely affected by restrictions that are not viewpoint-based. These limitations on the Court's equal access doctrine are illustrated by two recent cases, *Pleasant Grove City v. Summum*[47] and *Christian Legal Society v. Martinez*.[48]

In *Pleasant Grove City v. Summum*, decided in 2009, the Supreme Court considered the claim of Summum, a religious organization, that it had a free speech right to erect a monument in Pioneer Park, a public park in Pleasant Grove City, Utah. The park already contained a number of permanent monuments and displays, including a privately donated Ten Commandments monument. The city had denied Summun permission to erect a monument containing the Seven Aphorisms of Summum,[49] and the group

---

board's reasonable fear of violating the Establishment Clause. *See Bronx Household of Faith v. Board of Educ.*, 650 F.3d 30 (2d Cir. 2011).

[46] *Rosenberger*, 515 U.S. at 830. The Court emphasized this distinction in *Locke v. Davey*, 540 U.S. 712 (2004), ruling that *Rosenberger* did not extend to a state-sponsored college scholarship program that excluded students who majored in devotional theology. According to the Court, the scholarship program was "not a forum for speech" because it was designed to assist students with the cost of their education, "not to ' "encourage a diversity of views from private speakers." ' " *Id.* at 720 n.3 (citations omitted). We will consider *Locke* later in this chapter, in discussing the Free Exercise Clause.

[47] 555 U.S. 460 (2009).

[48] 561 U.S. 661 (2010).

[49] Founded in 1975, Summum "incorporates elements of Gnostic Christianity.... According to Summum doctrine, the Seven Aphorisms were inscribed on the original tablets handed down by God to Moses on Mount Sinai.... Because Moses believed that the Israelites were not ready to receive the Aphorisms, he shared them only with a select group of people. In the Summum Exodus account, Moses then destroyed the original tablets, traveled back to Mount Sinai, and returned with a second set of tablets containing the Ten Commandments." *Summum*, 555 U.S. at 465 n.1 (citation omitted). The Summum aphorisms include the following principles, among others: "SUMMUM is MIND; the universe is a mental creation.";

contended that the city had violated the Free Speech Clause by accepting the Ten Commandments monument but rejecting its own. The Supreme Court unanimously rejected Summum's claim.

As Justice Alito explained for eight Justices,[50] permanent monuments on public property—even in the setting of a traditional public forum such as a park—are government speech even if the monuments were originally donated by private groups. As to such monuments, there can be Establishment Clause challenges (as we will see in Chapter 8),[51] but there generally is no forum for private speech and therefore no right of equal access. More broadly, government speech is largely immune from the Free Speech Clause. Thus, with respect to its own expression, the government generally is free to engage in content- and viewpoint-based decisionmaking.[52] Accordingly, subject to the Establishment Clause, the government is free to commission or select whatever permanent monuments it believes will express the message or messages it might wish to convey. And the government's decisions in this setting do not trigger a free speech right to nondiscriminatory treatment or equal access.[53]

In its 2010 decision in *Christian Legal Society v. Martinez*,[54] the Court addressed the claim of a student group, the Christian Legal Society (CLS), that the University of California's Hastings College of the Law had violated the First Amendment by excluding CLS from the law school's "Registered Student Organization" (RSO)

"Nothing rests; everything moves; everything vibrates."; "Gender is in everything; everything has its masculine and feminine principles; Gender manifests on all levels."

[50] Justice Souter agreed with the Court's decision but did not join Justice Alito's opinion. *See id.* at 485–87 (Souter, J., concurring in the judgment).

[51] There was no Establishment Clause challenge in *Summum*. If there had been such a challenge, the Ten Commandments monument might well have survived Establishment Clause scrutiny under the authority of *Van Orden v. Perry*, 545 U.S. 677 (2005). *See Summum*, 555 U.S. at 483 (Scalia, J., concurring). We will discuss *Van Orden* in Chapter 8.

[52] The Court has extended the reasoning of *Summum* to specialty automobile license plates, ruling that they constitute government speech, not a forum for private expression, and that the government therefore is free to accept or reject proposed plates without fear of violating the Free Speech Clause. *See Walker v. Texas Div., Sons of Confederate Veterans, Inc.*, 135 S. Ct. 2239 (2015).

[53] In *Summum*, the Supreme Court distinguished *Capitol Square Review & Advisory Bd. v. Pinette*, 515 U.S. 753 (1995), in which the Court had applied equal access principles to temporary, unattended private displays in a traditional public forum. *See Summum*, 555 U.S. at 480. In *Capitol Square*, the Court held that the Free Speech Clause precluded the State of Ohio from barring the temporary display of a privately sponsored Latin cross in the state-owned plaza surrounding the Ohio State Capitol. Noting that the state had permitted other unattended displays in the plaza, the Court ruled that it could not exclude the cross because of its religious content.

[54] 561 U.S. 661 (2010).

program. Through the RSO program, Hastings offered official recognition, access to certain law school facilities, and other benefits to a wide variety of student groups, thus creating a limited public forum. But Hastings restricted the program to groups that complied with an "all-comers" nondiscrimination policy, according to which they were required to accept any and all students as both members and leaders, regardless of the students' status or beliefs. For example, the Hastings Democratic Caucus could not exclude Republicans. CLS objected to this policy, noting that the Free Speech Clause protects not only speech itself, but also expressive association.

Indeed, as CLS argued, the First Amendment protects the right of a group to associate for expressive purposes, and also its right *not* to associate with individuals who would undermine the group's expressive message. For instance, the Supreme Court had ruled in an earlier case, *Boy Scouts of America v. Dale*,[55] that the Boy Scouts had a First Amendment right to ignore a nondiscrimination law that would have required the group to accept, as an assistant scoutmaster, an individual who was both openly gay and a gay rights activist. According to the Court, accepting the gay scout leader would have undermined the Boy Scouts' expressive message, which included opposition to homosexual conduct. As a result, the Court invoked strict scrutiny, which the government could not satisfy. In *Christian Legal Society*, CLS relied on the reasoning of *Dale*. Protecting its expressive message as an evangelical Christian group, CLS contended, required it to restrict itself to students who adhered to a particular set of beliefs and practices. In particular, the group sought to reserve membership and leadership to individuals who signed a prescribed statement of Christian faith and who agreed not to engage in sexual activity outside the setting of traditional marriage. To this extent, CLS argued, it should be exempt from Hastings' all-comers requirement.

In a five-to-four ruling, the Supreme Court rejected the CLS claim. With Justice Ginsburg writing for the majority, the Court agreed that freedom of expressive association is protected by the First Amendment. But it concluded that in the context of a limited public forum, this freedom warrants no greater protection than speech itself, meaning that restrictions on access are broadly permissible in the absence of viewpoint discrimination. Distinguishing *Dale*, the majority noted that Hastings was not demanding, by regulation, that CLS include unwanted students. Rather, in offering potential access to the RSO program, a limited public forum, Hastings was "dangling the carrot of subsidy, not

---

[55]   530 U.S. 640 (2000).

wielding the stick of prohibition."[56] Because the all-comers policy
applied to all groups, religious or otherwise, whatever their message
or perspective, the policy was "textbook viewpoint neutral."[57] As a
result, the policy did not trigger strict scrutiny but instead was
subject only to a deferential test of minimal reasonableness. And
the policy readily survived this lenient review, in part on the
ground that Hastings reasonably believed that the policy opened
RSO leadership, educational, and social opportunities to all
students and encouraged tolerance, cooperation, and learning
among individuals with diverse backgrounds and beliefs.

Writing for the four dissenters, Justice Alito contended that the
all-comers policy was not reasonable and therefore was
unconstitutional. He argued that the policy undermined the
diversity of expression that Hastings claimed to be promoting
through the RSO program; that it seriously impaired expressive
association; and that it unfairly disadvantaged and marginalized
CLS and other religious groups that form precisely on the basis of
shared beliefs to which members and leaders are expected to
adhere.[58] Responding for the majority, however, Justice Ginsburg
maintained that arguments such as these went beyond an
appropriate inquiry into reasonableness and improperly addressed
a different question, "the *advisability* of Hastings' policy."[59] Viewed
deferentially, she concluded, the all-comers policy was sufficiently
reasonable to survive constitutional scrutiny in the limited public
forum context—even if it was not " 'the most reasonable or the only
reasonable' " policy that Hastings might have adopted.[60]

E. Religious Speech and the Free Speech Clause

As we have seen, one type of religious exercise—private
religious speech—has been accorded substantial protection under
the First Amendment, based mainly on the Free Speech Clause.
This protection extends to religious speech pure and simple as well
as religiously motivated speech on political and social issues.

The prohibition on compelled speech sometimes benefits
religious objectors. More important, the Free Speech Clause

---

[56] *Christian Legal Society,* 561 U.S. at 683.

[57] *Id.* at 695. Indeed, the majority concluded, the policy was not merely
viewpoint-neutral but was more broadly content-neutral as well. *See id.* at 695–96.

[58] *See id.* at 729–35, 741 (Alito, J., dissenting); *see also id.* at 716–21. Justice
Alito's lengthy opinion offered other arguments as well. For example, he contended
that the parties' stipulation concerning the all-comers policy should not be read to
preclude a challenge to Hastings' written nondiscrimination policy, and he argued
that the written policy was viewpoint-based. *See id.* at 708–16, 723–27.

[59] *Id.* at 692 (majority opinion) (emphasis in original).

[60] *Id.* (quoting *Cornelius v. NAACP Legal Defense & Ed. Fund, Inc.,* 473 U.S.
788, 808 (1985)).

strongly disfavors governmental action that formally or deliberately discriminates against religious speech or religious speakers, even in the setting of a nonpublic or limited public forum. With respect to governmental action that is content-neutral, the Clause is far more forgiving, although it sometimes offers protection, notably in the setting of a traditional public forum. In the context of a nonpublic or limited public forum, by contrast, as *Christian Legal Society* attests, religious speech and expressive association may be disadvantaged, arguably in serious ways, as long as the governmental action does not deliberately target religious viewpoints.

The Supreme Court's speech decisions serve the value of religious free speech, which is a form of expressive liberty but also a form of religious liberty. In other words, freedom of religious speech promotes religious voluntarism in the context of speech. Under the Court's prevailing doctrine, this freedom is substantial and important; it represents a critical component of religious liberty. Even so, the Court's protection of religious speech is confined mainly to situations that implicate not only the value of religious free speech but also the value of religious equality, understood in formal as opposed to substantive terms. Thus, the Court's free speech doctrine strongly disfavors deliberate governmental discrimination against religion. This is important protection, because such discrimination directly undermines the important value of equality between religious and nonreligious speech. But this doctrine offers only limited protection against laws or policies that do not deliberately target religion for special disadvantage. This is so even if, as in *Christian Legal Society*, the laws or policies may impair expressive freedom in significant ways or have a discriminatory effect on particular religious groups, potentially implicating the value of substantive (as opposed to formal) religious equality. And the Free Speech Clause provides no protection, of course, for religious conduct that is neither speech nor speech-related.

III. The Free Exercise Clause

What, then, of the Free Exercise Clause? If it offers nothing more than freedom of belief and profession, it does little if anything that the Free Speech Clause does not. In early cases, the Supreme Court suggested that the Free Exercise Clause in fact does nothing more and that, in particular, it provides no protection for religious conduct (other than speech). Thus, in its 1879 decision in *Reynolds v. United States*,[61] the Court held that the Free Exercise Clause did not protect the Mormon practice of polygamy, which was forbidden

---

[61] 98 U.S. 145 (1879).

by a federal criminal statute. "Laws are made for the government of actions," the Court wrote, "and while they cannot interfere with mere religious belief and opinions, they may with practices," lest "every citizen . . . become a law unto himself."[62] According to *Reynolds*, citizens have the right to *believe* in a religious practice such as polygamy, and they have the freedom to express their opinion through speech. Yet they are not free to act on their belief by actually engaging in the religious conduct. Needless to say, this is an extremely narrow, if not barren, interpretation of the Free Exercise Clause. This narrow view was later abandoned by the Supreme Court and, despite more recent doctrinal retrenchment, the Clause today offers some additional protection.

A. Religious Conduct and Substantial Burdens

A more vibrant understanding of the Free Exercise Clause would protect religious conduct, that is, the freedom to act in accordance with one's religious beliefs. Unlike the protection of belief, this protection certainly could not be absolute. Imagine, for example, the act of religiously motivated human sacrifice. But as a matter of presumptive constitutional protection, the Free Exercise Clause would move beyond mere belief, granting individuals a much more meaningful liberty—the freedom not only to decide what they *should* do religiously, but also to do it. The constitutional value of religious voluntarism would seem to demand no less. This protection likewise would honor and respect the religious identity of individuals, a value that is closely related to voluntarism but that identifies an aspect of human dignity that does not necessarily require the exercise of autonomous choice. Indeed, many individuals do not believe that they independently "choose" their own religion; rather, it is chosen for them by God, or perhaps by another religious force. Respecting their religious identity, and according them religious equality, means that even if these citizens attribute their religious decisions and actions to a source beyond themselves, they should receive no less free exercise protection than citizens with a more autonomous belief structure. Protecting religious conduct also would further other constitutional values, including religious flourishing in the private domain and the autonomy of religious institutions in demanding or encouraging particular forms of religious behavior.

As we will discuss shortly, the contemporary Supreme Court does not give the Free Exercise Clause a forceful interpretation. Even so, the Court does recognize that the exercise of religion includes religious conduct: "The free exercise of religion means, first

---

[62] *Id.* at 166–67.

and foremost, the right to believe and profess whatever religious doctrine one desires. . . . But the 'exercise of religion' often involves not only belief and profession but the performance of (or abstention from) physical acts: assembling with others for a worship service, participating in sacramental use of bread and wine, proselytizing, abstaining from certain foods or certain modes of transportation."[63] As a matter of current doctrine, the exercise of religion thus includes religious conduct, including but not limited to religious speech.

This conclusion advances the inquiry but certainly does not end it. One must determine, more precisely, what type of religious conduct (or abstention)[64] qualifies as the exercise of religion. And even if religious conduct is the exercise of religion, it might still fall outside the scope of the Free Exercise Clause. As a textual matter, for example, one might say that not all religious "exercise" is within the constitutionally protected *"free* exercise" or (as the current Court prefers) that not all governmental intrusions qualify as "prohibitions." But this may be little more than semantics. However closely or cleverly one reads the text, it does not answer the key substantive questions. In particular, one must determine what a challenger must show in order to trigger presumptive constitutional protection under the Free Exercise Clause, and one then must determine the precise nature of that presumptive protection.

In the remainder of this discussion, we will focus on the Supreme Court's contemporary doctrine concerning what amounts to the first stage of the "triggering" inquiry. More specifically, we will examine each of two initial requirements that the challenger must satisfy in order to trigger presumptive protection under the Free Exercise Clause: first, the claimant must be engaging in religious conduct that qualifies as the exercise of religion within the scope of the Clause; and second, the governmental action must constitute a burden on this religious exercise that is substantial enough to be constitutionally cognizable. (Even if these initial requirements are met, as we will see later, there still is no presumptive constitutional protection, in general, unless the burden on religious exercise is discriminatory.)

1.   The Exercise of Religion

For conduct to qualify as the exercise of religion under the Free Exercise Clause, it must, at a minimum, be conduct that is sincerely motivated by religious beliefs. As discussed in Chapter 4, religious

---

[63] *Employment Div. v. Smith*, 494 U.S. 872, 877 (1990).

[64] For simplicity, this discussion will focus mainly on affirmative religious conduct. The concepts and principles are no different for religious abstention.

beliefs for this purpose at least include beliefs derived from conventional, theistic religion, but may also include a broader set of analogous beliefs, including deeply held moral convictions. In any event, the claimant must be sincere in two respects: he or she must sincerely accept the religious belief as true or genuine and, in addition, it must be that belief—and not secular self-interest, for example—that actually motivates the conduct in question.

The requirements of religious motivation and sincerity are important and necessary, but they may not be sufficient. Even assuming a conventional definition of religion, conduct is often motivated by religious beliefs, at least partially, and most religious claimants are undeniably sincere. Under these criteria, qualifying conduct might include not only such inherently religious acts as prayer, worship, and ritual, but also a much broader variety of conduct inspired by religious understandings of morality or ethics. Without additional limitations, the exercise of religion might be so expansively defined that meaningful constitutional protection would be unrealistic. As a result, it might be appropriate to impose additional requirements, requirements limiting the scope of religious exercise to conduct that is especially important to religious voluntarism, religious identity, and other constitutional values.

The Supreme Court has at times suggested two such additional requirements. First, it sometimes has suggested that the religious conduct protected by the Free Exercise Clause is that which is "central" to a religion, or at least that which the claimant sincerely believes to be central.[65] Second, it sometimes has spoken of conduct that is not merely religiously motivated, but that is *compelled* or *mandated* by the claimant's sincere understanding of religious duty or obligation. More recently, however, the Court has emphasized that any judicial inquiry into centrality is improper, stating that such an inquiry is no more permissible than a judicial inquiry into religious truth. Although the Court could still require a *sincere claim* of religious centrality, it has implied that it will not do so.[66] And it has continued to speak not only of conduct that is religiously compelled, but also of conduct that is religiously motivated, giving

---

[65] *See, e.g., Wisconsin v. Yoder*, 406 U.S. 205, 209–13, 215–19 (1972) (granting free exercise protection to Old Order Amish only after elaborating and emphasizing the importance and centrality of the Amish religious beliefs and practices that were at stake).

[66] *See Smith*, 494 U.S. at 886–88. *But cf. Hernandez v. Commissioner*, 490 U.S. 680, 699 (1989) (declaring that the judiciary cannot determine centrality, but implying that a sincere claim of centrality might be required); *Church of the Lukumi Babalu Aye, Inc. v. City of Hialeah*, 508 U.S. 520, 534 (1993) (affording free exercise protection to "the central element" of Santería worship).

no clear indication of how strong or substantial the religious motivation must be.[67]

As later portions of this chapter will show, the contemporary Supreme Court has severely limited the protection afforded by the Free Exercise Clause, but not through the device of defining religious exercise restrictively. Thus, like "religion," the "exercise" of religion has neither been clearly defined nor narrowly limited by the Supreme Court. Perhaps the best reading of the Court's uncertain constitutional doctrine is that the exercise of religion under the Free Exercise Clause requires neither centrality nor religious compulsion,[68] but that it does demand, implicitly, that a claimant be sincerely relying on a religious belief as the *primary* or *dominant* motivation for the conduct in question. If so, this would be a rather lenient requirement, and virtually any serious claimant could meet it.

The exercise of religion is not confined to individual actors. Religious organizations, including those organized as nonprofit corporations, plainly can exercise religion within the meaning of the Free Exercise Clause. More controversially, as the Supreme Court ruled in *Burwell v. Hobby Lobby Stores, Inc.*,[69] so can for-profit corporations, at least if they are closely held businesses that operate under religious principles.[70] *Hobby Lobby* was decided under the Religious Freedom Restoration Act of 1993 (RFRA),[71] not the First Amendment, but the Court's analysis on this point seems equally

---

[67] *See, e.g.*, *Smith*, 494 U.S. at 876, 877, 878, 888 (referring variously to "conduct required by . . . religion," "acts . . . engaged in for religious reasons," conduct grounded in "religious motivation," acts "require[d]" by religious belief, and "actions thought to be religiously commanded"); *Lukumi*, 508 U.S. at 524, 532, 546 (referring to ceremonies "command[ed]" by religion but also to "conduct motivated by religious beliefs" and "conduct with a religious motivation").

[68] As a matter of statutory as opposed to constitutional law, the Religious Freedom Restoration Act of 1993 (RFRA) and the Religious Land Use and Institutionalized Persons Act of 2000 (RLUIPA) clearly reject any requirement of centrality or religious compulsion. Instead, they extend their statutory protection to "any exercise of religion, whether or not compelled by, or central to, a system of religious belief." 42 U.S.C. § 2000bb–2(4), § 2000cc–5(7)(A). We will address these statutes in Chapter 6.

[69] 134 S. Ct. 2751 (2014).

[70] The corporate documents of Hobby Lobby, the lead challenger in the case, included a "statement of purpose" that committed the company's owners—David and Barbara Green and their three children—to "[h]onoring the Lord in all [they] do by operating the company in a manner consistent with Biblical principles." *See id.* at 2766. The Supreme Court reserved the question of whether publicly traded corporations could exercise religion, but it noted that practical obstacles made this improbable. *See id.* at 2774.

[71] 42 U.S.C. §§ 2000bb to 2000bb–4.

applicable to the Free Exercise Clause.[72] In particular, the Court noted that it previously had entertained claims under the Free Exercise Clause by individual commercial actors,[73] and it concluded that use of the corporate form should not lead to a different conclusion. Furthering the religious freedom of closely held corporations, the Court explained, in reality protects the individual religious freedom of their owners. Accordingly, if the owners of a closely held corporation satisfy the requirements of sincerity and sufficient religious motivation, so does the corporation.[74]

2. The Substantial Burden Requirement

Assuming that a claimant's conduct meets the conditions of sincerity and sufficient religious motivation, thus qualifying as the exercise of religion, what amounts to a constitutionally cognizable burden on that exercise? The Supreme Court has stated that the burden must be a "substantial burden,"[75] but, here again, the Court has not fully explained what this means. What is clear is that two different sorts of burdens can be substantial enough to be constitutionally cognizable: burdens that are "direct" and those that are "indirect."[76]

A direct burden arises when the exercise of religion unavoidably triggers a criminal sanction or other legal penalty. Typically, the effect of the law is to forbid the religious conduct, making it literally impossible for the religious claimant to honor both the law and the claimant's religious understandings. *Wisconsin v. Yoder*[77] provides an example. Wisconsin's compulsory education law required parents to send their children to school until the age of 16. Old Order Amish could not follow the law, however, without abandoning a religious obligation: protecting their children from the worldly influences of high school. As the Court noted, the law's impact on the Amish parents' religious exercise was "not only severe, but inescapable," because it "affirmatively compell[ed] them,

---

[72] *But cf. Hobby Lobby*, 134 S. Ct. at 2772–73 (noting that the "exercise of religion" under RFRA is not confined to specific interpretations of that concept in prior First Amendment case law).

[73] *See id.* at 2769–70 (citing and discussing *Braunfeld v. Brown*, 366 U.S. 599 (1961), and *United States v. Lee*, 455 U.S. 252 (1982)). According to the Court, it did not matter that the free exercise claims in these earlier cases had ultimately been rejected for other reasons.

[74] In her dissenting opinion, Justice Ginsburg argued that for-profit corporations, even if closely held, cannot be said to exercise religion and so should not be protected under either the Free Exercise Clause or RFRA. *See id.* at 2793–97 (Ginsburg, J., dissenting).

[75] *See, e.g., Hernandez v. Commissioner*, 490 U.S. 680, 699 (1989).

[76] This direct-versus-indirect dichotomy can be understood in various ways. What follows is one interpretation.

[77] 406 U.S. 205 (1972).

under threat of criminal sanction, to perform acts undeniably at odds with fundamental tenets of their religious beliefs."[78] The Court protected the Amish from this direct burden by recognizing a constitutionally required exemption from the law.

An indirect burden arises when the law does not unavoidably regulate or forbid religious exercise but does place a religious believer on the horns of a decisional dilemma, for example, by offering financial or other inducements under conditions that would require the believer to forego religious conduct. In *Sherbert v. Verner*,[79] for instance, unemployment compensation was available only to those who would accept Saturday employment. The Court granted free exercise protection to Adell Sherbert, a Seventh-Day Adventist and therefore a Saturday Sabbatarian, ruling that the Saturday-work condition could not be applied to her. The Court noted that although the burden might properly be described as "indirect," the law nonetheless exerted "unmistakable" pressure on the exercise of religion by forcing Sherbert "to choose between following the precepts of her religion and forfeiting benefits, on the one hand, and abandoning one of the precepts of her religion in order to accept work, on the other hand."[80] More recently, in *Locke v. Davey*,[81] a case to which we will return shortly, the Court addressed a free exercise challenge to a state-sponsored college scholarship program. The program denied funding to students who elected to major in devotional theology, thereby imposing an indirect burden on their religious decisionmaking. Unlike in *Sherbert*, however, the Court found the burden "relatively minor,"[82] and, for that reason among others, it rejected the free exercise challenge.

Direct and indirect burdens each can impair various constitutional values, but the Court's analysis of whether a burden is substantial enough to be constitutionally cognizable appears to rest primarily on the value of religious voluntarism and, more specifically, on the protection of religious conscience. A direct burden on the exercise of religion obviously intrudes upon religious conscience and voluntarism by impeding the freedom to make and implement religious choices. In certain circumstances, however, an indirect burden might exert as great, or potentially greater, coercive pressure on this religious decisionmaking. A restrictive condition can be attached to substantial financial benefits, whereas the

---

[78]   *Id.* at 218.

[79]   374 U.S. 398 (1963).

[80]   *Id.* at 403–04.

[81]   540 U.S. 712 (2004).

[82]   *Id.* at 725.

violation of a direct legal ban might lead to a minimal fine. In *Yoder*, for example, the Amish parents confronted a criminal sanction but had been fined only $5.00. Whatever the precise penalty, however, a direct burden can force nonconforming religious believers to defy the law, thus bearing the opprobrium of unlawful conduct and, in the case of a criminal law, the brand of criminality. In any event, a burden, whether direct or indirect, presumably qualifies as substantial if it dissuades or discourages the exercise of religion by exerting substantial coercive pressure on religious decisionmaking.

Conversely, the Supreme Court has suggested, controversially, that there is no constitutionally cognizable burden when governmental action does not impair religious voluntarism by influencing *religious decisionmaking*, even if the governmental action might significantly impede the exercise of religion in other ways. In *Lyng v. Northwest Indian Cemetery Protective Association*,[83] for example, the Court found that no cognizable burden would result from a proposed National Forest road that, according to the challengers, would have seriously damaged the sanctity of Native American sacred sites. The Court conceded that the proposed road would "have severe adverse effects" on the challengers' ability to practice their religion at the sacred sites, but it emphasized that they would not "be coerced by the Government's action into violating their religious beliefs."[84] In terms of religious voluntarism, the governmental action would not induce the Native American believers to make or forego any religious decision concerning the conduct in which they should engage—even if that conduct might no longer be religiously efficacious or even possible—and it therefore would not impede their exercise of religious conscience. This type of reasoning, however, ignores other constitutional values, including the protection of religious identity as an aspect of human dignity. Perhaps most important, it fails to accord religious equality to religious understandings that do not emphasize individual responsibility and personal choice.[85]

The Court in *Lyng* also relied on a related but distinctive—and more defensible—principle: the Free Exercise Clause does not restrict the government's internal operations and procedures, even if the government's administrative functioning violates a claimant's religious understandings. In other words, the exercise of religion includes the claimant's own behavior but not the government's, so

---

[83]   485 U.S. 439 (1988).

[84]   *Id.* at 447, 449.

[85]   *See* David C. Williams & Susan H. Williams, *Volitionalism and Religious Liberty*, 76 CORNELL L. REV. 769 (1991).

there is no cognizable free exercise burden in this situation. The Court may very well have misapplied this principle in *Lyng*, because the challengers' own religious behavior was indeed being threatened—not by internal governmental operations but by the external effects of the proposed road.[86] Properly applied, however, a limitation along these lines is all but required as a matter of pragmatism, simply to permit the government to function. In *Bowen v. Roy*,[87] for example, the Court was virtually unanimous in adopting this principle and in concluding, accordingly, that a Native American's religious belief that a Social Security number should not be attached to his daughter did not permit him to insist that the government use a different system in processing a benefit claim on her behalf.[88]

In *Hobby Lobby*,[89] the Supreme Court addressed not only the exercise of religion, but also the substantial burden requirement. Here again, the Court was applying RFRA, not the First Amendment, but the RFRA requirement is identical by its terms, and the Court gave no indication that the Free Exercise Clause would or should be interpreted differently. As noted in Chapter 4, the challengers in *Hobby Lobby* believed that their religion forbade them from providing their employees with insurance coverage for forms of contraception that could operate after fertilization. This coverage was mandated by the Affordable Care Act (ACA), which imposed heavy taxes and financial penalties for noncompliance. The ACA's burden on religious exercise arguably was indirect, because the companies could have avoided the coverage requirement by paying the financial assessments, but the Court found this choice unrealistic and thus concluded, with "little trouble," that the Act imposed a substantial burden on the exercise of religion.[90] Notably, as discussed in Chapter 4, the Court rejected the government's argument that the connection between the ACA's insurance coverage requirement and the potential destruction of an embryo was too attenuated to give rise to a substantial burden on the employers' religious freedom. According to the Court, the substantial burden inquiry evaluates the coercive pressure that the government is placing on religious objectors. It does not authorize the judiciary to second-guess the objectors' religious understandings, not even with respect to impermissible complicity.

---

[86] *Compare Lyng*, 485 U.S. at 448–49, 456, *with id.* at 469–72 (Brennan, J., dissenting).

[87]   476 U.S. 693 (1986).

[88]   *Id.* at 699–701. The Court's decision in *Roy* was fractured, but only Justice White dissented on this point.

[89]   *Burwell v. Hobby Lobby Stores, Inc.*, 134 S. Ct. 2751 (2014).

[90]   *See id.* at 2775–79.

The ACA's contraceptive coverage requirement also has generated numerous RFRA challenges by religious nonprofit organizations, including religiously affiliated colleges, hospitals, and charities. In these cases, the government has offered the organizations relief from the coverage requirement, but only if they inform the government of their objection, thus triggering the operation of alternative governmental regulations that require the organizations' insurance companies (or third-party administrators) to provide the contested coverage independently, without the organizations' direct participation or financial support. The religious objectors in these cases have said that even this degree of involvement makes them impermissibly complicit in the use of contraceptives to which they object. Most lower courts, including U.S. Courts of Appeals in various circuits, have rejected these challenges, largely on the ground that there is no substantial burden when the government does no more than require the reporting of religious objections in this manner and then employs alternative governmental action—action that itself is immune from challenge under the reasoning of *Bowen v. Roy*.[91] But the U.S. Court of Appeals for the Eighth Circuit has ruled otherwise, creating a circuit split by finding a substantial burden and a RFRA violation.[92] The Supreme Court now is poised to resolve this dispute in 2016, having granted review in multiple cases.[93] We will revisit this controversy when we examine RFRA in Chapter 6.

B. Nondiscriminatory Burdens on Religious Conduct

In its interpretations of the Free Exercise Clause (as opposed to RFRA), the Supreme Court in recent decades has followed two distinctive approaches in addressing nondiscriminatory burdens on religious conduct. Under the constitutional regime exemplified by *Wisconsin v. Yoder*[94] and *Sherbert v. Verner*,[95] a substantial burden on the exercise of religion was enough, without more, to trigger presumptive protection under the Free Exercise Clause, giving rise to searching judicial scrutiny even when the burden resulted from a nondiscriminatory, generally applicable law. If the government

---

[91] *See, e.g., Geneva College v. Secretary U.S. Dep't of Health & Human Services*, 778 F.3d 422, 435–42 (3rd Cir. 2015), *cert. granted*, 136 S. Ct. 444 (2015).

[92] *See Sharpe Holdings, Inc. v. U.S. Dep't of Health & Human Services*, 801 F.3d 927 (8th Cir. 2015) (approving preliminary injunction); *Dordt College v. Burwell*, 801 F.3d 946 (8th Cir. 2015) (approving preliminary injunction).

[93] The Court has granted review in seven cases, which it has consolidated. The cases probably will be decided under the name *Zubik v. Burwell*, which was the first of these cases to be filed in the Supreme Court. *See Zubik v. Burwell*, 136 S. Ct. 444 (2015), *granting cert. to Geneva College*, 778 F.3d 422.

[94] 406 U.S. 205 (1972).

[95] 374 U.S. 398 (1963).

could not satisfy this scrutiny in defending the law's application to the challenger's religious conduct, an exemption from the law was constitutionally required. This regime prevailed from 1963, when the Supreme Court decided *Sherbert*, until 1990, when the Court decided *Employment Division v. Smith.*[96]

The Court's language in *Sherbert* and *Yoder* suggested a test of strict scrutiny similar to the test that we have seen applied (in certain contexts) under the Free Speech Clause. In particular, the Court stated that the Free Exercise Clause demanded an exemption unless the law's application to the challenger's religious conduct was necessary to serve a "compelling state interest"[97] or an "interest[ ] of the highest order."[98] The government could not satisfy this test in *Sherbert* or *Yoder*. In *Yoder*, for instance, the Court concluded that the state's admittedly strong interest in compulsory education did not preclude an exemption for the Amish, in part because only a year or two of formal education was at stake. State law required school attendance until age 16, and the Amish, objecting only to high school, willingly sent their children through the eighth grade. The Justices also found that the state's educational interest was not being seriously undermined because the Amish themselves, through informal vocational training, effectively equipped their youth for productive lives, even if they chose to leave the Amish community. The state thus failed to satisfy strict scrutiny because application of the law to the Amish was not necessary. As a result, the Free Exercise Clause demanded an exemption.

In other cases during this period, however, even as it applied the strict scrutiny test of *Sherbert* and *Yoder*, the Court sometimes found the test satisfied and accordingly rejected exemption claims. In *United States v. Lee*,[99] for example, the Court, distinguishing *Yoder*, refused to excuse an Amish employer from paying Social Security taxes for his Amish employees. The Amish recognize a religiously based, communal obligation to care for their own elderly and needy individuals, and the employer therefore believed that participation in the Social Security system would violate the Amish faith. The Court agreed that the law imposed a burden that triggered strict scrutiny under the Free Exercise Clause, but, expressing reluctance to exempt objectors from the payment of taxes, it found that the government had shown that requiring the Amish employer to pay the tax was "essential to accomplish an

---

[96]   494 U.S. 872 (1990).

[97]   *Sherbert*, 374 U.S. at 403.

[98]   *Yoder*, 406 U.S. at 215.

[99]   455 U.S. 252 (1982).

overriding governmental interest."[100] Likewise, in *Bob Jones University v. United States*,[101] the Court found that the governmental interest in eradicating racial discrimination in education was compelling and that it justified denying tax exempt status even to religious colleges whose racially discriminatory policies were grounded in religious understandings.[102]

During the doctrinal reign of *Sherbert* and *Yoder*, the Court's strict scrutiny test thus created a strong—but not insurmountable—presumption in favor of religious exemptions. This approach did not extend to military and prison regulations, which were evaluated under a reasonableness or rational-basis standard, a lenient test that permitted the government to deny exemptions with minimal justification.[103] Outside those exceptional areas, however, the Court endorsed the strict scrutiny standard for more than a quarter century, from the 1960s through the 1980s. In so doing, it offered constitutional protection to the exercise of religion even from nondiscriminatory burdens, thus protecting a variety of constitutional values, but most of all the value of religious voluntarism. As suggested earlier, that value is seriously impaired whenever there is a substantial burden on the exercise of religion, and it matters not whether the burden results from a discriminatory law.

The Supreme Court's 1990 decision in *Employment Division v. Smith*[104] marked a dramatic turn in doctrine. In *Smith*, the Court was asked to recognize a free exercise exemption for the sacramental use of an otherwise illegal drug, peyote, by members of the Native American Church. Not only did the Court refuse to do so,[105] but, over the vigorous objection of four Justices,[106] it also declined to apply the scrutiny that *Sherbert* and *Yoder* appeared to

---

[100] *Id.* at 257–58; *see id.* at 258–61.

[101] 461 U.S. 574 (1983).

[102] *See id.* at 602–04.

[103] *See Goldman v. Weinberger*, 475 U.S. 503, 507–08 (1986) (military); *O'Lone v. Estate of Shabazz*, 482 U.S. 342, 348–50 (1987) (prisons).

[104] 494 U.S. 872 (1990).

[105] The Court held that the Free Exercise Clause did not require an exemption from an Oregon criminal law that prohibited the use of peyote. The Court reached this issue through a somewhat circuitous route, because the case arose from a denial of unemployment compensation. Two members of the Native American Church, Alfred Smith and Galen Black, had been fired from their jobs for using peyote, but they argued that they could not be denied unemployment compensation on the basis of their sacramental use of the drug. The Court rejected this argument, finding that the state was free to deny them benefits precisely because their conduct was illegal under a general criminal prohibition that, the Court concluded, permissibly extended—despite the Free Exercise Clause—to the religious use of peyote.

[106] *See Smith*, 494 U.S. at 891–907 (O'Connor, J., concurring in the judgment); *id.* at 907–21 (Blackmun, J., joined by Brennan and Marshall, JJ., dissenting).

demand. Although the Court purported to distinguish and preserve its particular holdings in those cases, it essentially renounced their fundamental teaching. Thus, the Court declared that general laws affecting religious conduct do not require any form of heightened scrutiny and therefore do not require religious exemptions.

Giving a narrow reading to the word "prohibiting" in the Free Exercise Clause, the Court rejected the argument "that 'prohibiting the free exercise [of religion]' includes requiring any individual to observe a generally applicable law that requires (or forbids) the performance of an act that his religious belief forbids (or requires)."[107] Harkening back to its 1879 opinion in *Reynolds v. United States*,[108] the Court suggested that to grant a free exercise exemption from a general law would be to permit the religious believer, "by virtue of his beliefs, 'to become a law unto himself,' " a result that "contradicts both constitutional tradition and common sense."[109] The Court especially objected to the prospect of balancing religious claims against competing state interests in a wide variety of possible contexts, a task for which, according to the Court, judges are not well-suited.

As discussed previously, the initial requirements for triggering presumptive free exercise protection are twofold: the challenger's conduct must qualify as the exercise of religion, and the challenged governmental action must constitute a substantial burden on that religious exercise. Under the doctrine of *Smith*, however, these showings are merely preliminary, because a nondiscriminatory burden on the exercise of religion, no matter how substantial, generally does not implicate the Free Exercise Clause. As we will see shortly, there are some exceptions to this general rule. And as we will discuss in the next chapter, *Smith*'s interpretation of the First Amendment does not apply under the statutory regimes of RFRA and similar laws, nor, in some states, to claims based on state constitutional law. But as far as the Free Exercise Clause itself is concerned, *Smith* confines the Clause mainly to discriminatory burdens. Moreover, it appears that such burdens arise only from laws that formally or deliberately discriminate against religion. By immunizing most nondiscriminatory burdens from scrutiny under the Free Exercise Clause, *Smith* severely undermines the constitutional value of religious voluntarism. At the same time, it dramatically elevates the value of religious equality, understood in a strictly formal sense.

---

[107] *Id.* at 878 (majority opinion) (bracketed language provided by the Court).

[108] 98 U.S. 145 (1879).

[109] *Smith*, 494 U.S. at 885 (quoting *Reynolds*, 98 U.S. at 167).

C. Discriminatory Burdens on Religious Conduct

Under the doctrine of *Smith*, a burden on the exercise of religion triggers presumptive constitutional protection if the burden is not only substantial, but also discriminatory. According to the Supreme Court, a burden is discriminatory if it results from a law that is tainted by "the unconstitutional object of targeting religious beliefs and practices."[110] This language—and most of the Court's reasoning in *Smith* and later cases—suggests that the touchstone is formal or deliberate discrimination, directed either against a particular religion or against religion in general. Under this approach, the Free Exercise Clause is reduced to a provision analogous to the Fourteenth Amendment's Equal Protection Clause, which protects against purposeful discrimination based on impermissible criteria.[111] At least in the contemporary period, however, it is difficult to find laws that purposefully target the exercise of religion for special burdens, leading critics to charge that under the doctrine of *Smith*, the Free Exercise Clause has little if any practical significance.

In fact, *Smith* severely reduced, but did not eliminate, the practical significance of the Free Exercise Clause. As rare as discriminatory burdens may be, they are not nonexistent, as became clear in *Church of the Lukumi Babalu Aye, Inc. v. City of Hialeah*,[112] a case decided only three years after *Smith*. *Lukumi* invalidated a series of ordinances that had been adopted by the City of Hialeah, Florida, in direct response to the proposed establishment of a Santería church in Hialeah. Santería, which developed in Cuba in the Nineteenth Century, is a religion that combines elements of the traditional Yoruba religion, brought to Cuba by African slaves, with elements of Roman Catholicism.[113] Notably, a central feature of Santería is animal sacrifice, which serves as a principal form of devotion.[114] In a transparent attempt to stop the establishment and spread of Santería, the Hialeah city council made it a crime to "sacrifice" an animal, defined to mean "unnecessarily kill, torment,

---

[110] *City of Boerne v. Flores*, 521 U.S. 507, 529 (1997).

[111] *Cf. Ashcroft v. Iqbal*, 556 U.S. 662, 676 (2009) (suggesting that claims under the Free Exercise Clause, like equal protection claims of invidious discrimination, require proof of "discriminatory purpose") (citing *Church of the Lukumi Babalu Aye, Inc. v. City of Hialeah*, 508 U.S. 520 (1993), a free exercise case, and *Washington v. Davis*, 426 U.S. 229 (1976), an equal protection case).

[112] 508 U.S. 520 (1993).

[113] *See* Kenneth L. Karst, *The Stories in* Lukumi: *Of Sacrifice and Rebirth*, in FIRST AMENDMENT STORIES 437, 443–51 (Richard W. Garnett & Andrew Koppelman eds., 2012).

[114] Animals are sacrificed to spirits, known as Orishas, which sometimes are associated with Roman Catholic Saints. "Santería" is Spanish for "The Way of the Saints."

torture, or mutilate an animal in a public or private ritual or ceremony not for the primary purpose of food consumption." Taken together, the city's overlapping ordinances effectively outlawed the Santería practice of animal sacrifice even as the ordinances left other animal killings unaffected—including not only secular killings, but also the Orthodox Jewish practice of Kosher slaughter (in part because Kosher slaughter *is* "for the primary purpose of food consumption").

"At a minimum," the Supreme Court wrote in *Lukumi*, "the protections of the Free Exercise Clause pertain if the law at issue discriminates against some or all religious beliefs or regulates or prohibits conduct because it is undertaken for religious reasons."[115] Unlike, for example, a general ban on animal killing (which, under *Smith*, would raise no free exercise issue), the Hialeah ordinances specifically targeted Santería religious exercise and, as such, imposed a burden that was not only direct and substantial, but also discriminatory. This discriminatory burden triggered presumptive constitutional protection and demanded "the most rigorous of scrutiny."[116] *Lukumi* involved sectarian discrimination— discrimination not against religion in general but against the particular religion of Santería. The Court's reasoning, however, extended to all discriminatory burdens, whether sectarian or nonsectarian in nature.[117] The Court noted that a "compelling governmental interest" and a "narrowly tailored" law conceivably might justify a discriminatory burden, but it went on to state that these requirements would be satisfied "only in rare cases."[118] In reality, it is hard to imagine why the government would ever find it necessary to target religious exercise for discriminatory treatment, at least in the imposition of a direct burden. Indeed, a law that imposes a direct and discriminatory burden on the exercise of religion typically has no constitutional applications, rendering the law invalid on its face.

What about indirect burdens? As *Sherbert*'s unemployment compensation ruling makes clear,[119] conditions on the award of financial or other benefits can pressure would-be recipients to forego religious choices, placing them on the horns of a decisional dilemma and creating a substantial burden on the exercise of religion. Even after *Smith*, moreover, *Lukumi* would appear to

---

[115] *Lukumi*, 508 U.S. at 532.

[116] *Id.* at 546.

[117] *Cf. McDaniel v. Paty*, 435 U.S. 618 (1978) (invalidating a state law that prohibited the clergy of any denomination from holding designated public offices).

[118] *See Lukumi*, 508 U.S. at 531–32, 546–47.

[119] *See Sherbert v. Verner*, 374 U.S. 398 (1963).

demand vigorous judicial review if such an indirect burden is discriminatory—that is, if the government is formally or deliberately discriminating against religion by refusing benefits precisely because the would-be recipients are religious or because they would be using the benefits to pursue religious activities. To be sure, not all indirect burdens exert substantial coercive pressure on religious decisionmaking. But when the government deliberately discriminates against religion in the selective award of benefits, it impairs not only religious voluntarism but also religious equality. As a result, one could argue that virtually any burden, if discriminatory, should be treated as sufficiently substantial to trigger presumptive protection under the Free Exercise Clause.

An argument along these lines persuaded the United States Court of Appeals for the Ninth Circuit,[120] but, to the surprise of many, a seven-Justice Supreme Court majority reversed the Ninth Circuit in *Locke v. Davey*,[121] decided in 2004. In *Locke*, the Court considered a State of Washington program that provided merit- and income-based scholarships, ranging from about $1,000 to about $1,500 per year, to students at public and private colleges, but that denied the scholarships to otherwise eligible students at religious colleges if they were majoring in devotional theology, typically to prepare for careers in the ministry. For reasons we will address in Chapter 8, this discriminatory, religion-based denial of funding was not required by the Establishment Clause, which would have permitted Washington to extend the scholarships to the ministry students who were excluded. But the state relied on a provision in Washington's state constitution, which mandated a stronger separation of church and state, and the Supreme Court permitted the state's anti-establishment policy to prevail.

According to the Court, " 'there is room for play in the joints' " between the Establishment and Free Exercise Clauses,[122] meaning that states sometimes are free, if they choose, to promote anti-establishment policies that go beyond what the Establishment Clause demands. Here, Washington's discriminatory denial of scholarship funding created an obvious disincentive—a "financial penalty," in the words of Justice Scalia's dissent[123]—for any student otherwise inclined to pursue a religious calling. Even so, in a finding seemingly at odds with *Sherbert*, the Court concluded that the burden on religious exercise was "relatively minor."[124] As a

---

[120] *See Davey v. Locke*, 299 F.3d 748 (9th Cir. 2002), *rev'd*, 540 U.S. 712 (2004).

[121] 540 U.S. 712 (2004).

[122] *Id.* at 718 (quoting *Walz v. Tax Comm'n*, 397 U.S. 664, 669 (1970)).

[123] *Id.* at 731 (Scalia, J., dissenting).

[124] *Id.* at 725 (majority opinion). The Court claimed that unlike in *Sherbert*, individuals were not required "to choose between their religious beliefs and receiving

result, the Court rejected the strict scrutiny of *Lukumi* in favor of a far more lenient balancing approach. And under that approach, the state's denial of funding was justified by historical anti-establishment concerns about taxpayer-supported clergy, concerns that were reflected in a number of state constitutions.

The scope of *Locke* remains to be seen. It might be limited to the selective denial of funding for the devotional religious work and training of clergy and other religious professionals. Under this interpretation, the Free Exercise Clause might still preclude, in other settings, the exclusion of religious options from otherwise general programs of funding, such as voucher-based programs for education or social services. But the Court's emphasis on "play in the joints" might suggest a broader interpretation of *Locke*, one that would give the states considerable leeway.[125]

Whatever its scope, *Locke* permits governmental action that dissuades and discriminates against religious choices. Perhaps anti-establishment considerations are sufficient to justify this result, but, as we will see in Chapter 8, the Supreme Court itself has reasoned otherwise. Thus, in its interpretations of the Establishment Clause, the Court has determined that constitutional values—especially religious voluntarism and religious equality, both formal and substantive—support the nondiscriminatory extension of funding to religious recipients in settings such as this. Thus, it seems that *Locke* is simply giving deference to state-law policymaking in this context, regardless of whether that policymaking fully honors the values of the Religion Clauses.

To summarize, substantial and discriminatory burdens on the exercise of religion trigger an extremely strong presumption of invalidity and extremely strong strict scrutiny. This doctrine applies to direct burdens, as in *Lukumi*. The values of religious voluntarism and religious equality would support an extension of

---

a government benefit" because students majoring in devotional theology still could receive a scholarship, albeit only if they were simultaneously pursuing a secular degree at a separate educational institution. *Id.* at 720–21 & n.4.

[125] For lower court decisions interpreting *Locke* broadly and extending its reasoning to uphold state-law exclusions of religious schools from voucher programs for elementary and secondary education, see *Eulitt v. Maine*, 386 F.3d 344 (1st Cir. 2004); *Bush v. Holmes*, 886 So. 2d 340 (Fla. Dist. Ct. App. 2004) (en banc), *aff'd on other grounds*, 919 So. 2d 392 (Fla. 2006). For a critique of *Locke* and an argument that the decision should be interpreted narrowly, see Thomas C. Berg & Douglas Laycock, *The Mistakes in* Locke v. Davey *and the Future of State Payments for Services Provided by Religious Institutions*, 40 TULSA L. REV. 227 (2004).

As we will discuss in Chapter 8, the Supreme Court may clarify the scope of *Locke* in a pending case, *Trinity Lutheran Church v. Pauley*, 788 F.3d 779 (8th Cir. 2015), *cert. granted*, 2016 WL 205949 (U.S. Jan. 15, 2016) (No. 15-577).

this doctrine to indirect burdens as well, but *Locke* suggests that the Supreme Court may be disinclined to find that indirect burdens, even if discriminatory, are sufficiently substantial to trigger presumptive constitutional protection under the Free Exercise Clause.

D. Protection for Religious Conduct Even in the Absence of Formal or Deliberate Discrimination?

In the context of indirect burdens, contemporary constitutional protection under the Free Exercise Clause is confined by *Locke*. More generally, even in the context of direct and substantial burdens, the controlling doctrine is that of *Smith* and *Lukumi*. This doctrine is designed primarily to redress discriminatory burdens on religious exercise, that is, burdens that are formally or purposefully directed to religious conduct as such. This restrictive approach, which emphasizes nondiscrimination and formal religious equality, clearly is the heart of the Supreme Court's doctrine. Even so, the Court has not foreclosed the possibility of additional free exercise protection, which might serve other constitutional values. In particular, it has suggested that even in the absence of formal or deliberate discrimination, substantial burdens on the exercise of religion might trigger presumptive constitutional protection in each of two contexts: laws that are not "generally applicable"; and "hybrid" cases combining free exercise and other constitutional arguments. We will discuss these suggestions here. (In addition, the Court has clearly ruled that the institutional autonomy of religious organizations is a constitutional value that warrants protection from certain types of nondiscriminatory burdens; we will discuss that doctrine subsequently.)

1. Smith, Lukumi, and "General Applicability"

In *Smith*, the Court referred to the nondiscriminatory burdens that are immune from challenge under the Free Exercise Clause as those that result from "neutral law[s] of general applicability."[126] At first glance, it would seem that this phrase, taken as a whole, simply describes laws that do not target religious exercise and that therefore do not reflect formal or deliberate discrimination. According to a more complex interpretation, however, the word "neutral" captures the presumptive prohibition on purposeful discrimination, and "general applicability" means something else. According to this second interpretation, a law that imposes a substantial burden on the exercise of religion can escape Free Exercise Clause scrutiny only if it is not only "neutral," that is, free

---

[126] *Employment Div. v. Smith*, 494 U.S. 872, 879 (1990) (quoting *United States v. Lee*, 455 U.S. 252, 263 n.3 (1982) (Stevens, J., concurring in the judgment)).

from formal or deliberate discrimination, but also "generally applicable," understood as a separate requirement.

Most of the Court's opinion in *Smith* supports the first interpretation of this phrase. Yet one aspect of the Court's reasoning implied that "general applicability" might indeed be a separate requirement. Thus, in its creative attempt to distinguish *Sherbert* and similar cases concerning unemployment compensation,[127] the Court noted that they involved "a context that lent itself to individualized governmental assessment of the reasons for the relevant conduct."[128] The unemployment cases, the Court stated, "stand for the proposition that where the State has in place a system of individual exemptions, it may not refuse to extend that system to cases of 'religious hardship' without compelling reason."[129] The Court thus suggested that laws requiring at least some sorts of "individualized assessment" do not qualify as generally applicable laws and therefore are not immune from free exercise challenge. The Court's opinion in *Lukumi* went further, explicitly discussing "general applicability" as a separate requirement and concluding that the Hialeah ordinances did not qualify. The Court noted that the city had legitimate interests in public health and animal protection, but that the ordinances pursued those interests so selectively and "underinclusively" that they reached little if any conduct other than Santería animal sacrifice.[130]

Relying especially on *Lukumi* and reading "general applicability" as a separate and robust requirement, advocates have argued—and some lower courts have agreed—that the Supreme Court's free exercise doctrine can be read to protect religious exercise from certain laws that do not purposefully discriminate against it. In particular, they contend that even if a law regulates secular and religious conduct alike, it is presumptively invalid if it imposes a substantial burden on religious exercise and if the law, on its face or as applied, includes secular exceptions that undermine the government's interest in uniformity. Strict scrutiny would follow, and it typically could not be satisfied. Under this interpretation, "[i]f there are exceptions for secular interests, the religious claimant has to be treated as favorably as those who

---

[127] *See Sherbert v. Verner*, 374 U.S. 398 (1963); *Thomas v. Review Bd.*, 450 U.S. 707 (1981); *Hobbie v. Unemployment Appeals Comm'n*, 480 U.S. 136 (1987); *Frazee v. Illinois Dep't of Employment Sec.*, 489 U.S. 829 (1989).

[128] *Smith*, 494 U.S. at 884.

[129] *Id.*

[130] *See Church of the Lukumi Babalu Aye, Inc. v. City of Hialeah*, 508 U.S. 520, 542–46 (1993).

benefit from the secular exceptions."[131] Notably, the most prominent lower court opinion supporting this view is an opinion by then-Judge Alito, before his elevation to the Supreme Court. Speaking for the U.S. Court of Appeals for the Third Circuit, Judge Alito, observing that a police department's no-beard policy exempted officers who had medical excuses, ruled that the Free Exercise Clause demanded similar accommodation for beards worn by Muslim officers as a matter of religious obligation.[132]

This interpretation would extend the Free Exercise Clause beyond purposeful discrimination to redress laws that do not target religion, but that reflect selective indifference or selective inattention to religious interests.[133] It would thus move beyond formal equality and at least in the direction of substantive equality. By opening a broader range of laws to free exercise challenges, this interpretation also would promote, to that extent, religious voluntarism and other constitutional values.

This robust interpretation of "general applicability" is plausible and potentially attractive, but it probably is reading too much into the Supreme Court's doctrine.[134] In *Smith*, the Court's discussion of "individualized assessment" was designed to preserve, and to narrowly confine, the Court's prior holdings in the unemployment

---

[131] Douglas Laycock, *The Supreme Court and Religious Liberty*, 40 CATH. LAW. 25, 35 (2000); *see also* Richard F. Duncan, *Free Exercise is Dead, Long Live Free Exercise: Smith, Lukumi, and the General Applicability Requirement*, 3 U. PA. J. CONST. L. 850 (2001).

[132] *Fraternal Order of Police v. City of Newark*, 170 F.3d 359 (3d Cir. 1999) (Alito, J.). Then-Judge Alito invoked a similar interpretation of the Free Exercise Clause in *Blackhawk v. Pennsylvania*, 381 F.3d 202 (3d Cir. 2004) (Alito, J.) (granting an exemption from a wildlife permit fee requirement to a Native American owner of black bears, which were used by the owner in religious ceremonies, after finding that the permit fee requirement had secular exceptions rendering the law not generally applicable). *See also Rader v. Johnston*, 924 F. Supp. 1540 (D. Neb. 1996) (holding that a state university that exempted students from mandatory campus housing for various secular reasons was required by the Free Exercise Clause to accord similar accommodation to a religious objector who sought to live off campus in a Christian housing facility); Laycock, *supra* note 131, at 32–34 (discussing *Fraternal Order of Police* and *Rader*).

[133] This selective indifference or selective inattention might be seen to suggest at least the *possibility* of purposeful discrimination. As the Court's discussion in *Smith* implies, this risk may be especially prominent when laws call for "individualized assessment," but the risk may also arise, more generally, when laws include secular but not religious exceptions. *Cf. Fraternal Order of Police*, 170 F.3d at 365 ("[W]e conclude that the Department's decision to provide medical exemptions while refusing religious exemptions is sufficiently suggestive of discriminatory intent so as to trigger heightened scrutiny under *Smith* and *Lukumi*.").

[134] *See, e.g., Stormans, Inc. v. Wiesman*, 794 F.3d 1064, 1079–84 (9th Cir. 2015) (rejecting a broad reading of the "general applicability" requirement and finding that the existence of secular exceptions, including some entailing a degree of governmental discretion, did not undermine the general applicability of regulations requiring pharmacies to fill all lawfully prescribed drugs, including emergency contraceptives).

compensation cases. And in *Lukumi*, the Court did no more than invalidate laws whose disparate impact on religion was so overwhelming that it compelled an inference of purposeful discrimination, that is, the deliberate targeting of a particular religious practice.[135] The Court specifically found that "[t]he record in this case compels the conclusion that suppression of the central element of the Santería worship service was the object of the ordinances."[136] Thus, as the Court later explained, the fundamental teaching of *Smith* and *Lukumi* is that governmental action violates the Free Exercise Clause when it has "the unconstitutional object of targeting religious beliefs and practices."[137] Even so, the Court's unemployment compensation cases themselves remain valid, and there is room to argue for a broader and more vigorous understanding of general applicability.

2. "Hybrid" Claims

In *Smith*, the Court suggested that "hybrid" claims—claims that implicate not only the exercise of religion, but also some other constitutional interest—might be viable even against laws that are concededly nondiscriminatory and generally applicable. The Court utilized this theory to distinguish *Wisconsin v. Yoder*,[138] which it described as a "hybrid" case involving not only the Free Exercise Clause, but also the constitutional right of parents to control the education of their children.[139] Like its revisionist interpretation of the unemployment compensation cases, the Court's hybrid-claim theory and its explanation of *Yoder* are tenuous and decidedly post hoc,[140] making one question whether the theory has broader

---

[135] For analogous cases in the context of racial discrimination, see *Yick Wo v. Hopkins*, 118 U.S. 356 (1886); *Gomillion v. Lightfoot*, 364 U.S. 339 (1960). Because the purposeful discrimination was so obvious in *Lukumi*, the Court did not need to inquire directly into the underlying or subjective "motivation" for the city council's actions. *Compare Lukumi*, 508 U.S. at 540–42 (opinion of Kennedy, J.) (conducting such an inquiry nonetheless, and concluding that it further demonstrated the existence of purposeful discrimination), *with id.* at 558–59 (Scalia, J., concurring in part and concurring in the judgment) (objecting to this portion of Justice Kennedy's opinion).

[136] *Lukumi*, 508 U.S. at 534 (majority opinion); *cf. id.* at 557 (Scalia, J., concurring in part and concurring in the judgment) (suggesting that *Smith*'s "neutrality" and "general applicability" requirements "substantially overlap" and that laws violating the "general applicability" requirement are those that "through their design, construction, or enforcement target the practices of a particular religion for discriminatory treatment").

[137] *City of Boerne v. Flores*, 521 U.S. 507, 529 (1997).

[138] 406 U.S. 205 (1972).

[139] *See Employment Div. v. Smith*, 494 U.S. 872, 881–82 (1990). The Court cited the substantive due process case of *Pierce v. Society of Sisters*, 268 U.S. 510 (1925), and it noted that *Yoder* had cited *Pierce* as well. *Smith*, 494 U.S. at 881 & n.1.

[140] *See Lukumi*, 508 U.S. at 566–67 (Souter, J., concurring in part and concurring in the judgment).

doctrinal significance.[141] If it does, however, it might mean that a substantial burden on the exercise of religion, even if nondiscriminatory, can trigger heightened scrutiny if the law also burdens or impairs another constitutional interest, such as freedom of speech or freedom of association.

For the Free Exercise Clause to be doing any work in a hybrid case, of course, the other constitutional claim would have to be inadequate, standing alone, to trigger the same degree of scrutiny. The Supreme Court has done nothing to explain the appropriate constitutional arithmetic, nor has it otherwise elaborated the hybrid-claim theory that it advanced in *Smith*. Some lower courts have suggested that the theory might be viable if the companion constitutional claim is "colorable," but most have either rejected the theory as dicta or else have required that the companion claim be independently viable, an approach that effectively negates the theory by making the free exercise claim superfluous.[142] By all indications, the hybrid-claim theory has very little practical significance. In any event, the Supreme Court's doctrine concerning such claims is incomplete and uncertain.

E.   The Institutional Autonomy of Religious Organizations

At least to date, neither the general applicability requirement nor the hybrid-claim theory has made serious inroads on the basic doctrine of *Smith*, according to which the Free Exercise Clause is implicated only by discriminatory burdens on religious exercise. Conversely, one particular type of religious exercise—that involving the internal functioning and governance of religious organizations— has given rise to a more clear-cut exception to the rule of *Smith*, albeit an exception of uncertain scope. In *Smith* itself, the Court, citing earlier cases, noted that government may not "lend its power to one or the other side in controversies over religious authority or dogma."[143] More recently, in 2012, the Court confirmed and applied this principle in its unanimous decision in *Hosanna-Tabor*

---

[141] *See* Michael W. McConnell, *Free Exercise Revisionism and the* Smith *Decision*, 57 U. CHI. L. REV. 1109, 1121–24 (1990).

[142] *See Combs v. Homer-Center Sch. Dist.*, 540 F.3d 231, 244–47 (3d Cir. 2008) (rejecting hybrid-claim theory as dicta after discussing alternative approaches); *cf.* IRA C. LUPU & ROBERT W. TUTTLE, SECULAR GOVERNMENT, RELIGIOUS PEOPLE 187– 88 & n.33, 196 (2014) (arguing that *Smith*'s discussion of hybrid claims refers merely to situations in which religious freedom is protected by other constitutional liberties, that is, "situations in which religious freedom is subsumed in other, more general rights" and "in which a broader, secular conception of rights (speech, parental rights, etc.) does the constitutionally relevant work").

[143] *Smith*, 494 U.S. at 877 (citing *Presbyterian Church in the United States v. Mary Elizabeth Blue Hull Memorial Presbyterian Church*, 393 U.S. 440, 445–52 (1969); *Kedroff v. Saint Nicholas Cathedral*, 344 U.S. 94, 95–119 (1952); *Serbian Eastern Orthodox Diocese v. Milivojevich*, 426 U.S. 696, 708–25 (1976)).

Evangelical Lutheran Church and School v. EEOC.[144] In *Hosanna-Tabor*, the Court held that the First Amendment grants religious organizations a "ministerial exception" to otherwise applicable employment discrimination laws. The Court distinguished *Smith*, finding it irrelevant in this setting. More broadly, *Hosanna-Tabor* suggests that *Smith* does not apply to the internal affairs of religious organizations. Instead, with respect to these internal matters, the First Amendment may offer considerable protection for the institutional autonomy of religious organizations, even from laws that are nondiscriminatory and generally applicable.

The institutional autonomy of religious organizations is a constitutional value that is distinct from, but related to, the religious voluntarism of individuals. In fact, religious organizations take life through the voluntary decisions of individuals, who come together to pursue shared religious beliefs and practices. The content and character of these beliefs and practices are determined collectively, through a process of institutional self-governance. At a minimum, the First Amendment precludes courts from interfering with this process by determining that one side or another within a religious organization has the better religious argument. As discussed in Chapter 4, courts have no authority to decide the truth or reasonableness of competing religious claims. More generally, the process of institutional self-governance itself is entitled to constitutional protection, in order to facilitate the organization's—and therefore its members'—exercise of religion. Individuals can leave the religious body if they wish, of course. But as long as they remain members, they necessarily remain subject—based on implied if not express consent—to the collective decisionmaking of the organization that they have joined.[145] Otherwise, the religious freedom of the organization would be impaired, which in turn would undermine the religious freedom of its members as a whole. Accordingly, as the Supreme Court has suggested, the institutional autonomy of religious organizations warrants constitutional protection, at least with respect to internal disputes. This reasoning supports the view, endorsed in *Hosanna-Tabor*, that the First Amendment sometimes bars dissenters from pursuing legal claims against their own religious organization, claims that would undermine the institutional autonomy of the organization and

---

[144] 132 S. Ct. 694 (2012).

[145] *Cf. Watson v. Jones*, 80 U.S. (13 Wall.) 679, 729 (1872) ("All who unite themselves to [an ecclesiastical] body do so with an implied consent to [its] government, and are bound to submit to it.").

therefore the religious freedom of its other, non-dissenting members.[146]

In *Hosanna-Tabor*, Cheryl Perich filed a complaint against her church, for which she had worked as a parochial school teacher, claiming that she had been dismissed from her job in violation of the Americans with Disabilities Act (ADA). Prior to her dismissal, Perich mainly taught secular subjects, but she also taught religion classes, led her students in prayer, and performed other religious duties. Indeed, she had completed special theological training and had accepted the church's call as a "commissioned minister." Even so, under the rule of *Smith*, the Free Exercise Clause would have had no bearing on her claim, because, as the Supreme Court conceded, the ADA is a neutral law of general applicability. Nonetheless, the Justices ruled unanimously for the church, finding that it was free to fire Perich because her claim—whatever its merits under the ADA—was categorically barred. According to the Court, the First Amendment demands a "ministerial exception" to otherwise applicable employment discrimination laws, and, based on the particular facts of the case at hand, Perich qualified as a "minister" for this purpose. More generally, the ministerial exception permits churches and other religious bodies (but not nonreligious organizations) to select their leaders as they see fit. As such, the exception does not merely protect a church's decision "when it is made for a religious reason" but also ensures, more broadly, "that the authority to select and control who will minister to the faithful—a matter 'strictly ecclesiastical'—is the church's alone."[147]

The Court cited not only the Free Exercise Clause but also the Establishment Clause, noting that "the Establishment Clause ... prohibits government involvement in such ecclesiastical decisions."[148] But the ministerial exception rests first and foremost on the Free Exercise Clause, protecting "a religious group's right to shape its own faith and mission through its appointments."[149] As such, it represents an exception not only to the ADA and to other employment discrimination laws (whether federal or state), but also to the rule of *Smith*. Moreover, the ministerial exception generates absolute constitutional protection, as opposed to presumptive

---

[146] *See* Michael A. Helfand, *Religious Institutionalism, Implied Consent, and the Value of Voluntarism*, 88 S. CAL. L. REV. 539, 563–71 (2015).

[147] *Hosanna-Tabor*, 132 S. Ct. at 709 (quoting *Kedroff*, 344 U.S. at 119).

[148] *Id.* at 706.

[149] *Id.*; *cf.* Helfand, *supra* note 146, at 564 (arguing that the institutional autonomy of religious organizations, linked as it is to the religious voluntarism of individuals, warrants protection under the Free Exercise Clause "because it promotes the voluntary free exercise of religion").

protection under a test of strict scrutiny. As a result, it cannot be overcome by the government, not even if the government asserts a compelling justification. This exception thus grants religious institutions complete autonomy in hiring and firing their religious leaders,[150] free from the usual legal prohibitions on illicit discrimination.[151]

In distinguishing *Smith*, the Court in *Hosanna-Tabor* stated that "*Smith* involved government regulation of only outward physical acts" (albeit religious in character), whereas the case at hand "concern[ed] government interference with an internal church decision that affects the faith and mission of the church itself."[152] More broadly, the Court stated that the First Amendment "gives special solicitude to the rights of religious organizations,"[153] granting them a degree of institutional autonomy that does not extend to nonreligious groups. As the Court explained, our legal system has long reflected " 'a spirit of freedom for religious organizations, an independence from secular control or manipulation—in short, power to decide for themselves, free from state interference, matters of church government as well as those of faith and doctrine.' "[154] This reasoning supports not only the ministerial exception but also other facets of institutional

---

[150] The Court declined to adopt a specific test or formula for determining when an employee qualifies as a "minister" for purposes of the "ministerial exception," concluding that it was enough to say that "the exception covers Perich, given all the circumstances of her employment." *Hosanna-Tabor*, 132 S. Ct. at 707. In a concurring opinion, Justice Thomas argued that courts should "defer to a religious organization's good-faith understanding of who qualifies as its minister." *Id.* at 710 (Thomas, J., concurring). In a separate concurrence, Justice Alito emphasized that the ministerial exception, despite its name, extends to all religious groups, not merely those that use the term "minister" to describe their religious leaders. Advocating a functional approach, he argued that the exception should apply to any employee "who leads a religious organization, conducts worship services or important religious ceremonies or rituals, or serves as a messenger or teacher of its faith." *Id.* at 712 (Alito, J., concurring).

[151] The Court in *Hosanna-Tabor* made no mention of its decision two years earlier in *Christian Legal Society v. Martinez*, 561 U.S. 661 (2010). As discussed previously in this chapter, the Court in *Christian Legal Society*, interpreting the Free Speech Clause, refused to exempt a student religious group from an "all-comers" nondiscrimination policy that extended to the group's selection of its leaders. There is obvious tension between *Christian Legal Society* and *Hosanna-Tabor*, but the cases are not difficult to distinguish. Most importantly, the all-comers policy in *Christian Legal Society*, unlike the employment discrimination laws addressed in *Hosanna-Tabor*, entailed no direct legal compulsion. Instead, it applied only as a condition to the student group's participation in a limited public forum.

[152] *Hosanna-Tabor*, 132 S. Ct. at 707; *see id.* at 706 (noting that the ministerial exception protects "the internal governance of the church").

[153] *Id.* at 706.

[154] *Id.* at 704 (quoting *Kedroff v. Saint Nicholas Cathedral*, 344 U.S. 94, 116 (1952) (discussing the Supreme Court's opinion in *Watson v. Jones*, 80 U.S. (13 Wall.) 679 (1872)).

autonomy, at least with respect to a religious organization's internal affairs.

One such internal matter is the resolution of property disputes. When religious bodies or denominations splinter in the face of controversies over leadership or religious doctrine, the competing factions each may assert ownership of the religious organization's property, including local places of worship. In recent decades, for example, Protestant denominations have fractured over issues including sexual morality and same-sex relationships, leading to litigation concerning church property. In the typical situation, a local religious group, even as it withdraws in protest from its existing denomination, attempts to retain the building in which it has worshiped. In *Hosanna-Tabor*, the Court noted and reaffirmed earlier decisions addressing the institutional autonomy of religious organizations in this setting. In this line of cases, the Court has ruled that the First Amendment permits states, as a matter of state law, to adopt either of two approaches.

Under the "deference" approach of *Watson v. Jones*,[155] courts respect the institutional autonomy of religious organizations by deferring to their preexisting organizational structure.[156] If the religious organization is hierarchical—that is, if the local religious group operates within a broader, hierarchical structure of governance—the hierarchy's decision about the property is controlling.[157] Conversely, if the religious organization is congregational—if the local group operates independently—then the local congregation decides, following its usual method of decisionmaking.[158] In *Jones v. Wolf*,[159] the Court endorsed an alternative approach, permitting states to resolve property disputes, if they wish, according to "neutral principles of law," using "objective, well-established concepts of trust and property law" that govern property disputes generally.[160] This alternative permits

---

[155] 80 U.S. (13 Wall.) 679 (1872). The Court's decision did not rest on the First Amendment, which had not yet been applied to the states, but it has been read in later cases to reflect First Amendment considerations. *See, e.g., Presbyterian Church in the United States v. Mary Elizabeth Blue Hull Memorial Presbyterian Church*, 393 U.S. 440, 445 (1969).

[156] As Professor Douglas Laycock has observed, religious groups have adopted different organizational structures on the basis of "deep theological disagreements; the wars of religion were fought in part over these choices of whether to have a Pope, whether to have bishops, whether to have elected assemblies, or whether to have no authority at all higher than the local congregation." Douglas Laycock, *Church Autonomy Revisited*, 7 GEO. J.L. & PUB. POL'Y 253, 258 (2009).

[157] *See Watson v. Jones*, 80 U.S. (13 Wall) at 726–34.

[158] *See id.* at 724–26.

[159] 443 U.S. 595 (1979).

[160] *Id.* at 602–03.

religious bodies, through their ordinary institutional mechanisms, to craft and adopt legal documents, such as deeds and trusts, allocating the organization's property as they see fit.[161] Thus, each of the two permissible approaches to property disputes, in its own way, honors the institutional autonomy of religious organizations.[162]

The First Amendment's protection of institutional autonomy extends to other internal disputes, beyond those relating to employment discrimination and property. But the precise scope of this exception to the doctrine of *Smith* remains to be seen. In *Hosanna-Tabor*, the Court confined itself to the ministerial exception to employment discrimination laws, explicitly reserving other questions, even in the setting of employment.[163] But the logic of *Hosanna-Tabor*—and the underlying arguments for protecting institutional autonomy—support a broader First Amendment doctrine, one that would preclude "insiders" from suing their religious organizations in other situations as well. Indeed, consistent with this view, lower courts—before and after *Hosanna-Tabor*—have protected religious organizations from a variety of member-initiated lawsuits, including claims of "clergy malpractice"; challenges to church discipline, including excommunication or "shunning"; and certain other claims as well.[164]

IV. Constitutional Values, Freedom of Speech, and the Free Exercise Clause

There is deep and continuing controversy concerning the meaning of the Free Exercise Clause and the constitutional values it should be read to protect. Under the prevailing doctrine of *Employment Division v. Smith*,[165] the Supreme Court confines itself largely to the enforcement of nondiscrimination and formal religious equality. As *Locke v. Davey*[166] attests, moreover, even these minimal

---

[161] *See id.* at 603–04.

[162] *But cf. id.* at 610–21 (Powell, J., dissenting) (arguing that a proper understanding of the First Amendment would permit only one approach, the deference approach of *Watson v. Jones*); Laycock, *supra* note 156, at 256–58 (describing *Jones v. Wolf* as "an important loss for church autonomy" and contending that the increasingly prevalent neutral-principles approach has often been applied with a bias favoring local congregations, thus undermining the internal governance of hierarchical churches).

[163] *Hosanna-Tabor Evangelical Lutheran Church & Sch. v. EEOC*, 132 S. Ct. 694, 710 (2012).

[164] *See* Christopher C. Lund, *Free Exercise Reconceived: The Logic and Limits of Hosanna-Tabor*, 108 NW. U. L. REV. 1183 (2014). According to Professor Lund, *Hosanna-Tabor* and these lower court decisions suggest the following principle: "absent some compelling governmental interest, the First Amendment precludes insiders from suing their churches over matters of significant religious concern." *Id.* at 1203.

[165] 494 U.S. 872 (1990).

[166] 540 U.S. 712 (2004).

standards do not always extend to indirect burdens. At the same time, the Court's unanimous ruling in *Hosanna-Tabor Evangelical Lutheran Church and School v. EEOC*[167] strongly affirms the institutional autonomy of religious organizations, at least with respect to their internal affairs. Apart from the Free Exercise Clause, moreover, the Free Speech Clause provides important additional protection. But the Court's free speech doctrine likewise focuses mainly on nondiscrimination and formal equality—in protecting private religious speech from discriminatory treatment.

As already noted, and as we will discuss in the next chapter, legislative enactments such as the Religious Freedom Restoration Act, as well as comparable approaches under state constitutional law, sometimes protect religious conduct from nondiscriminatory burdens. But as for the Free Exercise Clause itself, the doctrine of *Smith* continues to govern in most settings. One can argue that this restrictive approach is inadequate and that the Supreme Court should give greater weight to religious voluntarism and other constitutional values. This argument might someday prevail, but it appears that a majority of the Court supports the current approach, and there is no indication that any major doctrinal change is in the offing.

---

[167] 132 S. Ct. 694 (2012).

Chapter 6

FREE EXERCISE: STATUTORY AND STATE-LAW PROTECTION

As we saw in the last chapter, the Supreme Court's interpretation of the Free Exercise Clause has varied over time. In the contemporary period, the Court's doctrine, although multifaceted, is dominated by *Employment Division v. Smith*.[1] According to *Smith*, the Free Exercise Clause generally is implicated only by discriminatory burdens on religious exercise. This restrictive approach is controlling constitutional doctrine under the First Amendment. But in a variety of settings, the First Amendment is supplemented by alternative sources of religious freedom, including federal and state statutes as well as state constitutional law. In this chapter, we move beyond the First Amendment to consider these alternative fonts of religious freedom, which often protect the exercise of religion even when the First Amendment does not. In particular, unlike *Smith*, they often demand religious exemptions from otherwise neutral laws of general applicability.

Even as it announced its decision in *Smith*, the Supreme Court made it clear that its ruling did not preclude legislatures from granting religious exemptions. On the particular matter at issue in *Smith*, for instance, the Court noted with approval that "a number of States have made an exception to their drug laws for sacramental peyote use."[2] "But to say that a nondiscriminatory religious-practice exemption is permitted, or even that it is desirable," the Court continued, "is not to say that it is constitutionally required, and that the appropriate occasions for its creation can be discerned by the courts."[3] *Smith* thus approved and invited specific statutory accommodations, crafted by legislatures to identify and protect particular aspects of religious exercise, such as the sacramental use of peyote. As we will see shortly, specific statutory accommodations are common in a wide range of settings.

Although the *Smith* Court contemplated specific statutory accommodations, adopted in the context of particular laws, Congress had a more ambitious idea: undoing the effect of *Smith* altogether. Concluding that the Court's new doctrine gave

---

[1]   494 U.S. 872 (1990).

[2]   *Id.* at 890.

[3]   *Id.*

inadequate protection to the exercise of religion, Congress attempted to "restore" the Court's prior doctrine by enacting the Religious Freedom Restoration Act of 1993 (RFRA).[4] Under the terms of RFRA, strict scrutiny once again was required for substantial burdens on the exercise of religion, including nondiscriminatory burdens—now as a matter of statutory rather than constitutional right. As explained below, however, the Supreme Court soon ruled that RFRA itself was unconstitutional as applied to state and local laws and governmental practices. Conversely, the Court left RFRA intact for federal laws and practices, and, indeed, it has applied the law vigorously in this context. Meanwhile, Congress adopted an additional statute, the Religious Land Use and Institutionalized Persons Act of 2000 (RLUIPA),[5] which reimposed the RFRA standard on state and local laws and practices in two discrete settings: land use regulations; and regulations affecting institutionalized persons, including prisoners.

Beyond these congressional actions, states have responded to the Supreme Court by enhancing religious freedom as a matter of state law. A large number of state legislatures have adopted state-law RFRAs modeled on the federal statute. And some state courts, interpreting their own constitutions, have rejected the approach of *Smith*, opting instead for a state constitutional doctrine along the lines of the Supreme Court's pre-*Smith* approach.

In recent years, critics have argued that RFRAs—and presumably state constitutional law—should categorically preclude religious exemptions from laws that forbid discrimination on prohibited grounds, or at least should preclude such exemptions for commercial businesses. These critics have been especially concerned that state-law RFRAs might be used to justify discrimination against gays and lesbians, a concern that has become especially pronounced with the advent of same-sex marriage. As a result, recent state-law proposals have generated heated political controversy.

More broadly, some have contended that statutes providing religious exemptions, although designed to accommodate the free exercise of religion, in fact confer an impermissible benefit on religion and thereby violate the Establishment Clause. This sort of Establishment Clause argument might be directed to specific statutory accommodations, to RFRA and RLUIPA, to similar state laws, or even to state constitutional doctrine. For example, Justice

---

4   42 U.S.C. §§ 2000bb to 2000bb–4.

5   42 U.S.C. §§ 2000cc to 2000cc–5.

Stevens once argued, in an opinion speaking only for himself, that RFRA violates the Establishment Clause.[6] More recently, by contrast, in *Cutter v. Wilkinson*,[7] the Supreme Court unanimously rejected an Establishment Clause challenge to RLUIPA's recognition of prisoner claims. *Cutter* and other precedents likewise suggest that the Establishment Clause does not threaten RLUIPA's land use provisions, nor does it undermine RFRA, RFRA's state-law counterparts, or analogous state constitutional law. Subject to certain limitations, specific statutory accommodations also are constitutionally permissible. We will return to these issues in the next chapter, when we address the concept of accommodation as it relates to the Establishment Clause.

In this chapter, we will put aside the Establishment Clause questions and focus on the scope and application of these various legal sources of religious exemptions. We first will address specific statutory accommodations. We then will discuss the federal statutes, RFRA and RLUIPA. Thereafter we will turn to state constitutional law and state-law RFRAs.

I.   Specific Statutory Accommodations

In a broad range of settings, statutes accommodate religious objectors by granting them specific exemptions from otherwise applicable laws, thus protecting their religious freedom. And there is nothing new about this practice. As Professor Douglas Laycock has observed, "From the late seventeenth century to the present, there is an unbroken tradition of legislatively enacted regulatory exemptions."[8]

Specific legislative accommodations initially emerged even while colonies and states continued to maintain established religions. Thus, religious dissenters sometimes were excused from worshiping in the established church or from paying taxes to support it. Other common exemptions during this period protected religious believers who objected to oath-taking or to military service. In addition, for example, North Carolina and Maryland excused religious objectors from courtroom rules that required the removal of hats, and Rhode Island permitted Jews to marry under Jewish standards even when the marriage would violate the state's usual affinity and consanguinity restrictions.[9]

---

[6]   *City of Boerne v. Flores*, 521 U.S. 507, 536–37 (1997) (Stevens, J., concurring).

[7]   544 U.S. 709 (2005).

[8]   Douglas Laycock, *Regulatory Exemptions of Religious Behavior and the Original Understanding of the Establishment Clause*, 81 NOTRE DAME L. REV. 1793, 1837 (2006).

[9]   *See id.* at 1803–08.

In the contemporary period, specific statutory accommodations are commonplace. Responding to the Supreme Court's invitation in *Smith*, for instance, the State of Oregon amended its criminal drug law to exempt the religious use of peyote.[10] Likewise, Congress responded to another restrictive decision under the Free Exercise Clause[11] by permitting members of the military, despite general dress-code requirements, to wear Jewish yarmulkes and other items of religious apparel that are "neat and conservative" and that do not interfere with the performance of military duties.[12]

Two important accommodation provisions appear in Title VII of the Civil Rights Act of 1964, which generally forbids employment discrimination on the basis of religion.[13] The first provision exempts religious organizations from this prohibition by permitting them to prefer members of their own faith, even for nonreligious jobs.[14] The second is designed to protect religious employees who work for nonreligious employers, including government agencies as well as private businesses. This provision supplements Title VII's basic prohibition on religious discrimination by requiring employers to "reasonably accommodate" their employees' religious observances and practices, such as attending worship services or wearing religious apparel, if the employer can do so "without undue hardship on the conduct of the employer's business."[15]

More generally, federal, state, and local laws are peppered with specific statutory accommodations. Legal surveys have suggested that there may be two thousand or more such laws.[16] As Professors John Witte, Jr., and Joel A. Nichols have reported, these include religious exemptions in federal laws "governing all manner of subjects," including "laws of evidence and civil procedure, taxation and bankruptcy, disability, labor, employment, unions, civil rights, interstate commerce, ERISA, workplace, military, immigration and naturalization, food and drugs, prisons, hospitals, land use, and much more."[17] Likewise, state and local laws "create sundry special religious rights for some of these same topics, as well as for local

---

[10] *See* OR. REV. STAT. § 475.752(4).

[11] *Goldman v. Weinberger*, 475 U.S. 503 (1986).

[12] *See* 10 U.S.C. § 774.

[13] 42 U.S.C. § 2000e–2(a).

[14] 42 U.S.C. § 2000e–1(a); *see Corporation of the Presiding Bishop v. Amos*, 483 U.S. 327 (1987); *see also* 42 U.S.C. § 2000e–2(e)(2).

[15] 42 U.S.C. § 2000e(j). It is not particularly difficult for employers to show an "undue burden," which has been construed to include anything more than a *de minimis* cost or burden on business operations. *See Trans World Airlines, Inc. v. Hardison*, 432 U.S. 63, 84 (1977).

[16] *See* JOHN WITTE, JR., & JOEL A. NICHOLS, RELIGION AND THE AMERICAN CONSTITUTIONAL EXPERIMENT 161 (3d ed. 2011).

[17] *Id.*

issues like property tax, zoning, nonprofit organizations, education, charity, and the like."[18] These specific statutory accommodations—federal, state, and local—offer important protection for the free exercise of religion. Although the accommodations are not a matter of constitutional right, they can be seen to support constitutional values, including the religious voluntarism of individuals and the institutional autonomy of religious organizations.

II. The Religious Freedom Restoration Act

A.   RFRA, Congress, and the Supreme Court

Unlike other legislative responses to restrictive judicial decisions under the Free Exercise Clause, the Religious Freedom Restoration Act of 1993 (RFRA) did not merely enact a specific statutory accommodation. Instead, through its adoption of RFRA, Congress forthrightly rejected the general constitutional doctrine that emerged from *Employment Division v. Smith*[19] in favor of the Court's earlier approach, as reflected in *Sherbert v. Verner*[20] and *Wisconsin v. Yoder*.[21] RFRA offers statutory protection for the free exercise of religion, but it does so through a general legal standard that previously was a matter of constitutional law. As such, it is a remarkable, and remarkably important, religious freedom statute.

Congress was not shy in expressing its disagreement with the Supreme Court. Thus, in RFRA's formal statement of findings and purposes, Congress referred to the First Amendment's protection of "free exercise of religion as an unalienable right;"[22] declared that "governments should not substantially burden religious exercise without compelling justification;"[23] and noted that "in *Employment Division v. Smith*, the Supreme Court virtually eliminated the requirement that the government justify burdens on religious exercise imposed by laws neutral toward religion."[24] Asserting that "the compelling interest test as set forth in prior Federal court rulings is a workable test for striking sensible balances between religious liberty and competing prior governmental interests,"[25] Congress declared that the purpose of the Act was "to restore the compelling interest test as set forth in *Sherbert v. Verner* and *Wisconsin v. Yoder* and to guarantee its application in all cases

---

[18] *Id.*

[19] 494 U.S. 872 (1990).

[20] 374 U.S. 398 (1963).

[21] 406 U.S. 205 (1972).

[22] 42 U.S.C. § 2000bb(a)(1).

[23] 42 U.S.C. § 2000bb(a)(3).

[24] 42 U.S.C. § 2000bb(a)(4) (citation omitted).

[25] 42 U.S.C. § 2000bb(a)(5).

where free exercise of religion is substantially burdened."[26] To effectuate this purpose, RFRA's primary substantive provision reinstated the Court's earlier approach, albeit as a matter of statutory rather than constitutional right. Thus, this provision states that "Government shall not substantially burden a person's exercise of religion even if the burden results from a rule of general applicability," unless the government can "demonstrate[ ] that application of the burden to the person—(1) is in furtherance of a compelling governmental interest; and (2) is the least restrictive means of furthering that compelling governmental interest."[27]

At the time of its adoption, RFRA was a broadly bipartisan measure that garnered overwhelming political support. It was promoted by a wide and diverse array of groups—secular and religious, liberal and conservative. This "Coalition for the Free Exercise of Religion" included well over fifty organizations, with membership "spann[ing] the theological and ideological spectrum from the Southern Baptist Convention to the National Council of Churches, from the Christian Legal Society to the ACLU, from the Traditional Values Coalition to People for the American Way."[28] According to Senator Orrin Hatch, it was "one of the broadest coalitions ever assembled to support a bill before Congress."[29] Reflecting this wide-ranging consensus, the House of Representatives passed the Act by voice vote without objection,[30] and the Senate approved the measure by a vote of 97 to 3.[31] RFRA was signed into law by President Bill Clinton, who later praised Congress for "reaffirming our solemn commitment to protect the first guarantee of our Bill of Rights."[32]

Despite the broad political support for RFRA, it tested the limits of congressional power, and, just four years after its enactment, the Supreme Court ruled that Congress had gone too far. In *City of Boerne v. Flores*,[33] the Court did not conclude or suggest that RFRA violated the Establishment Clause.[34] Instead, it

---

[26] 42 U.S.C. § 2000bb(b)(1) (citations omitted).

[27] 42 U.S.C. § 2000bb–1.

[28] Forest D. Montgomery, *Common Adversity Works for Common Good*, CHRISTIAN LEGAL SOC'Y Q., Winter 1993, at 9.

[29] 139 CONG. REC. S14352 (daily ed. Oct. 26, 1993) (statement of Sen. Hatch).

[30] 139 CONG. REC. H2363 (daily ed. May 11, 1993) (adopting House bill); *id.* at H8715 (daily ed. Nov. 3, 1993) (concurring in Senate amendment).

[31] 139 CONG. REC. S14471 (daily ed. Oct. 27, 1993).

[32] Proclamation No. 6646, 59 Fed. Reg. 2925 (1994) (presidential proclamation declaring January 16, 1994, "Religious Freedom Day").

[33] 521 U.S. 507 (1997).

[34] As noted earlier, Justice Stevens took that position, but no other Justice shared his view. *See id.* at 536–37 (Stevens, J., concurring).

declared that RFRA exceeded the scope of Section 5 of the Fourteenth Amendment, which gives Congress the power to "enforce" the provisions of that amendment against state and local governments. This power extends to the Fourteenth Amendment's incorporation of Bill of Rights standards, including those of the Free Exercise Clause. As the Court made clear in *Boerne*, however, the congressional power is remedial, not substantive. Thus, Section 5 permits Congress to enforce, with some discretion, the relevant constitutional provision—in this case, the Free Exercise Clause—as it has been interpreted by the Supreme Court. But Congress cannot impose restrictions on state and local governments that are based upon its own, more capacious interpretation of what the Constitution demands. Because RFRA was designed to expand, not enforce, the Free Exercise Clause as interpreted in *Smith*, it exceeded the scope of congressional power under Section 5, and it therefore was invalid as applied to state and local laws and governmental practices. With respect to state and local governments, *Boerne* thus returned the federal law of religious free exercise to the restrictive constitutional standard of *Smith*.

By every indication, however, RFRA remains valid and controlling as applied to federal laws and practices. To be sure, *Boerne* relied in part on separation-of-powers considerations. In rebuking Congress for rejecting the Supreme Court's interpretation of the Free Exercise Clause, for instance, the Court cited *Marbury v. Madison* and declared that interpreting the Constitution, as it had done in *Smith*, falls "within the province of the Judicial Branch, which embraces the duty to say what the law is."[35] In summarizing its reasoning, moreover, the Court stated that "RFRA contradicts vital principles necessary to maintain separation of powers and the federal balance."[36] It seems clear from the opinion as a whole, however, that it was the *combination* of separation-of-powers and federalism concerns that led the Court to interpret Section 5 as it did. In the federal-law setting, of course, there is no federalism issue, and RFRA does not rest on Congress's Section 5 power. Rather, it amounts to a congressional decision to protect religious freedom by pulling back, to the extent specified by RFRA, from exercising whatever enumerated power otherwise supports the particular federal lawmaking that is at issue. Lower courts have concluded that Congress is free to restrict the operation of its own lawmaking in this fashion, and that, accordingly, RFRA remains

---

[35] *Id.* at 536 (majority opinion) (citing *Marbury v. Madison*, 5 U.S. (1 Cranch) 137, 177 (1803)).

[36] *Id.*

valid as applied to federal laws and practices.[37] The Supreme Court has not directly confronted the issue, but it has applied RFRA in the federal setting and has strongly implied that the law to this extent is within the scope of congressional power.[38]

In the federal sphere, where it continues to govern, RFRA "adopts a statutory rule comparable to the constitutional rule rejected in *Smith*."[39] In two respects, RFRA clarifies, and arguably strengthens, the Supreme Court's pre-*Smith* doctrine. First, through a 2000 amendment, RFRA covers "any exercise of religion, whether or not compelled by, or central to, a system of religious belief."[40] Prior to the amendment, RFRA referred simply to "the exercise of religion under the First Amendment to the Constitution."[41] Second, RFRA makes it clear that when strict scrutiny is triggered, it includes a "least restrictive means" requirement.[42] Pre-*Smith* case law did not always use that precise language. In reality, however, these two provisions of RFRA do little more than clarify or confirm legal principles that were largely if not entirely embedded in the Court's pre-*Smith* constitutional doctrine, as discussed in Chapter 5.[43]

More generally, RFRA reinstates the various components of the Court's pre-*Smith* approach. Thus, although neither compulsion nor centrality is required, the objector still must show that he or she indeed is exercising religion—that is, acting on the basis of a sincerely held religious belief—and that the government is imposing

---

[37] The leading case is *Christians v. Crystal Evangelical Free Church (In re Young)*, 141 F.3d 854 (8th Cir. 1998). In this case, bankruptcy debtors invoked RFRA to prevent the bankruptcy trustee from reclaiming, as avoidable transactions, religious tithes that they had given to their church. According to the court, RFRA had "effectively amended the Bankruptcy Code," and this was within the power of Congress "under the Bankruptcy Clause and the Necessary and Proper Clause of Article I of the Constitution." *Id.* at 861, 856.

[38] *See Burwell v. Hobby Lobby Stores, Inc.*, 134 S. Ct. 2751, 2761 (2014) ("As applied to a federal agency, RFRA is based on the enumerated power that supports the particular agency's work.") (citing lower court decisions upholding RFRA's validity in the federal context).

[39] *Gonzales v. O Centro Espírita Beneficente União do Vegetal*, 546 U.S. 418, 424 (2006).

[40] 42 U.S.C. § 2000cc–5(7)(A); *see* 42 U.S.C. § 2000bb–2(4) (cross-referencing 42 U.S.C. § 2000cc–5). This amendment to RFRA was included in the Religious Land Use and Institutionalized Persons Act of 2000 (RLUIPA). *See also* 42 U.S.C. § 2000cc–3(g) (calling for "a broad protection of religious exercise").

[41] 42 U.S.C. § 2000bb–2(4) (1994 ed.) (no longer in effect).

[42] 42 U.S.C. § 2000bb–1.

[43] The Justices debated the significance of these two RFRA provisions in *Burwell v. Hobby Lobby Stores, Inc.*, 134 S. Ct. 2751 (2014). In his majority opinion, Justice Alito contended that they suggested a significant expansion of religious freedom, whereas Justice Ginsburg, in her dissenting opinion, argued that they did not. *Compare id.* at 2761 n.3, 2761–62, 2767 & n.18, 2772–73 (majority opinion) *with id.* at 2791–93 (Ginsburg, J., dissenting).

a substantial burden on that religious exercise. To this extent, RFRA calls for the same analysis as the Free Exercise Clause, as elaborated in Chapter 5. Since RFRA rejects the rule of *Smith*, however, the objector need not show (as the Free Exercise Clause generally requires) that the burden is discriminatory. Indeed, in the typical RFRA case, the objector is seeking an exemption from a neutral law of general applicability. And if the Court finds that the law imposes a substantial burden on religious exercise, the government is required to grant an exemption unless it satisfies strict scrutiny. To make this showing, the government must prove that applying the law to the objector—that is, denying the exemption—is necessary to serve a compelling governmental interest. Accordingly, as stated earlier, RFRA's core provision declares that government cannot "substantially burden a person's exercise of religion" unless it "demonstrates that application of the burden to the person" furthers "a compelling governmental interest" by "the least restrictive means."[44]

The Supreme Court has applied RFRA in only two cases. In these two cases, however, the Court not only has applied the law without doubting its constitutionality in the federal realm but also has given the law a robust interpretation. In both cases, the Court ruled that RFRA mandated religious exemptions, thus honoring the congressional goal of protecting religious freedom even from nondiscriminatory laws. In the first case, *Gonzales v. O Centro Espírita Beneficente União do Vegetal*,[45] the Court explained and applied RFRA's statutory strict scrutiny. *Gonzales* involved a situation much like *Smith* itself—the sacramental use of an otherwise illegal drug—but the Justices found that RFRA demanded a different result. In the second case, *Burwell v. Hobby Lobby Stores, Inc.*,[46] the Court ruled that RFRA relieved some employers from a federal requirement that they provide their employees with insurance coverage for contraceptives. Going well beyond *Gonzales*, the Court offered an expansive interpretation of RFRA, extending its protection to certain for-profit corporations; allowing objectors to show a substantial burden even when asserting arguably attenuated, complicity-based claims; and making it even more clear, as *Gonzales* had suggested, that RFRA's strict scrutiny is quite demanding indeed.

In *Gonzales*, decided in 2006, the Court addressed the claim of O Centro Espírita Beneficente União do Vegetal (UDV) that RFRA entitled it to an exemption from the federal Controlled Substances

---

[44]   42 U.S.C. § 2000bb–1.

[45]   546 U.S. 418 (2006).

[46]   134 S. Ct. 2751 (2014).

Act. The UDV is a Christian Spiritist group, based in Brazil, that has a small branch of followers in the United States. The religion blends elements of Christianity with indigenous beliefs and practices. Members of the group receive communion by drinking hoasca (pronounced "wass-ca"), a sacramental tea brewed from plants native to the Amazon region. Hoasca contains dimethyltryptamine (DMT), an hallucinogenic substance, the importation and use of which are banned under Schedule I of the Controlled Substances Act. The government conceded that this ban, as applied to the UDV, substantially burdened the group's sincere exercise of religion, triggering strict scrutiny under RFRA. But it argued that it was justified in denying the requested exemption because the ban in fact served a compelling interest by the least restrictive means. In a unanimous decision, however, the Justices disagreed, ruling that RFRA bars application of the Controlled Substances Act to the UDV's sacramental use of hoasca.[47]

Speaking for the Court, Chief Justice Roberts emphasized that it was not enough that the Controlled Substances Act, in general, serves a compelling interest. Instead, "RFRA requires the Government to demonstrate that the compelling interest test is satisfied through application of the challenged law 'to the person'— the particular claimant whose sincere exercise of religion is being substantially burdened."[48] In the case at hand, this inquiry demanded an assessment of "the harms posed by the particular use at issue here—the circumscribed, sacramental use of hoasca by the UDV."[49] The federal government already offered a regulatory exemption from the Controlled Substances Act for the sacramental use of peyote, and the Court was not persuaded that providing an exemption here would be any more problematic. Because the government had "failed to demonstrate . . . a compelling interest in barring the UDV's sacramental use of hoasca,"[50] the group was entitled to the exemption that it sought.

B. Hobby Lobby and the Affordable Care Act

In its 2014 decision in *Burwell v. Hobby Lobby Stores, Inc.,*[51] the Supreme Court relied on RFRA in extending relief to Hobby Lobby and certain other employers who objected on religious

---

[47] More precisely, the Court affirmed the granting of a preliminary injunction in favor of the UDV, but its reasoning clearly supported the group's claim for permanent relief. *Gonzales* was an 8–0 decision. Justice Alito did not participate, having joined the Court after the case was argued.

[48] *Gonzales,* 546 U.S. at 430–31 (citing 42 U.S.C. § 2000bb–1(b)).

[49] *Id.* at 432.

[50] *Id.* at 439.

[51] 134 S. Ct. 2751 (2014).

grounds to provisions of the Affordable Care Act of 2010 (ACA) and related regulations. The ACA, as implemented by the Department of Health and Human Services (HHS), required the employers to provide their employees with insurance coverage for various contraceptives, without any cost-sharing requirements. The challengers were closely held for-profit corporations that operated under religious principles. The lead challenger, Hobby Lobby, operated a chain of 500 arts-and-crafts stores with more than 13,000 employees. Its corporate documents included a "statement of purpose" that committed the company's owners—David and Barbara Green and their three children—to "[h]onoring the Lord in all [they] do by operating the company in a manner consistent with Biblical principles."[52] Based on concededly sincere religious beliefs, Hobby Lobby and the other employers objected to providing coverage for four particular forms of contraception—two types of intrauterine devices (IUDs) and two types of "morning-after pills"— that the employers found morally objectionable because they could operate after fertilization, thus resulting in the destruction of human embryos. Unlike in *Gonzales*, the Justices were sharply divided in *Hobby Lobby*, but a five-Justice majority found that RFRA entitled the challengers to relief. In so doing, the Court resolved each of three issues in their favor, finding that the corporations in question were eligible to assert RFRA claims, that the ACA's contraceptive mandate imposed a substantial burden on the exercise of religion, and that the government could not satisfy strict scrutiny.

The initial question in *Hobby Lobby* was whether for-profit corporations were categorically excluded from the protection of RFRA. In her dissenting opinion, Justice Ginsburg argued that they were. She contended that for-profit corporations, even if closely held, cannot be said to exercise religion and so should not be protected under either the Free Exercise Clause or RFRA.[53] But a majority of the Court disagreed. Speaking through an opinion by Justice Alito, the Court relied in part on specific statutory language and in part on broader principles.

RFRA protects the exercise of religion by a "person." This term is not defined by RFRA itself, but it is defined by a more general federal statute, the "Dictionary Act," which governs "the meaning of

---

[52]   *Id.* at 2766.

[53]   *See id.* at 2793–97 (Ginsburg, J., dissenting). In this portion of her opinion, Justice Ginsburg spoke only for herself and Justice Sotomayor. The other two dissenters, Justices Breyer and Kagan, joined the remainder of her opinion, rejecting the RFRA claim on other grounds, but they did not reach the question of whether for-profit corporations were entirely excluded from the statute's coverage. *See id.* at 2806 (Breyer & Kagan, JJ., dissenting).

any Act of Congress, unless the context indicates otherwise."[54] The Dictionary Act states that "the wor[d] 'person' ... include[s] corporations, companies, associations, firms, partnerships, societies, and joint stock companies, as well as individuals."[55] In her dissenting opinion, Justice Ginsburg argued that because for-profit corporations cannot be said to exercise religion, the particular context of RFRA justified a departure from this general definition. But the Court, to the contrary, found "nothing in RFRA that suggests a congressional intent to depart from the Dictionary Act definition."[56]

According to the Court, "RFRA was designed to provide very broad protection for religious liberty,"[57] beyond that which is constitutionally required, and the "exercise of religion" under RFRA is not confined to specific interpretations of that concept in prior First Amendment case law.[58] Even so, the Court discussed its prior First Amendment doctrine and general principles of religious freedom. It noted that it had entertained claims under the Free Exercise Clause by individual commercial actors,[59] and it argued that use of the corporate form should not lead to a different conclusion. Protecting the religious freedom of organizations, the Court asserted, is important to the religious freedom of individuals. This certainly is true for religious organizations, including those that operate as nonprofit corporations. Such organizations plainly are protected by the Free Exercise Clause and RFRA. According to the Court, moreover, similar reasoning supports protection for the religious freedom of closely held for-profit corporations, because this protection, in reality, supports the religious freedom of their owners:

> Congress provided protection for people like the ... Greens by employing a familiar legal fiction: It included corporations within RFRA's definition of "persons." But it is important to keep in mind that the purpose of this fiction is to provide protection for human beings. ... [P]rotecting the free-exercise rights of corporations like

---

[54] 1 U.S.C. § 1.

[55] Id.

[56] Hobby Lobby, 134 S. Ct. at 2768.

[57] Id. at 2767.

[58] See id. at 2772–73.

[59] See id. at 2769–70 (citing and discussing Braunfeld v. Brown, 366 U.S. 599 (1961), and United States v. Lee, 455 U.S. 252 (1982)). According to the Court, it did not matter that the free exercise claims in these earlier cases had ultimately been rejected for other reasons.

> Hobby Lobby ... protects the religious liberty of the
> humans who own and control those companies.[60]

As discussed in Chapter 5, the Court's reasoning in *Hobby Lobby*
strongly suggests that closely held for-profit corporations can
exercise religion for purposes of the Free Exercise Clause. In any
event, they clearly qualify for protection under RFRA. Thus, at least
under RFRA, if the owners of a closely held corporation satisfy the
requirements of sincerity and sufficient religious motivation, as
explained in Chapter 5, so does the corporation.[61]

The second major issue in *Hobby Lobby* was whether the ACA's
contraceptive mandate, as applied to Hobby Lobby and the other
challengers, "substantially burdened" the exercise of religion. Here
again, this provision of RFRA mirrors the Free Exercise Clause,
which, as interpreted by the Supreme Court, also includes a
substantial burden requirement. As explained in Chapter 5,
burdens on religious exercise can be direct or indirect. A direct
burden, such as a criminal prohibition, makes it impossible for the
religious claimant to honor both the law and the claimant's religious
understandings. An indirect burden does not, but it nonetheless
exerts pressure on the religious claimant, in the form of financial or
other inducements. Either type of burden can be substantial, as
long as it imposes substantial coercive pressure, making it
difficult—even if not impossible—for the religious objector to follow
his or her religious beliefs.

In *Hobby Lobby*, the Court interpreted RFRA in a manner that
confirmed and clarified this understanding of the substantial
burden requirement. In particular, the Court made it clear that the
substantial burden inquiry evaluates the coercive pressure that the
government is placing on religious objectors. It does not authorize
the judiciary to second-guess the objectors' religious
understandings, not even with respect to impermissible complicity.
The government had argued that the connection between the ACA's
insurance coverage requirement and the potential destruction of an
embryo was extremely attenuated, so much so that it could not give
rise to a substantial burden on the employers' religious freedom. In
her dissenting opinion, Justice Ginsburg found this argument
persuasive. But the majority strongly disagreed.

As already discussed in Chapter 4, the Court maintained that
Justice Ginsburg's position entailed an improper judicial inquiry, a
forbidden judicial assessment of "whether the religious belief

---

[60] *Id.* at 2768.

[61] The Supreme Court reserved the question of whether publicly traded
corporations could exercise religion, but it noted that practical obstacles made this
improbable. *See id.* at 2774.

asserted in a RFRA case is reasonable."[62] Whether providing the contested insurance coverage constituted impermissible complicity, the Court explained, "implicates a difficult and important question of religion and moral philosophy, namely, the circumstances under which it is wrong for a person to perform an act that is innocent in itself but that has the effect of enabling or facilitating the commission of an immoral act by another."[63] That question, the Court concluded, is a "question that the federal courts have no business addressing."[64] The challengers "sincerely believe that providing the insurance coverage demanded by the HHS regulations lies on the forbidden side of the line, and it is not for us to say that their religious beliefs are mistaken or insubstantial."[65]

Evaluated purely in terms of coercive pressure to comply, the contraceptive mandate rather clearly imposed a substantial burden. The ACA levied heavy taxes and financial penalties for noncompliance, amounting to millions of dollars per year.[66] The burden arguably was indirect, because the companies could have avoided the coverage requirement by paying the assessments. Given the enormous sums of money that were at stake, however, this choice was not realistic; the coercive pressure on religious exercise plainly was substantial. As a result, the Court concluded, with "little trouble," that the Act imposed a substantial burden on the exercise of religion.[67]

Having ruled that the challengers were protected by RFRA and that the ACA imposed a substantial burden on their religious exercise, the Court turned to the third issue in the case: whether the contraceptive mandate, as applied to the challengers, satisfied RFRA's strict scrutiny standard by furthering a "compelling governmental interest" by "the least restrictive means." Speaking for the dissenters, Justice Ginsburg argued that it did, meaning that the challengers' RFRA claim should be rejected even if

---

[62] *Id.* at 2778.

[63] *Id.* (footnote omitted).

[64] *Id.*

[65] *Id.* at 2779.

[66] Companies providing group health plans without the contraceptive coverage were required to pay a tax of $100 per day per employee. For Hobby Lobby, the tax would have totaled about $475 million per year. Companies could avoid this tax by dropping employee health insurance altogether, but that approach generally would result in a different financial assessment, a penalty of $2,000 per employee per year—less substantial than the tax, but still hefty. For Hobby Lobby, this penalty would have amounted to roughly $26 million per year. In any event, as the Court noted, Hobby Lobby and the other challengers did not want to drop health-insurance coverage for their employees, a decision that itself would have violated their religious values. *See id.* at 2775–77.

[67] *Id.* at 2775.

(contrary to her view) strict scrutiny was indeed appropriate. Voicing concern for the "thousands of women" who might be affected by a RFRA exemption, Ginsburg concluded that the government had shown that the contraceptive mandate "furthers compelling interests in public health and women's well being . . . [and] there is no less restrictive, equally effective means that would . . . ensure that women employees receive, at no cost to them, the preventive care needed to safeguard their health and well being."[68] Employees should not be required to "relinquish benefits accorded them by federal law," she continued, "in order to ensure that their commercial employers can adhere unreservedly to their religious tenets."[69] And the ACA requires coverage "through the existing employer-based system of health insurance 'so that [employees] face minimal logistical and administrative obstacles.' "[70]

Here again, the majority disagreed. It "assume[d] that the interest in guaranteeing cost-free access to the four challenged contraceptive methods is compelling within the meaning of RFRA,"[71] but it found that the government had not satisfied RFRA's "least restrictive means" requirement. Describing this requirement as "exceptionally demanding," the Court ruled that "HHS has not shown that it lacks other means of achieving its desired goal without imposing a substantial burden on the exercise of religion by the objecting parties in these cases."[72] The Court cited two less restrictive, alternative means of providing the contraceptives in the circumstances at hand.

First, the government could directly assume the relatively modest cost of providing them to the affected employees. The Court suggested that excessive cost might render an alternative means impracticable, but it observed that RFRA sometimes may require the government to spend additional funds in order to accommodate religious freedom. Second, and more obviously, the government could extend an existing regulatory accommodation that HHS had already put in place for religious nonprofit organizations, such as religious colleges and charities.[73] If such an organization advised the government of its religious objection to the contraceptive

---

[68]   *Id.* at 2787, 2799, 2801–02 (Ginsburg, J., dissenting).

[69]   *Id.* at 2802.

[70]   *Id.* (citing 78 Fed. Reg. 39888 (July 2, 2013)).

[71]   *Id.* at 2780 (majority opinion).

[72]   *Id.*

[73]   In addition to this accommodation, HHS entirely exempted "religious employers" from the contraceptive mandate, a category of employers encompassing "churches, their integrated auxiliaries, and conventions or associations of churches," along with "the exclusively religious activities of any religious order." *See id.* at 2763 (majority opinion) (citations omitted).

mandate, it was excused from providing the insurance coverage, and its insurance company (or third-party administrator, if the organization was self-insured) was then required to provide the coverage separately, without imposing any cost-sharing requirements on the organization or its employees. According to the Court, this alternative would "not impinge on the plaintiffs' religious belief" and would "serve[ ] HHS's stated interests equally well" because "the plaintiffs' female employees would continue to receive contraceptive coverage without cost sharing . . . , and they would continue to 'face minimal logistical and administrative obstacles,' because their employers' insurers would be responsible for providing information and coverage."[74] As a result, "[t]he effect . . . on the women employed by Hobby Lobby and the other companies involved in these cases would be precisely zero."[75]

Speaking for the majority, Justice Alito resisted Justice Ginsburg's suggestion that the Court's reasoning might extend to a wide variety of religious objections.[76] He insisted that the decision was narrowly focused on the contraceptive mandate. In an important concurring opinion, Justice Kennedy agreed, and he emphasized that the decision hinged on the existing accommodation for religious nonprofits. The Court's decision, he explained, would not preclude the government from furthering what the Court assumed—and what Kennedy appeared to declare—to be "a legitimate and compelling interest in the health of female employees."[77] He noted that this interest, along with religious freedom, both warrant protection, but "the means to reconcile those two priorities are at hand in the existing accommodation," a circumstance that "might well suffice to distinguish the instant cases from many others in which it is more difficult and expensive to accommodate a governmental program to countless religious claims based on an alleged statutory right of free exercise."[78]

Despite the Court's reliance on the existing nonprofit accommodation as support for its ruling, it also hinted that the accommodation might itself be subject to challenge in certain circumstances, saying that it was not deciding "whether an approach of this type complies with RFRA for purposes of all religious claims."[79] The Court was well aware of pending cases in

---

[74] *Id.* at 2782 (citations omitted).

[75] *Id.* at 2760.

[76] *Compare id.* ("our holding is very specific") *with id.* at 2787 (Ginsburg, J., dissenting) (describing the Court's decision as one of "startling breadth").

[77] *Id.* at 2786 (Kennedy, J., concurring).

[78] *Id.* at 2787.

[79] *Id.* at 2782 (majority opinion).

which some religious organizations were contending that HHS's regulatory accommodation did not resolve their religious objection. The issues in these cases are complex, but the essence of the challengers' claim is that by objecting to the contraceptive mandate they trigger or bring into play the alternative governmental regulations requiring their insurance companies (or third-party administrators) to provide the contested coverage separately. And they assert that even this degree of involvement is enough to render them complicit in the use of contraceptives to which they object.[80]

These RFRA challenges by religious nonprofits have been rejected by various U.S. Courts of Appeals, largely on the ground that there is no substantial burden when the government does no more than require the reporting of religious objections and then employs alternative governmental action—action that itself is immune from challenge under the reasoning of *Bowen v. Roy*,[81] as discussed in Chapter 5.[82] And even if there were a substantial burden on the exercise of religion, RFRA's strict scrutiny test might very well be satisfied,[83] a conclusion that is at least suggested by the reasoning of Justice Kennedy in *Hobby Lobby,* whose vote was essential to the five-four decision. Even so, the U.S. Court of Appeals for the Eighth Circuit, rejecting the views of its sister circuits, has ruled in favor of RFRA challengers in this situation, finding that there is a substantial burden and that the government cannot satisfy strict scrutiny.[84] Faced with the resulting circuit split, the Supreme Court now is poised to resolve this dispute in

---

[80] Three days after deciding *Hobby Lobby*, the Supreme Court granted temporary and limited injunctive relief to one such challenger. *See Wheaton College v. Burwell*, 134 S. Ct. 2806 (2014). The Court ruled that, pending appeal, the religious nonprofit could inform the government of its religious objection without using a government-prescribed form and without sending copies of the form to its insurance providers. At the same time, the Court noted that it was expressing no view on the merits of the case and that nothing in its interim order would preclude the government from acting "to facilitate the provision of full contraceptive coverage under the [ACA]." *Id.* at 2807. Justice Sotomayor, joined by Justices Ginsburg and Kagan, filed a dissenting opinion. *See id.* at 2807–17 (Sotomayor, J., dissenting).

[81] 476 U.S. 693 (1986).

[82] *See, e.g., Geneva College v. Secretary U.S. Dep't of Health & Human Services*, 778 F.3d 422, 435–42 (3rd Cir. 2015) (concluding that the accommodation provision does not impose a substantial burden on the exercise of religion), *cert. granted*, 136 S. Ct. 444 (2015).

[83] *See Priests for Life v. U.S. Dep't of Health & Human Services*, 772 F.3d 229, 256–67 (D.C. Cir. 2014) (concluding that even if the accommodation provision imposes a substantial burden on the exercise of religion, it satisfies strict scrutiny because it is the least restrictive means for ensuring contraceptive coverage), *cert. granted*, 136 S. Ct. 446 (2015).

[84] *See Sharpe Holdings, Inc. v. U.S. Dep't of Health & Human Services*, 801 F.3d 927 (8th Cir. 2015) (approving preliminary injunction); *Dordt College v. Burwell*, 801 F.3d 946 (8th Cir. 2015) (approving preliminary injunction).

2016, having granted review in multiple cases.[85] Despite the hints that might be drawn from Justice Kennedy's opinion in *Hobby Lobby*, it is impossible to predict how the Justices will rule.[86]

III. The Religious Land Use and Institutionalized Persons Act

As we have seen, RFRA does not apply to state and local laws and governmental practices, having been declared unconstitutional to that extent by the Supreme Court's 1997 decision in *City of Boerne v. Flores*.[87] In response to *Boerne*, Congress considered new legislation, the Religious Liberty Protection Act (RLPA). RLPA was designed to sidestep the Court's conclusion that RFRA exceeded the scope of Congress's power under Section 5 of the Fourteenth Amendment by invoking Congress's powers under the Constitution's Spending and Commerce Clauses. Thus, RLPA would have reimposed RFRA's compelling interest test on state and local laws and practices if they substantially burdened a person's exercise of religion in a program or activity receiving federal financial assistance or if the substantial burden affected interstate commerce.[88] The House of Representatives passed a version of RLPA in 1999, but it did not become law. By then, the 1993 political coalition that had supported RFRA had fractured, with liberal and progressive groups, including the ACLU, expressing concerns about the possibility of religious exemptions from state and local antidiscrimination laws, including laws protecting unmarried couples, gays and lesbians, and other protected groups.

In the end, however, conservatives and liberals were able to agree on a more limited statute, one that did not raise these discrimination concerns. Thus was born the Religious Land Use and Institutionalized Persons Act of 2000 (RLUIPA).[89] RLUIPA applies

---

[85] The Court has granted review in seven cases, which it has consolidated. The cases probably will be decided under the name *Zubik v. Burwell*, which was the first of these cases to be filed in the Supreme Court. *See Zubik v. Burwell*, 136 S. Ct. 444 (2015), *granting cert. to Geneva College*, 778 F.3d 422.

[86] In the wake of the Supreme Court's *Hobby Lobby* decision and its interim order in *Wheaton College*, the government undertook new rulemaking. In July 2015, it issued final rules that revised and expanded the accommodation provision for religious objectors to the contraceptive mandate. The new regulations extend the accommodation to "closely held for-profit entities," which the regulations define. In addition, the new rules make the use of a government-prescribed form optional. If objectors prefer not to use the form, they can inform the government by letter, indicating their religious objection and providing the name and contact information for their insurance company or (if self-insured) for their third-party administrator. *See* 80 Fed. Reg. 41318–47 (July 14, 2015).

[87] 521 U.S. 507 (1997).

[88] *See* H.R. 1691, 106th Cong. § 2(a) (1999).

[89] 42 U.S.C. §§ 2000cc to 2000cc–5.

to state and local laws and practices in only two settings: land use regulations; and regulations affecting institutionalized persons, including prisoners. Congress was persuaded that land use regulations, including zoning laws, often threatened the ability of churches, synagogues, and other religious bodies to establish and maintain their places of worship. According to the leading Senate sponsors of RLUIPA, the congressional hearings "reveal[ed] a widespread pattern of discrimination against churches as compared to secular places of assembly, and of discrimination against small and unfamiliar denominations as compared to larger and more familiar ones."[90] With respect to prisoners, the law was supported in part by the conservative belief that permitting prisoners to practice their religion could further rehabilitation and in part by the liberal view that religious liberty warrants protection in the coercive prison setting. RLUIPA, like RFRA, was a broadly bipartisan measure. It passed without objection in both the House and the Senate, and, like RFRA, it was signed into law by President Bill Clinton.[91]

Like the more general RLPA proposal, RLUIPA relies primarily on the Spending and Commerce Clauses in extending its requirements to state and local governments. Some of the Act's land use provisions, which specifically address religious discrimination and exclusion, are grounded on Section 5 of the Fourteenth Amendment, but they are designed to comply with *Boerne*'s remedial understanding of that power.[92] Otherwise, RLUIPA applies if a substantial burden on the exercise of religion—in either the land use[93] or the prison setting[94]—"is imposed in a program or activity that receives Federal financial assistance" or if the

---

[90] Joint Statement of Senator Hatch and Senator Kennedy on the Religious Land Use and Institutionalized Persons Act of 2000, 146 Cong. Rec. S7774, S7775 (July 27, 2000) [hereinafter Joint Statement of Senator Hatch and Senator Kennedy].

[91] President Clinton's signing statement obliquely reflected the legislative debate that preceded RLUIPA's enactment: "The Religious Land Use and Institutionalized Persons Act will provide protection for one of our country's greatest liberties—the exercise of religion—while carefully preserving the civil rights of all Americans." William J. Clinton, Statement on Signing the Religious Land Use and Institutionalized Persons Act of 2000 (Sept. 22, 2000).

[92] These provisions address discrimination and exclusion, along with the risk of discrimination in schemes of land use regulation that depend upon individualized assessment. *See* 42 U.S.C. § 2000cc(a)(2)(C), (b). As such, they arguably are permissible under Section 5 on the ground that they enforce, rather than supplant, the Supreme Court's understanding of the First Amendment. This argument links these provisions primarily to the Court's interpretations of the Free Exercise Clause in *Church of the Lukumi Babalu Aye, Inc. v. City of Hialeah*, 508 U.S. 520 (1993), and *Employment Division v. Smith*, 494 U.S. 872 (1990), including *Smith*'s explanation of *Sherbert v. Verner*, 374 U.S. 398 (1963), as a decision addressing an individualized-assessment situation. *See* Joint Statement of Senator Hatch and Senator Kennedy, *supra* note 90, 146 Cong. Rec. at S7775–76.

[93] *See* 42 U.S.C. § 2000cc(a).

[94] *See* 42 U.S.C. § 2000cc–1.

substantial burden or its removal "affects, or ... would affect, commerce with foreign nations, among the several States, or with Indian tribes."[95] As a practical matter, one or both of these conditions is easily satisfied in nearly every RLUIPA case (the commerce condition for land use regulations,[96] the funding condition for prisons), but the conditions apparently are enough to bring the Act within the scope of congressional power. Lower courts have rejected federalism-based constitutional challenges to the Act, and there is little reason to believe that the Supreme Court disagrees with these rulings. The Court has not considered a land use case, but it has discussed and applied RLUIPA's prisoner provision without doubting its constitutionality. More generally, the Court has noted, in matter-of-fact fashion, that RLUIPA "applies to the States and their subdivisions and invokes congressional authority under the Spending and Commerce Clauses."[97] The federalism issue has not been directly addressed by the Court and so is not entirely free from doubt.[98] As with RFRA in the federal domain, however, there is strong reason to believe that RLUIPA is within the scope of congressional power.

A. Institutionalized Persons

RLUIPA's prisoner provision in fact protects "institutionalized persons" more broadly, that is, individuals who are "residing in or confined to" state or local facilities or institutions, including not only prisons and jails but also juvenile facilities, mental hospitals, and nursing homes.[99] In reality, however, virtually all of the cases involve prisoner claims. Within the scope of its operation, this provision, mirroring RFRA, prohibits the government from imposing a "substantial burden" on a person's "religious exercise" unless it can demonstrate that "imposition of the burden on that person ... is in furtherance of a compelling governmental interest ... and ... is the least restrictive means of furthering that compelling governmental interest."[100]

---

[95] 42 U.S.C. § 2000cc(a)(2)(A), (B); 42 U.S.C. § 2000cc–1(b); *see also* 42 U.S.C. § 2000cc–2(g).

[96] Most land use regulations also satisfy the separate, individualized-assessment condition, which provides an independent basis for applying RLUIPA's "substantial burden" land use provision. *See* 42 U.S.C. § 2000cc(a)(2)(C).

[97] *Holt v. Hobbs*, 135 S. Ct. 853, 860 (2015); *see also Burwell v. Hobby Lobby Stores, Inc.*, 134 S. Ct. 2751, 2761 (2014).

[98] *See Cutter v. Wilkinson*, 544 U.S. 709, 718 n.7 (2005) (noting, but declining to address, federalism-based constitutional objections to RLUIPA's prisoner provision); *cf. id.* at 727 n.2 (Thomas, J., concurring) (suggesting, without deciding, that RLUIPA "may well exceed Congress' authority under either the Spending Clause or the Commerce Clause").

[99] 42 U.S.C. § 2000cc–1(a); *see* 42 U.S.C. § 1997.

[100] 42 U.S.C. § 2000cc–1(a).

The Supreme Court has considered this provision of RLUIPA on two occasions. In 2005, as noted earlier, the Justices unanimously upheld the provision against an Establishment Clause challenge. In *Cutter v. Wilkinson*,[101] the prisoners were adherents of Satanist, Wicca, and other non-mainstream religions who were seeking accommodation for their religious practices, including group worship, the wearing of religious apparel, and the use of ceremonial items. The Supreme Court, confining itself to the Establishment Clause issue, did not address the merits of these claims. But it did offer some general interpretive guidelines. It noted that RLUIPA protects authentically religious claims, not fraudulent assertions, and the statute therefore "does not preclude inquiry into the sincerity of a prisoner's professed religiosity."[102] With respect to authentic claims that do trigger RLUIPA's strict scrutiny, moreover, the Court emphasized that "prison security is a compelling state interest."[103] And the strict scrutiny standard in this setting, the Court added, should "be applied in an appropriately balanced way, with particular sensitivity to security concerns"[104] and "with 'due deference to the experience and expertise of prison and jail administrators in establishing necessary regulations and procedures to maintain good order, security and discipline, consistent with consideration of costs and limited resources.' "[105]

More recently, in 2015, the Court for the first time addressed the merits of a prisoner's claim, and it issued a unanimous decision in the prisoner's favor. In *Holt v. Hobbs*,[106] the Court considered a RLUIPA challenge to the application of an Arkansas prisoner grooming policy, which generally prohibited prisoners from wearing beards. The challenger was Gregory Holt, also known as Abdul Maalik Muhammad, who was a devout Muslim. He wished to wear a half-inch beard in accordance with his religious beliefs, and the Court ruled that RLUIPA entitled him to do so; that is, RLUIPA required that he be exempted from the no-beard rule. Although the Justices did not entirely abandon *Cutter*'s suggestion that the judgments of prison officials are entitled to respect, they made it clear that, even in the prison setting, strict scrutiny is not easily

---

[101] 544 U.S. 709 (2005).

[102] *Id.* at 725 n.13.

[103] *Id.*

[104] *Id.* at 722.

[105] *Id.* at 723 (quoting Joint Statement of Senator Hatch and Senator Kennedy, *supra* note 90, 146 Cong. Rec. at S7775); *see also id.* at 720 n.8 ("Directed at obstructions institutional arrangements place on religious observances, RLUIPA does not require a State to pay for an inmate's devotional accessories.").

[106] 135 S. Ct. 853 (2015).

satisfied. In so doing, they relied in part on *Hobby Lobby*'s interpretation of RFRA, calling it RLUIPA's "sister statute."

Speaking for the unanimous Court, Justice Alito noted that the challenging party—under RLUIPA's prisoner provision, as under RFRA—bears the initial burden of proving that his religious exercise is grounded in a sincerely held religious belief and that the challenged governmental action substantially burdens this religious exercise. In the case at hand, Holt's sincerity was not disputed, and the Court found that he clearly faced a substantial burden, because violating the grooming rule would subject him to disciplinary action. It was beside the point that Holt was free to practice his religion in other ways, and it did not matter that other Muslims might not share his view that Islam requires men to grow beards. Citing RLUIPA's broad definition of "religious exercise" (a definition that RLUIPA shares with RFRA), Alito explained that RLUIPA applies regardless of whether religious practices are "compelled" by a prisoner's faith.[107] Moreover, he continued, its protection "is 'not limited to beliefs which are shared by all of the members of a religious sect.' "[108]

Invoking RLUIPA's strict scrutiny, the Court agreed that the government had a compelling interest in prison safety and security. More specifically, it had two compelling interests: preventing prisoners from hiding contraband; and keeping them from disguising their identities. Like RFRA, however, RLUIPA requires the government to satisfy the compelling interest and least restrictive means requirements with respect to the particular claimant in the case at hand. Here, it was hard to see how the prison's concern about contraband was implicated by Holt's short beard, and, in any event, each of the prison's two interests could be served by less restrictive means, such as searching the beard if necessary and keeping photographs that showed Holt with and without the beard. Although the expertise of prison officials warrants respect, the Court explained, "RLUIPA ... does not permit ... unquestioning deference."[109] Moreover, the least restrictive means test, as the Court had stated in *Hobby Lobby*, is " 'exceptionally demanding,' " requiring the government to show, even in the prison setting, that " 'it lacks other means of achieving

---

[107] *See id.* at 862 (citing 42 U.S.C. § 2000cc–5(7)(A)); *see also id.* at 860 (noting that "Congress defined 'religious exercise' capaciously" and also noting 42 U.S.C. § 2000cc–3(g), which calls for "a broad protection of religious exercise").

[108] *Id.* at 863 (quoting *Thomas v. Review Bd.*, 450 U.S. 707, 715–16 (1981)).

[109] *Id.* at 864.

its desired goal without imposing a substantial burden on the exercise of religion by the objecting part[y].' "[110]

In a concurring opinion, Justice Sotomayor contended that the Court's decision in *Holt* did not undermine its discussion of deference in *Cutter*. She suggested that deference to prison officials is appropriate under RLUIPA "when prison officials offer a plausible explanation for their chosen policy that is supported by whatever evidence is reasonably available to them," but that here they had "offered little more than unsupported assertions in defense of [their] refusal of [Holt's] requested religious accommodation."[111] Justice Ginsburg, joined by Justice Sotomayor, submitted her own short concurrence, reaffirming her dissenting opinion in *Hobby Lobby* and noting that this case was different because accommodating Holt's religious belief "would not detrimentally affect others who do not share [his] belief."[112]

B. Religious Land Use[113]

As already noted, RLUIPA, in common with RFRA, defines "religious exercise" to include "any exercise of religion, whether or not compelled by, or central to, a system of religious belief."[114] But it goes on to provide, more specifically, that "[t]he use, building, or conversion of real property for the purpose of religious exercise shall be considered to be religious exercise of the person or entity that uses or intends to use the property for that purpose."[115] Through several overlapping provisions, RLUIPA protects this particular form of religious exercise from "land use regulation," which the statute defines as "a zoning or landmarking law, or the application of such a law, that limits or restricts a claimant's use or development of land."[116]

RLUIPA contains four substantive provisions addressing land use regulation. The first forbids outright "discriminat[ion] against any assembly or institution on the basis of religion or religious denomination,"[117] and the second bans any land use regulation that

---

[110] *Id.* (quoting *Burwell v. Hobby Lobby Stores, Inc.*, 134 S. Ct. 2751, 2780 (2014)). The Court noted that the federal government and most states permit prisoners to wear half-inch beards, suggesting that the Arkansas ban was not necessary. *See id.* at 866.

[111] *Id.* at 867, 868 (Sotomayor, J., concurring).

[112] *Id.* at 867 (Ginsburg, J., concurring).

[113] Kevin M. LeRoy provided helpful research assistance on this topic.

[114] 42 U.S.C. § 2000cc–5(7)(A).

[115] 42 U.S.C. § 2000cc–5(7)(B).

[116] 42 U.S.C. § 2000cc–5(5).

[117] 42 U.S.C. § 2000cc(b)(2). Lower courts have ruled that evidence of purposeful, "discriminatory intent" is required to support a claim under this provision, meaning that any violation of this provision also would violate the Free Exercise Clause, as

"totally excludes" or "unreasonably limits" religious assemblies, institutions, or structures within the jurisdiction in question.[118] These provisions have not been heavily litigated, perhaps because the protection that they offer is largely subsumed within the other two provisions, which have been invoked and applied in many more cases. RLUIPA's "substantial burden" land use provision mimics its prisoner provision, as well as RFRA, by prohibiting any land use regulation that "imposes a substantial burden on the religious exercise of a person, including a religious assembly or institution," unless the government can demonstrate that "imposition of the burden on that person, assembly, or institution . . . is in furtherance of a compelling governmental interest . . . and . . . is the least restrictive means of furthering that compelling governmental interest."[119] And the final provision, requiring "equal terms," bars land use regulation "that treats a religious assembly or institution on less than equal terms with a nonreligious assembly or institution."[120] The Supreme Court has not decided a RLUIPA land use case, but there has been considerable litigation in the lower courts, leading to mixed results.[121] Lacking guidance from the Supreme Court, the U.S. Circuit Courts of Appeals have offered their own interpretations of the statute, focusing mainly on the "substantial burden" and "equal terms" provisions.[122]

The substantial burden provision requires a fact-intensive investigation to determine whether the application of a land use regulation exerts substantial coercive pressure on a religious organization, inducing it to change its behavior in a manner that impairs its ability to exercise religion through property that it owns

---

interpreted in *Church of the Lukumi Babalu Aye, Inc. v. City of Hialeah*, 508 U.S. 520 (1993). *See, e.g., Chabad Lubavitch v. Litchfield Historic Dist. Comm'n*, 768 F.3d 183, 198 (2d Cir. 2014).

[118] 42 U.S.C. § 2000cc(b)(3).

[119] 42 U.S.C. § 2000cc(a)(1).

[120] 42 U.S.C. § 2000cc(b)(1).

[121] *See* Douglas Laycock & Luke W. Goodrich, *RLUIPA: Necessary, Modest, and Under-Enforced*, 39 FORDHAM URB. L.J. 1021 (2012) (reviewing the first twelve years of experience with RLUIPA's land use provisions).

[122] RLUIPA is subject to enforcement not only through private lawsuits, but also by the U.S. Department of Justice. *See* 42 U.S.C. § 2000cc–2(f). Utilizing this authority, the Department increasingly has acted on behalf of mosques and Islamic schools, often in situations involving blatant or barely concealed hostility and discrimination against Muslims. *See* Eric W. Treene, *Zoning and Mosques: Understanding the Impact of the Religious Land Use and Institutionalized Persons Act*, THE PUBLIC LAWYER, Winter 2015, at 2. As a result, "[a]lthough RLUIPA was not enacted with the rights of Muslims as a principal concern, in the wake of 9/11 it has become a critical tool in protecting the rights of Muslim communities throughout the United States." *Id.* at 7.

or controls.[123] This inquiry is similar to the substantial burden inquiry in other settings, adapted to the particular context of religious land use.[124] In the typical case, a religious body is seeking to alter, expand, or relocate its place of worship or religious mission, but it is denied permission to do so. Courts have considered a wide variety of factors, including "the arbitrariness of a denial ... [;] whether the denial was conditional; if so, whether the condition was itself a substantial burden; and whether the [religious organization] had ready alternatives."[125] If the organization had readily available, viable alternatives, such as modifying its building plans to comply with a condition or using another suitable location, the existence of those alternatives tends to negate a finding of substantial burden. Conversely, if the challenger had a reasonable expectation of receiving approval when it bought the property at issue, that weighs in favor of its substantial burden claim.[126] More generally, whether a particular burden is substantial may depend on the size and resources of the religious group; that is, it may depend on the burden's "magnitude in relation to the needs and resources of the religious organization in question."[127] If the claimant is able to demonstrate a substantial burden, it usually will prevail on its RLUIPA claim. The statute permits the government to justify a substantial burden, but only by satisfying strict scrutiny. And in the land use setting, the government generally will be unable to do so.[128]

RLUIPA's equal terms provision responds to congressional concerns about the disparate treatment of religious organizations in the land use context. It is designed to promote the value of religious

---

[123] *See, e.g., Bethel World Outreach Ministries v. Montgomery County Council,* 706 F.3d 548, 556 (4th Cir. 2013); *Westchester Day School v. Village of Mamaroneck,* 504 F.3d 338, 349 (2d Cir. 2007). To fall within the scope of RLUIPA, the land use must itself entail the exercise of religion, as opposed to, say, commercial activity that might be undertaken by a church or other religious body. *See* Laycock & Goodrich, *supra* note 121, at 1042–46.

[124] In this context, the religious organization normally is not being pressured to violate its religious beliefs (because religious beliefs typically do not demand a particular location or building structure), and RLUIPA should not be read to require such a showing. *See Bethel World Outreach Ministries,* 706 F.3d at 555–56.

[125] *Chabad Lubavitch v. Litchfield Historic Dist. Comm'n,* 768 F.3d 183, 195 (2d Cir. 2014).

[126] *See, e.g., Bethel World Outreach Ministries,* 706 F.3d at 557–58.

[127] *World Outreach Conference Ctr. v. City of Chicago,* 591 F.3d 531, 539 (7th Cir. 2009); *cf. id.* at 537 ("burden is relative to the weakness of the burdened").

[128] *See, e.g., Bethel World Outreach Ministries,* 706 F.3d at 558–59; *International Church of the Foursquare Gospel v. City of San Leandro,* 673 F.3d 1059, 1070–71 (9th Cir. 2011); *Westchester Day School,* 504 F.3d at 353; *cf. Petra Presbyterian Church v. Village of Northbrook,* 489 F.3d 846, 851 (7th Cir. 2007) (suggesting that serious inquiry at the substantial burden stage is essential precisely because the government rarely will prevail under strict scrutiny).

equality—at least in the sense of formal equality between religious and nonreligious groups and to some extent, perhaps, also in the sense of substantive equality. Thus, unlike RLUIPA's less frequently litigated nondiscrimination provision,[129] the equal terms provision does not require proof of deliberate or purposeful discrimination on the basis of religion. Instead, it states that government cannot "impose or implement a land use regulation in a manner that treats a religious assembly or institution on less than equal terms with a nonreligious assembly or institution."[130]

The equal terms provision does not require the challenger to show a substantial burden on the exercise of religion. Likewise, it does not refer to strict scrutiny. As a result, an equal terms violation is categorical, not merely presumptive; there is no room for the government to defend a violation by contending that it can satisfy strict scrutiny.[131] Although seemingly straightforward, the equal terms provision has given rise to difficult issues of interpretation and differing approaches in the various U.S. Circuit Courts of Appeals. The fundamental problem is that treating a religious use of property *differently* than a secular use is not necessarily to treat it *unequally*. Excluding churches and synagogues from a zoning district that permits nonreligious private clubs and lodges is likely to violate the equal terms provision.[132] Conversely, treating a church differently than a school, under different regulatory processes, may amount to merely *"different treatment, not unequal treatment"* in violation of RLUIPA.[133] Likewise, the exclusion of churches from a commercial district, when nonreligious community centers, meeting halls, and libraries are also excluded, probably does not violate the equal terms requirement.[134]

The circuit courts have expressed divergent views concerning the evidence that is required to show an equal terms violation. More

---

[129] 42 U.S.C. § 2000cc(b)(2).

[130] 42 U.S.C. § 2000cc(b)(1).

[131] The U.S. Court of Appeals for the Eleventh Circuit has ruled to the contrary, declaring that the government can justify an equal terms violation by satisfying strict scrutiny. See *Midrash Sephardi, Inc. v. Town of Surfside*, 366 F.3d 1214, 1232, 1235 (11th Cir. 2004). But this interpretation of RLUIPA is not supported by the statute's text, is not followed in other circuits, and is almost certainly wrong.

[132] See *Midrash Sephardi*, 366 F.3d at 1230–31, 1235.

[133] *Primera Iglesia Bautista Hispana of Boca Raton, Inc. v. Broward County*, 450 F.3d 1295, 1313 (11th Cir. 2006) (emphasis in original). In this case, the church was seeking a zoning "variance," whereas the school had been granted "rezoning." The Court ruled that the school was "not a valid comparator here because the 'rezoning' process is an entirely different form of relief from obtaining a 'variance.' " *Id.* at 1310.

[134] See *River of Life Kingdom Ministries v. Village of Hazel Crest*, 611 F.3d 367, 373 (7th Cir. 2010) (en banc).

specifically, they have divided on the question of whether an equal terms claim requires evidence of a "similarly situated" secular "comparator," and, if it does, how the determination of "similarly situated" is to be made.[135] One approach is to read the equal terms provision more or less literally, using dictionary definitions to determine what counts as an "assembly or institution" and finding a violation if any nonreligious "assembly or institution" is permitted when a religious one is not.[136] But most courts have rejected this approach, reasoning that equal treatment, properly understood, can be evaluated only in "relation to relevant concerns."[137] Under this view, unequal treatment occurs only when the proposed religious use is treated differently than secular uses that are otherwise comparable, in light of the regulatory purposes or criteria that undergird the land use regulation in question. Some courts have asked, in one manner or another, whether the land use regulation treats religious assemblies or institutions less well than nonreligious assemblies or institutions that are similarly situated with respect to the government's "regulatory purpose."[138] Adopting a somewhat different approach, the U.S. Court of Appeals for the Seventh Circuit, in a notable en banc opinion by Judge Posner, has called for a comparative evaluation that focuses on objectively determined "accepted zoning *criteria*," derived from commonplace zoning practices and classifications, as opposed to "regulatory *purpose*," which Posner contends is subject to manipulation and "self-serving testimony by zoning officials and hired expert witnesses."[139] The Supreme Court may eventually weigh in with its own, authoritative interpretation of the equal terms provision, but it has yet to do so.

IV. State Constitutional Law and State Religious Freedom Statutes

The federal law of religious free exercise derives mainly from the Free Exercise Clause, RFRA, and RLUIPA. Due to *City of Boerne v. Flores*,[140] RFRA no longer applies to state and local laws and practices. RLUIPA does, but only in two discrete settings: institutionalized persons and land use. Otherwise, the federal law

---

[135] *See Chabad Lubavitch v. Litchfield Historic Dist. Comm'n*, 768 F.3d 183, 196 (2d Cir. 2014).

[136] *See Midrash Sephardi*, 366 F.3d at 1230–31; *see also* Laycock & Goodrich, *supra* note 121, at 1058–66 (endorsing and elaborating this sort of "plain-language" approach).

[137] *River of Life*, 611 F.3d at 371.

[138] *See, e.g., Lighthouse Institute for Evangelism, Inc. v. City of Long Branch*, 510 F.3d 253, 266 (3d Cir. 2007).

[139] *River of Life*, 611 F.3d at 371 (emphasis in original).

[140] 521 U.S. 507 (1997).

of religious free exercise, as applied to state and local governments, is based on the Free Exercise Clause, as interpreted by the Supreme Court. And the Court's interpretation is dominated by the doctrine of *Employment Division v. Smith*.[141] Under that doctrine, the Free Exercise Clause generally is implicated only by discriminatory burdens on religious exercise, and, accordingly, the Clause generally does not require state and local governments to grant religious exemptions from neutral laws of general applicability. This is so even if a law imposes a substantial burden on the exercise of religion and even if the government cannot justify the burden under strict scrutiny or any other type of serious judicial review.

This restrictive regime of religious freedom is sufficient to satisfy the First Amendment. Depending on the state, it might or might not be sufficient under state law. Every state has its own constitution, and every state constitution includes one or more provisions protecting religious freedom.[142] State courts, not federal, have the final word concerning the meaning of these provisions. In addition, state legislatures, if they wish, are free to adopt religious freedom statutes.

With respect to state constitutional law in the aftermath of *Smith*, states fall into three general categories. In some states, the scope of state constitutional protection remains unresolved, with no clear indication of whether state constitutional law merely tracks the Free Exercise Clause, as construed in *Smith*, or instead goes beyond it. In a second group of states, courts have adhered to the *Smith* approach as a matter of state as well as federal law, interpreting their state constitutions to do no more than mirror the Free Exercise Clause, as interpreted in *Smith*. In a third group of states, by contrast, courts have ruled that their state constitutions offer independent protection, beyond that provided by the First Amendment, and that the doctrine of *Smith* is inadequate to satisfy state constitutional guarantees. In most of the states in this third group, courts have formulated state constitutional law that is generally similar to pre-*Smith* First Amendment doctrine, as reflected in *Sherbert v. Verner*[143] and *Wisconsin v. Yoder*.[144] In others, courts have crafted distinctive state constitutional doctrines that differ from the *Sherbert/Yoder* approach but that nonetheless

---

[141] 494 U.S. 872 (1990).

[142] For a complete compilation of state constitutional provisions relating to religion and religious freedom, see BORIS I. BITTKER, SCOTT C. IDLEMAN, & FRANK S. RAVITCH, RELIGION AND THE STATE IN AMERICAN LAW 880–909 (2015).

[143] 374 U.S. 398 (1963).

[144] 406 U.S. 205 (1972).

sometimes demand religious exemptions when the doctrine of *Smith* would not.[145]

The dynamic of independent state constitutional interpretation is well illustrated by *State v. Hershberger*,[146] a 1990 decision of the Minnesota Supreme Court. Several Old Order Amish, based on their understanding of the Bible, including its command that they "be not conformed to this world,"[147] had objected to a Minnesota slow-moving-vehicle law that required them to use fluorescent orange-red triangular emblems on their buggies. When it first considered the case, in 1989, the Minnesota Supreme Court had relied on the Free Exercise Clause in ruling that the state was required to accommodate the Amish by exempting them from this requirement and by permitting them to use reflective tape and lanterns instead.[148] But that was before *Smith*, which was decided in 1990. Less than a week after deciding *Smith*, moreover, the U.S. Supreme Court granted certiorari in the *Hershberger* case, vacating the judgment of the Minnesota Supreme Court and remanding the case for further consideration in light of *Smith*.[149] On remand, however, the Minnesota Supreme Court reaffirmed its earlier judgment in favor of the Amish, this time on the basis of state constitutional law. As the court explained, "Minnesotans are afforded greater protection for religious liberties against governmental action under the state constitution than under the first amendment of the federal constitution."[150] More specifically, the court ruled that a Minnesota constitutional provision protecting religious conscience required it to reject the approach of *Smith* and to apply strict scrutiny, which the government could not satisfy, even though the challenged law was a neutral law of general applicability.

Another state-law response to *Smith* and *Boerne* has been the enactment of state religious freedom statutes. Indeed, more than twenty states have enacted Religious Freedom Restoration Acts

---

[145] For a comprehensive survey of all fifty states, see Paul Benjamin Linton, *Religious Freedom Claims and Defenses Under State Constitutions*, 7 U. ST. THOMAS J. L. & PUB. POL'Y 103 (2013). According to Linton, state courts in roughly half the states, interpreting their state constitutions, appear to follow the doctrine of *Smith*. In the remaining states, courts either have rejected *Smith* as a matter of state constitutional law or else have yet to resolve the issue one way or the other. *See id.* at 188.

[146] 462 N.W.2d 393 (Minn. 1990) (*Hershberger II*).

[147] Romans 12:2 (King James Version).

[148] *See State v. Hershberger*, 444 N.W.2d 282 (Minn. 1989) (*Hershberger I*).

[149] *Minnesota v. Hershberger*, 495 U.S. 901 (1990) (mem.).

[150] *Hershberger II*, 462 N.W.2d at 397.

that are modeled on the federal RFRA.[151] As with state constitutional law, there are variations from state to state, but these state-law RFRAs generally adopt the same basic approach as the federal statute. Thus, they typically provide that the government cannot impose a substantial burden on the exercise of religion, even under a neutral law of general applicability, unless the government can demonstrate that application of the law to the religious objector is the least restrictive means of furthering a compelling governmental interest.

Because state RFRAs are creatures of state law, their interpretation is left primarily to state courts. The courts of each RFRA state have the final word concerning the meaning of that state's RFRA. They may, but need not, follow the RFRA interpretations of state courts in other RFRA states. Likewise, in interpreting their own RFRA, they are bound neither by the U.S. Supreme Court's interpretations of the federal RFRA nor by its interpretations of RFRA's sister statute, RLUIPA. Even so, the U.S. Supreme Court's interpretations of the federal statutes are certainly germane, as a matter of persuasive authority, to the interpretation of state RFRAs, because the federal and state statutes share the same general purpose and typically contain the same or similar statutory language. As a result, state courts are likely to consult the Supreme Court's precedents, including its recent decisions in *Burwell v. Hobby Lobby Stores, Inc.*[152] and *Holt v. Hobbs.*[153] And they might very well choose to follow the Court's interpretative analysis in these cases, as a matter of state law, even though (apart from the Court's constitutional reasoning) they are not required to do so.[154]

Generally speaking, state RFRAs have not been widely litigated. And when they have been invoked, the religious freedom

---

[151] *See* NATIONAL CONFERENCE OF STATE LEGISLATURES, STATE RELIGIOUS FREEDOM RESTORATION ACTS, at http://www.ncsl.org/research/civil-and-criminal-justice/state-rfra-statutes.aspx. One state, Alabama, has adopted its version of RFRA by state constitutional amendment. The others have acted by legislation. *See id.* We are calling all of these laws Religious Freedom Restoration Acts, or RFRAs, even though not every state uses that label.

[152] 134 S. Ct. 2751 (2014).

[153] 135 S. Ct. 853 (2015).

[154] A state RFRA cannot be interpreted in a manner that violates the First Amendment. For example, a state court cannot reject a RFRA claim by declaring that the religious belief of the challenger is, from a religious perspective, either wrong or unreasonable. As discussed in Chapter 4, this sort of judicial inquiry is constitutionally forbidden. This constitutional prohibition clearly played a role in the Supreme Court's refusal to second-guess the complicity claim in *Hobby Lobby* and its refusal to question Holt's understanding of Islam in *Holt v. Hobbs*. To the extent that the Court's reasoning was based on the First Amendment, it is binding on state courts.

claims have often been rejected. Courts have found that there is no substantial burden on religious exercise, for example, or that the government has satisfied strict scrutiny.[155] Conversely, there have been some notable victories for religious objectors. A Native American student, for instance, successfully invoked the Texas RFRA to obtain an exemption from a public school dress code, with the court protecting the student's right to follow his religion by wearing his hair long.[156] Likewise, a court relied on the Pennsylvania RFRA to protect the outreach ministry of a group of Philadelphia churches, ruling that the city could not bar them from feeding homeless individuals in the city parks.[157]

In recent years, state RFRA proposals have become increasingly controversial. Most of the opposition has come from liberal and progressive groups, who have worried that religious objectors might be exempted from laws that prohibit illicit discrimination. As noted earlier, this has been an issue at least since the late 1990s, when Congress was considering the Religious Liberty Protection Act, but the controversy has grown over time. Much of the debate has centered on state and local laws protecting gays, lesbians, and transgender individuals from discrimination. The advent of same-sex marriage, now protected as a constitutional right,[158] has made the controversy even more pointed.[159] Citing religious objections, for example, some wedding vendors, including photographers, florists, and bakers, have declined to provide services for same-sex weddings. If sued under a state or local antidiscrimination law, these objectors could request a religious exemption under a state RFRA. Likewise, they could request an exemption if their state follows a similar approach to religious freedom under its state constitution.

---

[155] See Christopher C. Lund, *Religious Liberty After* Gonzales: *A Look at State RFRAs*, 55 S. DAK. L. REV. 466 (2010) (discussing, as of 2010, the paucity of litigation in most RFRA states, the tendency of courts to reject state RFRA claims, and the sometimes dubious reasoning supporting such rulings).

[156] *A.A. v. Needville Indep. Sch. Dist.*, 611 F.3d 248 (5th Cir. 2010).

[157] *Chosen 300 Ministries, Inc. v. City of Philadelphia*, 2012 WL 3235317 (E.D. Pa. 2012) (granting preliminary injunction); *see also, e.g., Abbott v. City of Fort Lauderdale*, 783 So. 2d 1213 (Fla. App. 2001) (protecting homeless feeding program under Florida RFRA). The Texas and Pennsylvania cases were decided by federal courts, but they were applying state law.

[158] *See Obergefell v. Hodges*, 135 S. Ct. 2584 (2015).

[159] The controversy over religious freedom and same-sex marriage has extended to specific statutory accommodations as well. Some states, for example, have enacted or considered legislation protecting government employees who object on religious grounds to issuing same-sex marriage licenses or to performing same-sex weddings. Other states have passed or considered laws permitting faith-based adoption agencies to decline to place children with same-sex couples.

Wedding vendors in fact have asserted exemption claims, both under state RFRAs and under state constitutional law. To date, however, these claims have been rejected,[160] and similar claims in the future are likely to meet the same fate. More broadly, state RFRA or state constitutional objections to antidiscrimination laws (and objections to federal antidiscrimination laws under the federal RFRA) are unlikely to succeed. There is one notable exception: the religious objector might prevail if it is a religious organization acting to preserve its internal religious character and identity. For example, a religious organization might be granted an exemption from an antidiscrimination law if the law would preclude it from using religious or religiously based criteria to define its religious community and, in particular, to select its own members and employees.[161] Otherwise, especially in the commercial domain, courts generally have concluded, and are likely to conclude in future cases, that laws preventing discrimination, even as applied to religious objectors, satisfy strict scrutiny. That is, the laws further a compelling governmental interest, preventing illicit discrimination, that cannot be served by any less restrictive means. As a result, religious exemptions are not warranted.[162] Courts could find otherwise in the same-sex marriage context, but they are unlikely to do so. As a result, the concerns of RFRA opponents appear to be overstated. Even so, these concerns have led at least two states,

---

[160] *See Elane Photography, LLC v. Willock,* 309 P.3d 53, 76–77 (N.M. 2013) (rejecting exemption under state RFRA); *State of Washington v. Arlene's Flowers, Inc.,* No. 13–2–00871–5, slip op. at 15–16, 45–51 (Wash. Superior Ct. Feb. 18, 2015) (rejecting exemption under state constitutional law). In *Elane Photography,* the New Mexico Supreme Court not only rejected the exemption claim of a Christian wedding photographer, but also concluded that the New Mexico RFRA did not even apply, because the government was not a party in the case. The court relied upon specific language in the New Mexico RFRA, including a provision—mirroring similar language in the federal RFRA—declaring that a religious objector may assert a RFRA violation "as a claim or defense in a judicial proceeding and obtain appropriate relief against a government agency." *See Elane Photography,* 309 P.3d at 76; *see generally* Shruti Chaganti, Note, *Why the Religious Freedom Restoration Act Provides a Defense in Suits by Private Plaintiffs,* 99 VA. L. REV. 343 (2013) (discussing this statutory language and arguing that it should not be read to preclude RFRA defenses in private-party litigation).

[161] In some situations, an exemption along these lines might be provided by a specific statutory accommodation. For example, as discussed earlier in this chapter, religious organizations are specifically exempted from the federal prohibition on religious discrimination in employment under a provision that permits them to prefer members of their own faith, even for nonreligious jobs. *See* 42 U.S.C. § 2000e–1(a). Moreover, as discussed in Chapter 5, the First Amendment's "ministerial exception"—as explained in *Hosanna-Tabor Evangelical Lutheran Church and School v. EEOC,* 132 S. Ct. 694 (2012)—protects religious organizations from state as well as federal prohibitions on employment discrimination, but only with respect to employees who qualify as "ministers" for this purpose.

[162] *Cf. Burwell v. Hobby Lobby Stores, Inc.,* 134 S. Ct. 2751, 2783 (2014) (rejecting suggestion that federal RFRA would permit exemption from prohibition on racial discrimination in employment).

Texas and Indiana, to include specific statutory exclusions in their state RFRAs, exclusions that categorically preclude RFRA objections to certain antidiscrimination claims.[163]

As we have seen, the law of religious freedom varies from state to state. Due to the state-law developments that we have discussed, *Employment Division v. Smith* provides the controlling standard for state and local laws and practices in only a minority of states. In addition to the states with state-law RFRAs, a number of states have followed the lead of Minnesota, interpreting their state constitutions to protect religious freedom even from neutral laws of general applicability. All in all, some thirty or more states have either adopted a state RFRA or have interpreted their state constitution to afford similar protection. In the remaining states, state and local governments are bound by RLUIPA, and there may be specific statutory accommodations in particular settings. Otherwise, however, these states need only comply with the Free Exercise Clause. As a result, they generally are free to reject religious exemptions on the authority of *Smith*.

V. Constitutional Values, the First Amendment, and Other Sources of Free Exercise Protection

As explained in Chapter 5, the Free Exercise Clause—under the prevailing doctrine of *Employment Division v. Smith*[164]—has been confined largely to the enforcement of nondiscrimination and formal religious equality. In this chapter, we have seen how Congress and a majority of states have gone beyond the Free Exercise Clause, as interpreted by the Supreme Court, to promote not only religious equality but also other constitutional values. Some of RLUIPA's land use provisions, including its equal terms provision, are specifically designed to further religious equality. More generally, however, RFRA, RLUIPA, and comparable state law—in the form of state RFRAs and state constitutional law—protect the exercise of religion even from nondiscriminatory burdens. In so doing, they further the core constitutional value of religious voluntarism, protecting the freedom of individuals to make religious choices for themselves. They also promote other constitutional values, including respect for the religious identity of individuals, the institutional autonomy of religious organizations, and the flourishing of religion in the private domain. Specific

---

[163] *See* TEX. CIV. PRAC. & REM. CODE § 110.011; S.B. 50 (Ind. 2015) (enacted Apr. 2, 2015). In the case of Indiana, the exclusion was adopted in response to a political firestorm, complete with boycott threats, that had erupted after the state initially passed the law without this provision. *See* S.B. 101 (Ind. 2015) (enacted Mar. 26, 2015).

[164] 494 U.S. 872 (1990).

statutory accommodations, both in federal and state law, also protect religious practices from otherwise applicable laws, thus promoting these values as well, albeit in a more focused fashion.

Perhaps ironically, the constitutional values of religious free exercise are now furthered as much by statutory and state-law protections as they are by the First Amendment. Indeed, these alternative sources of free exercise protection arguably have eclipsed the Free Exercise Clause, at least to a significant degree. The result is a rich and complex regime of religious freedom. At the same time, it is important to note that statutes protecting religious freedom, including RFRA, RLUIPA, and their state-law analogues, are subject to legislative repeal or modification. State lawmaking, moreover, whether in the form of statutes or state constitutional law, does not offer comprehensive national protection. In short, these various sources of legal protection are extremely important, but they are not a complete response to *Employment Division v. Smith*, nor do they provide a complete substitute for the Supreme Court's pre-*Smith* constitutional doctrine.

Chapter 7

THE ESTABLISHMENT CLAUSE: GENERAL CONCEPTS AND TESTS

Like the Free Exercise Clause, the Establishment Clause was originally directed to Congress but today extends to the states as well. Its sparse text states that "Congress"—now understood to include the government generally—"shall make no law respecting an establishment of religion." These few words have given rise to a complex body of constitutional doctrine. We will examine the specifics in due course, but it is helpful to begin by briefly revisiting some of the basic concepts and principles that were introduced in Chapter 4.

I. Establishment Clause Fundamentals

To a large extent, the Establishment Clause has been interpreted to mirror the Free Exercise Clause. Thus, just as the Free Exercise Clause prevents the government from mistreating religion through the imposition of impermissible burdens, the Establishment Clause prohibits the government from advantaging religion through the conferral of impermissible benefits.[1] It is important to remember that the constitutional definition of religion remains an open question under each clause. At least for purposes of the Establishment Clause, however, a broad definition is unlikely, and we can assume that religion probably is confined to beliefs and practices that are conventionally religious, which generally means theistic in nature. On this assumption, the Clause forbids impermissible benefits to religion in its conventional sense, and we are left to determine what counts as an impermissible benefit.

We will focus primarily on the question of when a benefit to religion is "impermissible." As noted in Chapter 4, however, a preliminary question is whether there is an Establishment Clause "benefit" at all. Unlike the comparable issue of constitutionally cognizable burdens under the Free Exercise Clause, this usually is not a difficult issue, and, indeed, the Court rarely discusses it as such. Generally speaking, when the government promotes or assists religion in any way, whether by discriminatory or

---

[1] As discussed below, the Establishment Clause occasionally works alongside the Free Exercise Clause to protect the exercise of religion from laws that burden or disadvantage religious organizations or religious practices. But these situations are quite exceptional.

nondiscriminatory means, it has conferred a benefit that passes this preliminary constitutional threshold. There is a contrary argument, however, when the government is removing what would otherwise be a legal burden on religion, even when, in so doing, the government is discriminating in religion's favor. This argument would arise, for example, in the defense of a religious exemption to an otherwise general prohibition on the use of peyote. In this type of situation, one can argue that the religious exemption conforms to free exercise values and therefore should not be seen as a "benefit" to religion under the Establishment Clause. We will return to this issue later, when we discuss the concept of "accommodation." For now, suffice it to say that this argument is plausible only if the government is providing relief from what would otherwise qualify as a direct or indirect burden on the exercise of religion, as discussed in Chapter 5. Outside the context of accommodation, virtually any assistance to religion can be seen as a benefit under the Establishment Clause. The critical question is whether the benefit is impermissible.

This question is not easy, and the appropriate answer in any given context is unavoidably value-laden. Indeed, the inquiry potentially implicates each of the seven constitutional values or groups of values that were outlined in Chapter 3. The first three values should be familiar by now, because they were emphasized in Chapters 5 and 6, where we discussed the Free Exercise Clause as well as alternative sources of free exercise protection. These values are important to the Establishment Clause as well. Thus, the Establishment Clause can be read, first, to disfavor governmental benefits that jeopardize religious voluntarism, for example, by inducing individuals to modify their religious beliefs or practices in order to qualify. Second, the Clause might be seen to protect the religious identity of dissenters, whether religious or irreligious, whose sense of self can be threatened when the government promotes or endorses religious beliefs they do not share. Third, religious equality, whether understood in a formal or more substantive sense, is obviously an important constitutional value— no less so here, in the context of legal benefits, than in the free exercise context of legal burdens.

The next three sorts of constitutional values, although also relevant to the Free Exercise Clause and religious free exercise, play distinctive roles under the Establishment Clause. These values relate less to individual rights than to structural, institutional, or cultural considerations. Thus, the fourth set of constitutional values are the political values of promoting a religiously inclusive political community and protecting the government from improper religious involvement. When the conferral of benefits denigrates the religious identity of dissenters, for example, it might also create religious divisiveness that could threaten the unity of the political community itself. The fifth set of values are religious values, protecting religion from government and protecting the autonomy of religious institutions, values that can be impaired when governmental benefits have the perverse effect of compromising the vitality of religion and the independence of the organizations that promote it. The sixth value, preserving traditional governmental practices, acts as a potential counterweight in the Establishment Clause context. This value might support the constitutionality of certain traditional practices—for example, our national motto, "In God We Trust"—that appear to benefit religion in a way that might otherwise be impermissible.

The seventh and final constitutional value—that of religious free speech—protects and promotes religious voluntarism in the particular context of speech. As discussed in Chapter 5, the Free Speech Clause strongly protects private religious speech from censorship or discriminatory treatment at the hands of government, even when the speech occurs in governmental settings. Private speech is not subject to the Establishment Clause. Governmentally sponsored speech (including symbolism), by contrast, is a very different matter. It is not protected by the Free Speech Clause, and it is constrained by the Establishment Clause. When religious speech takes place in governmental settings, however, it may be the combined product of private and governmental action, complicating the issue of sponsorship and potentially putting the value of religious free speech in tension with competing constitutional values. As a result, the value of religious free speech, like that of tradition, sometimes may support the validation of governmental practices that otherwise might be seen to violate the Establishment Clause.

In the course of this chapter and the next, we will see how the interpretation, implementation, and weighing of these various constitutional values have influenced the development of the Supreme Court's Establishment Clause doctrine. In recent years, the Court's decisionmaking under the Establishment Clause, like its decisionmaking under the Free Exercise Clause, has emphasized the value of religious equality and has increasingly understood that value in formal rather than substantive terms. The other values have not disappeared from view, however, and the Court's Establishment Clause doctrine is considerably more complex than a simple prohibition on formal or deliberate discrimination.

In our attempt to elucidate the Supreme Court's decisionmaking, we will begin by highlighting the basic and important distinction between discriminatory and nondiscriminatory benefits to religion. Thereafter, in the remainder of this chapter, we will discuss the broad framework of the Court's Establishment Clause doctrine, examining the general constitutional tests and concepts that the Court has invoked. These include the test of *Lemon v. Kurtzman*,[2] the endorsement test, a coercion test, and the concepts of tradition and accommodation. In Chapter 8, with this general doctrinal framework in mind, we will turn to each of several, more specific areas of concern: religion and the public schools; religious symbolism in other public contexts; and public aid to religious schools, organizations, and individuals.

II. Discriminatory and Nondiscriminatory Benefits to Religion

Just as the Free Exercise Clause generally forbids discriminatory burdens on the exercise of religion, so, too, does the Establishment Clause generally forbid discriminatory benefits to religion, at least if the discrimination amounts to formal or deliberate discrimination in religion's favor. As we will see shortly, this prohibition is implemented through general constitutional tests requiring a secular, nonreligious purpose for lawmaking and forbidding governmental action that is adopted precisely for the purpose of promoting or endorsing religion. The prohibition also is reflected in the Court's specific rulings, including numerous decisions invalidating the deliberate and discriminatory promotion of religion over irreligion in the public schools—for example, through the schools' sponsorship of prayer or other religious practices. As explained in Chapter 4, the Establishment Clause prohibition on discriminatory benefits is all but absolute if the discrimination is sectarian, favoring one religion over another. Nonsectarian discrimination, favoring religion generally over irreligion, is usually unconstitutional as well, although there appears to be an exception for certain governmental practices that are traditional.[3] Apart from this tradition-based exception, however,

---

[2] 403 U.S. 602 (1971). As explained below, the *Lemon* test considers the purpose and effect of the challenged governmental action, as well as the potential for excessive entanglement between religion and government. *See id.* at 612–13.

[3] As we will see, legislative prayer, a longstanding practice, is permissible even if the prayer is sectarian. At first glance, this seems to present a tradition-based exception not only to the usual prohibition on nonsectarian discrimination but also to the "all but absolute" prohibition on sectarian discrimination. As discussed below, however, it is the individual prayer-giver who determines the specific content of his or her prayer, and, accordingly, the governmental role in this setting arguably is nonsectarian, favoring religion generally but not promoting or endorsing the particular religion of the prayer-giver.

the prohibition on discriminatory benefits is broadly applied, and it is a well-established feature of the Court's doctrine. This prohibition obviously furthers formal religious equality. At the same time, it generally tends to promote substantive religious equality and other constitutional values as well.

The Court's general doctrinal tests, which we are about to discuss, imply that the Establishment Clause is concerned not only with deliberately discriminatory benefits, but also with other benefits to religion. These tests, for example, speak not only about the government's purpose, but also about the "primary effect" of its actions and possible impressions of governmental endorsement. They also speak about the risk of entanglement between religion and government. In the past, these sorts of considerations led to the invalidation of various programs of financial aid that did not formally discriminate in religion's favor. More recent decisions, however, have abandoned much of the reasoning and some of the holdings of these prior cases. According to the current Supreme Court, just as formal discrimination generally leads to invalidation, the absence of such discrimination generally is sufficient to satisfy the Establishment Clause. This position further elevates the value of formal equality, but, as we will see, it may jeopardize other constitutional values. Even so, these other values have not been entirely abandoned, and, indeed, some types of nondiscriminatory benefits to religion are still regarded as unconstitutional.

III. General Doctrinal Tests and Concepts

Remarkably enough, the current Supreme Court simultaneously recognizes three general Establishment Clause tests, each with different elements: the *Lemon* test, the endorsement test, and a coercion test. In addition, the Court's doctrine recognizes or considers two other general factors or concepts—tradition and accommodation—that are not explicit in any of the three general tests. This section will attempt to explain the development and content of these tests and concepts, their current significance, their relationship to each other, and their linkage to constitutional values.

The final concept, that of accommodation, connects this chapter to the last two by addressing the relationship between the Establishment Clause and the Free Exercise Clause. More specifically, it confronts the question of whether and to what extent the Establishment Clause permits the government to advance free exercise values, for example, by adopting specific statutory accommodations or more general religious liberty statutes, such as those discussed in Chapter 6. Accommodation is important not only for its general doctrinal significance, but also as a specialized, complicated, and contested field of Establishment Clause decisionmaking in its own right. As a result, accommodation will require substantially more elaboration than the other tests and concepts discussed in this section.

A. Lemon

In its 1947 decision in *Everson v. Board of Education*,[4] the Supreme Court announced a broad and strict interpretation of the Establishment Clause. The Court's interpretation appeared to require not merely formal equality between and among religions and between religion and irreligion, nor even substantive equality, but also a separation of religion and government. Quoting Thomas Jefferson, the Court declared that "the clause against establishment of religion by law was intended to erect 'a wall of separation between church and State.'"[5] In the years following *Everson*, the Court articulated doctrinal standards that were designed to implement this philosophy. In 1971, the Court consolidated these standards in *Lemon v. Kurtzman*[6] by announcing a general, three-pronged test for Establishment Clause cases. To survive judicial scrutiny, the Court stated, a statute (or other governmental action) must satisfy each of three requirements: "First, the statute must have a secular legislative purpose; second, its principal or primary effect must be one that neither advances nor inhibits religion . . . ; finally, the statute must not foster 'an excessive governmental entanglement with religion.'"[7]

Since 1971, the Supreme Court has applied the *Lemon* test in a wide variety of Establishment Clause cases. In recent years, the test has been harshly criticized by various Justices, but the Court has never repudiated the test and continues to use it, albeit less often than in the past and sometimes in modified form. In a 2000 school prayer case, for example, and again in a 2005 decision concerning public displays of the Ten Commandments, a majority— much to the chagrin of the dissenting Justices—cited the *Lemon* test and relied upon its first prong in finding constitutional violations.[8] Likewise, the Court has utilized the *Lemon* factors in financial aid cases even as its decisions have substantially relaxed

---

[4]   330 U.S. 1 (1947).

[5]   *Id.* at 16.

[6]   403 U.S. 602 (1971).

[7]   *Id.* at 612–13.

[8]   *Santa Fe Indep. Sch. Dist. v. Doe*, 530 U.S. 290, 314–16 (2000); *McCreary County v. ACLU*, 545 U.S. 844, 859–74 (2005). For the dissenters' objections to the Court's use of *Lemon*, see *Santa Fe*, 530 U.S. at 319–20 (Rehnquist, C.J., dissenting); *McCreary*, 545 U.S. at 889–92, 900–03 (Scalia, J., dissenting).

the Establishment Clause barriers in that context. Thus, the Court has stated that it "continue[s] to ask whether the government acted with the purpose of advancing or inhibiting religion" and "continue[s] to explore whether the aid has the 'effect' of advancing or inhibiting religion."[9] At least in the financial aid context, however, the Court has indicated that it no longer regards entanglement as a separate prong, treating it instead as one aspect of the effect inquiry and thereby weakening its doctrinal significance.[10] Outside the Supreme Court, moreover, lower courts often invoke the *Lemon* test in full or in part.

We need not dwell long on the Court's references to "inhibiting religion," but this language does merit comment. It suggests that the Establishment Clause not only precludes certain benefits to religion, but also certain disadvantages. Relatedly, *Lemon*'s concern about "entanglement" can be understood to support the institutional separation of religion and government in settings of disadvantage as well as benefit, thus protecting the institutional autonomy of religious organizations from burdensome or intrusive governmental regulations. To date, however, considerations along these lines have borne fruit in only one Supreme Court decision, *Hosanna-Tabor Evangelical Lutheran Church and School v. EEOC*.[11] As explained in Chapter 5, *Hosanna-Tabor* held that the First Amendment grants religious organizations a "ministerial exception" to employment discrimination laws, permitting them to hire and fire their religious leaders as they see fit. In support of this ruling, the Court did not cite or discuss *Lemon*, but it did rely in part on the Establishment Clause, noting that "the Establishment Clause . . . prohibits government involvement in such ecclesiastical decisions."[12] Even so, the ministerial exception rests first and foremost on the Free Exercise Clause, protecting "a religious group's right to shape its own faith and mission through its appointments."[13] To the extent that the Establishment Clause supports the Free Exercise Clause in this setting, it likewise might support the Free Exercise Clause in protecting the internal governance of religious bodies in other settings as well.[14] But the

---

[9] *Agostini v. Felton*, 521 U.S. 203, 222–23 (1997).

[10] *See id.* at 232–33.

[11] 132 S. Ct. 694 (2012).

[12] *Id.* at 706.

[13] *Id.*

[14] *See* Michael W. McConnell, *Reflections on* Hosanna-Tabor, 35 HARV. J. L. & PUB. POL'Y 821, 833–34 (2012); *see generally* Carl H. Esbeck, *Establishment Clause Limits on Governmental Interference with Religious Organizations*, 41 WASH. & LEE L. REV. 347 (1984).

Free Exercise Clause, properly understood, may itself provide sufficient grounding for such protection.[15]

In any event, the Free Exercise Clause—not the Establishment Clause—normally is the relevant provision when the government is hindering or burdening religion. In the typical Establishment Clause case, by contrast, the government is attempting to benefit religion. For the most part, then, we can put aside the "inhibiting religion" language and limit the *Lemon* test to governmental attempts to benefit religion.[16] So understood, the *Lemon* test precludes governmental action that has the non-secular purpose of advancing religion (either one religion or religion generally) or the primary effect of so doing. Whether separately or as a part of the effect prong, the test also precludes benefits that create an excessive entanglement between religion and government.

The first prong of *Lemon*, precluding the government from acting with the purpose of advancing religion, essentially embodies a requirement of formal equality between and among religions and between religion and irreligion. This prong prevents the government from purposefully discriminating in favor of religion (either one religion or religion generally) through the award of deliberately discriminatory benefits. The second prong, focusing on the actual effect of the governmental action, may reflect a more substantive understanding of religious equality, one that might be informed by religious voluntarism and other values. The entanglement inquiry suggests a concern for institutional separation, a concern that may point to structural constitutional values, both political and religious. In any event, the very existence of the effect and entanglement elements of the *Lemon* test, whatever their precise meanings, clearly implies that formal equality is not always sufficient under the Establishment Clause.

B. Endorsement

In 1984, in her influential concurring opinion in *Lynch v. Donnelly*,[17] Justice O'Connor introduced the endorsement test by proposing a "clarification" of *Lemon* that was later embraced by the

---

[15] *See* Michael A. Helfand, *Religious Institutionalism, Implied Consent, and the Value of Voluntarism*, 88 S. CAL. L. REV. 539, 564 (2015) (arguing that the institutional autonomy of religious organizations, linked as it is to the religious voluntarism of individuals, warrants protection under the Free Exercise Clause "because it promotes the voluntary free exercise of religion").

[16] This is not to deny that in the examination of governmentally conferred benefits, the Court might appropriately consider the risks that the benefits might pose for the vitality of religion and of religious institutions. To this extent, unintended disadvantages to religion may play a role in the Court's Establishment Clause analysis.

[17] 465 U.S. 668, 687–94 (1984) (O'Connor, J., concurring).

Court as a separate doctrinal tool. O'Connor argued that *Lemon* should be understood to forbid the government from endorsing religion, either deliberately or in effect, and that the first two prongs of *Lemon* should be modified accordingly:

> The purpose prong of the *Lemon* test asks whether government's actual purpose is to endorse or disapprove of religion. The effect prong asks whether, irrespective of government's actual purpose, the practice under review in fact conveys a message of endorsement or disapproval. An affirmative answer to either question should render the challenged practice invalid.[18]

As this language indicates, Justice O'Connor interpreted the Establishment Clause to preclude not only governmental "endorsement" of religion, but also governmental "disapproval." Like *Lemon*'s reference to "inhibiting" religion, however, O'Connor's concern about "disapproval" is largely (but not entirely) inconsequential. Only in rare cases—none reaching the Supreme Court—has governmental action been challenged under the Establishment Clause on the ground that it disapproved religion.[19] Instead, like the *Lemon* test, the endorsement test almost always concerns governmental attempts to benefit religion, not to disadvantage it. This is the typical Establishment Clause situation, and we will confine our discussion accordingly.

Under the endorsement test, the government violates the Establishment Clause if it intends to communicate a message that endorses religion (either one religion or religion generally) or if, whatever the government's intention, its action has the effect of communicating such a message. (The endorsement test does not separately address the issue of entanglement.) As a practical matter, the modified first prong adds little to the original *Lemon* formulation, because it is difficult to find purposeful advancement of religion without purposeful endorsement, and vice versa. The

---

[18] *Id.* at 690.

[19] *See, e.g., Catholic League for Religious & Civil Rights v. City & County of San Francisco,* 624 F.3d 1043 (9th Cir. 2010) (en banc) (fractured decision rejecting Establishment Clause challenge to San Francisco resolution that harshly denounced a Vatican directive barring Catholic adoption agencies from placing children with same-sex couples); *Awad v. Ziriax,* 754 F. Supp. 2d 1298, 1306 (W.D. Okla. 2010) (granting preliminary injunction against "Save Our State Amendment," which would have amended state constitution to forbid courts from considering Sharia law, in part because it likely violated the Establishment Clause by "conveying a message of disapproval" toward Islam), *aff'd on other grounds,* 670 F.3d 1111 (10th Cir. 2012); *see generally* Jay Wexler, *Government Disapproval of Religion,* 2013 BYU L. Rev. 119 (defending and elaborating the disapproval portion of the endorsement test, arguing that it should be confined to explicitly negative references, and suggesting that it may become increasingly important in the years that lie ahead).

second prong of the endorsement test, however, suggests a potentially important shift of focus. This prong examines the effect of the challenged governmental action symbolically, looking in particular at its objective meaning. Thus, the Court is to determine whether a "reasonable observer," properly informed of the relevant history and context, would find in the government's action a message that endorses religion.[20] Even if, in the language of *Lemon*, governmental action might have the primary effect of advancing religion, it is not unconstitutional under the second prong of the endorsement test unless it carries this impermissible message. Conversely, it is at least possible that governmental action could convey a message of governmental endorsement even if it does not appreciably advance religion, at least not in any tangible way. The modified second prong requires qualitative and sensitive judgments about symbolic meaning, whereas the original second prong arguably contemplates a more quantitative inquiry into the nature and degree of concrete legal benefits.

In various Establishment Clause settings, the Supreme Court has adopted and utilized one or both prongs of Justice O'Connor's endorsement reformulation, often in conjunction with the original *Lemon* test. Indeed, the Court has extended the endorsement test's "reasonable observer" or "objective observer" perspective—a concept originally linked to the second prong of the endorsement analysis—by invoking it to help inform the first prong of the *Lemon* and endorsement tests as well. As the Court explained, this is a fitting perspective because the investigation of governmental purpose is an objective inquiry, not a search for hidden or secret motivations.[21]

As with the *Lemon* test, the endorsement test has encountered significant opposition among the Justices. But it has been and remains a part of the Court's Establishment Clause doctrine, and, like the *Lemon* test, it continues to guide lower court decisionmaking. As we will discuss in Chapter 8, the endorsement test has been especially important in the context of religious symbolism, including public displays that include religious elements. More broadly, it provides a general standard that supplements and complements the conventional *Lemon* inquiry.[22]

To some extent, the endorsement test reflects the same constitutional values as those of *Lemon* itself. Thus, its first prong

---

[20] *See, e.g., Capitol Square Review & Advisory Bd. v. Pinette*, 515 U.S. 753, 778–82 (1995) (O'Connor, J., concurring in part and concurring in the judgment).

[21] *See McCreary County v. ACLU*, 545 U.S. 844, 861–63 (2005).

[22] *See, e.g., County of Allegheny v. ACLU*, 492 U.S. 573, 592–94 (1989); *Santa Fe Indep. Sch. Dist. v. Doe*, 530 U.S. 290, 301–10 (2000); *Zelman v. Simmons-Harris*, 536 U.S. 639, 654–55 (2002).

promotes formal religious equality, and its second prong may tend to serve substantive equality and perhaps religious voluntarism. The test's specific focus on governmental messages of endorsement, however, gives special attention to two other values: respecting the religious identity of dissenting citizens and promoting a religiously inclusive political community. Governmental endorsements of religion, without more, may have little or no influence on religious beliefs and practices and therefore may not meaningfully impair religious voluntarism. But they are quite likely to affront and alienate dissenting citizens, whether religious or irreligious, who are conspicuously excluded from the government's symbolic favor. As Justice O'Connor wrote in her *Lynch* concurrence, "Endorsement sends a message to nonadherents that they are outsiders, not full members of the political community. . . ."[23] As to these dissenters, the government's action, endorsing religious beliefs they do not share, may constitute not only an insult, but also a psychological assault on the core of their self-identity. By denigrating the dissenters' identity, moreover, the governmental action is likely to create resentment and religious divisiveness that could threaten the unity of the political community itself.[24]

C.   Coercion

Critics of *Lemon* and of the endorsement test long have argued that those tests are too restrictive. They contend that the government should have greater leeway to support religion and to do so deliberately, at least if the support is nonsectarian, not favoring any particular religion over others. According to one version of this argument, the only appropriate limit on nonsectarian support is a test of coercion. Under such a test, governmental action would not violate the Establishment Clause unless it coerced dissenting citizens. Otherwise, the government would be perfectly free to advance or endorse religion over irreligion.

The proper inquiry under a coercion test is subject to debate, but it might mirror the inquiry into substantial burdens on the exercise of religion, as discussed in Chapter 5. As we learned in that chapter, the Free Exercise Clause protects against direct and indirect burdens on the exercise of religion, at least if the burdens are both substantial and discriminatory. In like fashion, when the government is discriminating in religion's favor, the Establishment Clause might protect dissenters from direct and indirect coercive pressure on their desire *not* to engage in religious conduct. Under

---

[23]   *Lynch*, 465 U.S. at 688 (O'Connor, J., concurring).

[24]   For an elaboration of these themes, see Daniel O. Conkle, *Toward a General Theory of the Establishment Clause*, 82 Nw. U. L. REV. 1113, 1172–79 (1988).

this analysis, governmental action would violate the Establishment Clause either if it required individuals to engage in religious conduct or if it placed dissenters on the horns of a decisional dilemma, for example, by offering financial or other benefits only to those who were willing to acquiesce in the conduct. Indirect coercion, at least, is a matter of degree. As in the analogous free exercise context, however, a finding of illicit coercion presumably would be appropriate if the governmental action exerted substantial pressure on the dissenters' decisionmaking process.

Whatever its precise meaning, the coercion test is linked specifically and narrowly to the value of religious voluntarism. Standing alone, it reads the Establishment Clause to disfavor nonsectarian benefits to religion only if the governmental action substantially impedes the freedom of individuals to make and implement religious choices, including especially the choice not to participate in religious conduct. Clearly, such a serious intrusion on religious voluntarism should be seen as a core violation of the Establishment Clause. But the coercion test largely ignores other constitutional values. In the absence of coercion, it does not require the government to respect the self-identity of dissenters. Nor does it honor the value of religious equality, either formal or substantive, insofar as that value calls for equality between religion and irreligion. It also gives very little weight to structural values, including those that protect the government and the political community and those that protect religion and religious institutions.

Despite its limited perspective, an approach emphasizing coercion had attracted considerable support on the Supreme Court by the late 1980s, and, in 1992, there was speculation that a majority might move in this direction in *Lee v. Weisman*.[25] In fact, the Court in *Weisman* did utilize a coercion analysis of sorts, but, over the vigorous dissent of four Justices,[26] the Court nonetheless concluded that it was unconstitutional for a public school to sponsor a clergy-led, nonsectarian prayer at a graduation ceremony. Unlike the dissenting Justices, the Court took an extremely broad view of illicit governmental coercion. Noting the "subtle coercive pressure" of the public school environment and the role of "public pressure, as well as peer pressure," the Court found that the school had placed objecting students in an "untenable position" of "indirect coercion."[27] This coercion did not necessarily induce objecting students to actively join the prayer, even silently. But it did subject them to

---

[25] 505 U.S. 577 (1992).

[26] *See id.* at 631–46 (Scalia, J., dissenting).

[27] *Id.* at 590, 592–93 (majority opinion).

"pressure, though subtle and indirect," to "participate" in a more passive way.[28] Thus, they felt obliged to attend the ceremony despite their objection, and, once there, they felt obliged to quietly acquiesce in the prayer, giving others the impression that they either were joining or approving it.[29] This analysis suggests that it is unconstitutional for the government to coerce individuals, even by indirect and subtle means, into a situation that creates the *appearance* that they are participating in or approving religious conduct to which they actually object. Notably, the Court in *Weisman* explicitly declined to reconsider *Lemon*, and its overall analysis—including its capacious understanding of coercion—suggested a continuing reliance on elements of the *Lemon* and endorsement approaches.[30]

In the aftermath of *Weisman*, coercion has become a more explicit part of the Supreme Court's Establishment Clause doctrine, but not as a replacement for the Court's other tests. Instead, the coercion test—in the broad form expounded in *Weisman*—has become yet another doctrinal tool, one that stands alongside *Lemon* and the endorsement test. Thus, in a 2000 school prayer decision, the Court used all three tests, including a *Weisman*-like analysis of coercion, in the course of invalidating a public school policy that promoted student-led prayers before high school football games.[31] In reality, however, the coercion test in most settings is largely superfluous. Whenever there is coercion favoring religion, however subtle and indirect, there also is advancement or endorsement in violation of the Court's other Establishment Clause tests. As a matter of current doctrine, that advancement or endorsement generally is enough, in itself, to render the governmental action unconstitutional, meaning that coercion is not an essential element of an Establishment Clause claim.[32] Accordingly, as long as *Lemon* and the endorsement test continue to govern, it seems that the presence of coercion simply provides an additional basis for finding a constitutional violation and, perhaps, for finding the violation especially egregious. (As we are about to see, there appears to be an

---

[28] *Id.* at 593, 599.

[29] *See id.* at 590–99.

[30] *See* Daniel O. Conkle, Lemon *Lives*, 43 CASE W. RES. L. REV. 865 (1993).

[31] *Santa Fe Indep. Sch. Dist. v. Doe*, 530 U.S. 290 (2000).

[32] In *Van Orden v. Perry*, 545 U.S. 677 (2005), a Ten Commandments case to which we will return in Chapter 8, a four-Justice plurality adopted a lenient approach, rejecting the *Lemon* test (and implicitly the endorsement test) in the context of "passive" religious symbolism outside the public school context, in part precisely because such symbolism is passive as opposed to coercive. *See id.* at 686–92 (plurality opinion). This opinion arguably moves in the direction of making coercion an essential element of an Establishment Clause claim, but the scope of the opinion is limited, and, in any event, it did not command majority support.

implicit exception to *Lemon* and the endorsement test, an exception based on tradition. In the context of that limited exception, the presence or absence of coercion may have considerably greater relevance.)

D. Tradition

Although the *Lemon* and endorsement tests provide the dominant general framework for Establishment Clause cases, the Supreme Court has indicated that the Clause permits some governmental practices that would appear to violate these tests. In its 1983 decision in *Marsh v. Chambers*,[33] for example, the Court upheld the practice of legislative prayer by publicly paid chaplains. At that time, *Lemon* was the governing Establishment Clause test, the endorsement test having not yet arisen as a separate doctrinal tool. Under any serious application of *Lemon*, however, it is difficult to deny that legislative prayer has both the purpose and effect of advancing religion. The practice might also be seen as a quintessential entanglement of religion and government. Perhaps not surprisingly, therefore, the Court in *Marsh* made no pretense of applying the *Lemon* test, which it ignored altogether. Instead, the Court emphasized that legislative prayer goes back to the First Congress and is such a longstanding tradition that it is "part of the fabric of our society."[34]

In dicta in other cases, the Court likewise has approved other traditional practices that, by every indication, not only advance and endorse religion, but do so deliberately. It has cited with approval, for example, each of the following: presidential Thanksgiving proclamations that, since the time of George Washington, have included religious references and appeals; the Supreme Court's own opening cry, "God Save the United States and this Honorable Court," which dates to the tenure of Chief Justice John Marshall; our national motto, "In God We Trust," which became official in 1956, and the inclusion of this phrase on our money, a practice that began in the 1800s and that has extended to all currency since the 1950s; and the statutorily prescribed language, "one nation under God," which has been part of the Pledge of Allegiance since 1954.[35]

If a governmental practice dates back to the founding, one might contend, as did the Court in *Marsh*, that its constitutionality is supported not only by tradition, but also by the original

---

[33] 463 U.S. 783 (1983).

[34] *Id.* at 792.

[35] *See, e.g., Lynch v. Donnelly*, 465 U.S. 668, 674–78 (1984).

understanding of the First Amendment.[36] As noted in Chapter 2, however, this sort of selective reliance on the original understanding is problematic and unpersuasive.[37] Using an alternative argument, the Court sometimes has implied that the traditional practices it approves actually can satisfy *Lemon* and the endorsement test because they merely "acknowledge" or "recognize" religion without advancing or endorsing it.[38] Going one step further, some Justices have suggested that these practices, despite their references and appeals to God, have lost their religious meaning over time and now serve symbolic purposes that are secular in nature.[39] These various arguments may or may not be persuasive, but a more straightforward explanation is available, one that does not ignore the religious character of these practices and that is willing to concede that they do promote religion. This explanation relies directly on tradition as a source of constitutional meaning, and it identifies what amounts to a tradition-based exception to the *Lemon* and endorsement tests.

The contours of this implicit exception are quite uncertain, in part because the Supreme Court has been reluctant to confirm its existence. In its 2014 decision in *Town of Greece v. Galloway*,[40] for instance, the Court reaffirmed *Marsh*, but it denied that the decision was constitutionally exceptional. Noting that *Marsh* could be viewed "as 'carving out an exception' to the Court's Establishment Clause jurisprudence, because it sustained legislative prayer without subjecting the practice to 'any of the formal "tests" that have traditionally structured' this inquiry,"[41] the Court nonetheless insisted that "*Marsh* must not be understood as permitting a practice that would amount to a constitutional violation if not for its historical foundation."[42] Rather, "[t]he case teaches instead that the Establishment Clause must be interpreted 'by reference to historical practices and understandings.' "[43] In reality, however, the Court's point may be a matter of semantics. The Court is making it clear that *Marsh* is not an exception to the Establishment Clause, but it appears to be conceding that *Marsh is* an exception to the *Lemon* and endorsement tests, which typically

---

[36] In *Marsh*, the Court emphasized that the First Congress, the same Congress that framed the First Amendment, specifically approved the practice of legislative prayer.

[37] See the final footnote of Chapter 2.

[38] *See, e.g., Lynch*, 465 U.S. at 674–78.

[39] *See, e.g., id.* at 716–17 (Brennan, J., dissenting).

[40] 134 S. Ct. 1811 (2014).

[41] *Id.* at 1818 (citing *Marsh*, 463 U.S. at 796, 813 (Brennan, J., dissenting)).

[42] *Id.* at 1819.

[43] *Id.* (citing *County of Allegheny v. ACLU*, 492 U.S. 573, 670 (1989) (Kennedy, J., concurring in the judgment in part and dissenting in part)).

govern Establishment Clause cases but do not govern the issue of legislative prayer. And that is precisely because "*Marsh* found those tests unnecessary because history supported the conclusion that legislative invocations are compatible with the Establishment Clause."[44]

In any event, as a matter of current doctrine, it appears that there is a tradition-based exception to the *Lemon* and endorsement tests. Again, the precise parameters of this exception are not clear, but it seems that the exception generally requires that three criteria be satisfied. First, the governmental practice must represent a widely accepted and longstanding American tradition. The tradition need not date back to the founding, but the deeper and the older it is, the stronger the case for upholding it. Second, the government's promotion of religion must be nonsectarian, not favoring any particular religion over others.[45] And third, the governmental support for religion must be primarily and fundamentally symbolic, rather than tangible or coercive. Thus, it must not involve significant financial support for religion or religious institutions, and it must not improperly coerce dissenting citizens. The question of improper coercion leads back to some form of the coercion test, giving that inquiry special significance in this context.

The tradition-based exception is informed by other considerations as well, beyond these three criteria. In *Town of Greece*, for instance, the Court relied on tradition and the absence of coercion—essentially, the first and third criteria (financial support was not an issue)—in reaffirming the constitutionality of legislative prayer. Going beyond *Marsh*, however, the Court ruled that legislative prayer need not be nonsectarian but instead, for example, can be explicitly Christian.[46] At first glance, this holding appears to depart from the second criterion, which generally

---

[44] *Id.* at 1818; *see id.* at 1819 ("*Marsh* stands for the proposition that it is not necessary to define the precise boundary of the Establishment Clause where history shows that the specific practice is permitted.").

[45] Even general references to "God," including "In God We Trust" and "one nation under God," may not embrace all religions. But they are treated as nonsectarian because they do not promote any particular religion and because they are broadly inclusive of various religious perspectives.

[46] *Marsh* arguably had approved the practice of legislative prayer on the assumption that it would be nonsectarian, and, in dicta in a later decision, the Court had described the case accordingly. *See County of Allegheny*, 492 U.S. at 603 (stating that "history cannot legitimate practices that demonstrate the government's allegiance to a particular sect or creed" and that the prayers in *Marsh* were acceptable "because the particular chaplain had 'removed all references to Christ' ") (quoting *Marsh*, 463 U.S. at 793 n.14); *but see Town of Greece*, 134 S. Ct. at 1821 (rejecting this statement from *County of Allegheny* as "irreconcilable with the facts of *Marsh* and with its holding and reasoning").

confines the tradition-based exception to governmental action that promotes religion in a nonsectarian manner. Under a more complex and nuanced understanding of legislative prayer, however, it may be that the "government," in a sense, is not violating the second condition even if a specific prayer is sectarian. On this view, the government, as distinct from the prayer-giver it has authorized to speak, is not favoring any particular religion over others.

As the Court explained in *Town of Greece*, the tradition of legislative prayer, dating back to the First Congress and continuing to the present day, has included prayers that are explicitly Christian or otherwise sectarian. Moreover, even though the prayers are sponsored by the government, it is the individual prayer-givers who determine their particular content, a factor that implicates the value of religious free speech and the First Amendment's aversion to censorship. In *Town of Greece*, the prayer-givers were private citizens, who volunteered to serve as "chaplains of the month." But even a publicly paid chaplain, as in *Marsh*, has a free speech interest in determining the content of his or her prayer. In other words, legislative prayer can be understood to reflect a mixture of governmental sponsorship and private or quasi-private religious speech.[47] Under this bifurcated understanding of legislative prayer, the governmental role arguably is nonsectarian, sponsoring the practice of legislative prayer but not promoting or endorsing the particular content of any given prayer. In any event, as the Court noted in *Town of Greece*, "[t]o hold that invocations must be nonsectarian would force the legislatures that sponsor prayers and the courts that are asked to decide these cases to act as supervisors and censors of religious speech," a prospect at odds with the First Amendment principle that "government may not seek to define permissible categories of religious speech."[48] Rejecting that approach, the Court ruled instead that prayer-givers, within extremely broad limits, should be free to craft their prayers as they see fit. "Once it invites prayer into the public sphere," the Court stated, "government must permit a prayer giver to address his or her own God or gods as conscience dictates, unfettered by what an administrator or judge considers to be nonsectarian."[49] We will have

---

[47] *See generally* Daniel O. Conkle, *The Establishment Clause and Religious Expression in Governmental Settings: Four Variables in Search of a Standard*, 110 W. VA. L. REV. 315, 324 (2007) (arguing that governmental sponsorship of religious expression can be a matter of degree and that "[t]he greater the governmental involvement, the greater the potential injury to Establishment Clause values," whereas "[t]he greater the private involvement . . ., the greater the risk to religious free speech").

[48] *Town of Greece*, 134 S. Ct. at 1822.

[49] *Id.* at 1822–23.

more to say about *Town of Greece* in Chapter 8, when we return to the issue of legislative prayer.

As another possible variation or addendum to the three basic criteria, the government's promotion of a general religious reference or declaration, other things equal, may be more acceptable than its promotion of a prayer or other act of religious worship. If so, the tradition-based exception might permit the Supreme Court, despite its school prayer rulings, to approve school-sponsored recitations of the Pledge of Allegiance, complete with its "under God" language. The Court confronted—but avoided—this Establishment Clause issue in its 2004 decision in *Elk Grove Unified School District v. Newdow*,[50] ruling that the question was not justiciable because the challenger (a parent with limited and disputed custodial rights) lacked "prudential standing" to bring the case in federal court. But three Justices would have reached the merits, and each would have rejected the Establishment Clause claim. Two of them, Chief Justice Rehnquist and Justice O'Connor, cited reasons generally consistent with an implicit exception along the lines we have discussed.[51]

The "under God" language in the Pledge of Allegiance dates back to 1954, and the religious reference is nonsectarian, but what about the exception's third condition, in particular, the requirement that there be no improper coercion? In *West Virginia State Board of Education v. Barnette*,[52] the Supreme Court held that public schools cannot directly compel objecting students to recite the Pledge. But in the face of an Establishment Clause challenge, this freedom from direct coercion might or might not be sufficient. The Court's school prayer decisions make it clear that the risk of indirect and subtle coercion, as discussed in *Lee v. Weisman*,[53] is reason enough to reject a tradition-based exception for school-sponsored nonsectarian prayer in the public school setting, even if the prayer is formally voluntary. But as Chief Justice Rehnquist and Justice O'Connor emphasized in *Newdow*, the Pledge of Allegiance is not a prayer or religious exercise. It is a patriotic exercise that includes a brief and general religious reference or declaration.[54] Moreover, a student who objects only to the "under God" language is free to remain silent during that portion of the Pledge. These factors mitigate the

---

[50] 542 U.S. 1 (2004).

[51] See *id.* at 25–33 (Rehnquist, C.J., concurring in the judgment); *id.* at 33–45 (O'Connor, J., concurring in the judgment). Justice Thomas was the third Justice, but he urged a broader modification of Establishment Clause doctrine. See *id.* at 45–54 (Thomas, J., concurring in the judgment).

[52] 319 U.S. 624 (1943).

[53] 505 U.S. 577 (1992).

[54] See *Newdow*, 542 U.S. at 31 (Rehnquist, C.J., concurring in the judgment); *id.* at 39–43 (O'Connor, J., concurring in the judgment).

risk of coercion, thus reducing the threat to religious voluntarism. To be sure, there is a lingering potential for indirect and subtle coercion, but perhaps the weight of tradition is sufficient to overcome this concern. If so, then it may be enough that students cannot be directly or substantially coerced to actively join the recitation.[55] In any event, the Pledge of Allegiance issue tests the scope of the implicit exception, and, in light of the Court's justiciability ruling in *Newdow*, the Establishment Clause question remains open.[56]

Whatever the precise scope of the implicit exception and however the Supreme Court might describe its reasoning, it seems that tradition informs the Court's doctrine by acting as a partial counterweight to other constitutional values.[57] As long as the exception does not permit any serious coercion, it does not meaningfully impair religious voluntarism. It does limit the value of religious equality in this context, however, to equality between and among religions, because the exception allows the government to favor religion over irreligion. And the Court's holding in *Town of Greece*, permitting sectarian legislative prayer—albeit under the influence of free speech considerations—is in tension with the value of religious equality even as it relates to equality between and among religions. The tradition-based exception is in tension with other constitutional values as well. It permits governmental action that disrespects the religious identity of dissenting citizens and that, as a result, might undermine the religious inclusiveness of the political community. Even so, these various harms are lessened by the intangible and non-coercive character of the government's

---

[55] *See* Conkle, *supra* note 47, at 336–40 (discussing this issue and explaining that its proper resolution is difficult precisely because it depends upon the evaluation and weighing of competing constitutional values).

[56] In the aftermath of *Newdow*, lower courts generally have rejected Establishment Clause challenges to the Pledge and to its recitation in the public schools. One such ruling came from the U.S. Court of Appeals for the Ninth Circuit, in renewed litigation involving the same challenger whose case had reached the Supreme Court. *See Newdow v. Rio Linda Union Sch. Dist.*, 597 F.3d 1007 (9th Cir. 2010). The court's two-to-one decision provoked a lengthy dissent. *See id.* at 1042–1116 (Reinhardt, J., dissenting).

[57] Beyond the implicit exception as such, tradition sometimes may lead the Court to apply its conventional doctrine less strictly than usual. For possible examples, see *McGowan v. Maryland*, 366 U.S. 420, 431–53 (1961) (upholding traditional Sunday closing laws, despite their religious origins, on the ground that they no longer have either the purpose or effect of aiding religion); *Walz v. Tax Comm'n*, 397 U.S. 664, 672–80 (1970) (finding that the extension of nonprofit tax-exempt status to religious organizations does not sponsor or advance religion and emphasizing that this longstanding governmental practice "is not something to be lightly cast aside"); *Lynch v. Donnelly*, 465 U.S. 668, 675–76, 678–85 (1984) (finding no violation of *Lemon* in a city's inclusion of a nativity scene in a Christmas display, but only after noting with approval the government's traditional recognition of both Christmas and Thanksgiving as holidays with religious significance).

action, and tradition is a competing value that properly is relevant to constitutional interpretation. Moreover, the very fact that the practices reflect traditional policies, not new ones, might further mitigate the impairment of other constitutional values. In particular, dissenters might be somewhat more willing to accept the practices as imbedded features of the status quo, not contemporary statements of inequality or disrespect, and this in turn might reduce the likelihood of their alienation from the political community.[58]

E. Accommodation

The term "accommodation" has more than one meaning. For instance, it sometimes is used as a generic description for relaxed interpretations of the Establishment Clause, interpretations permitting the government to accommodate or even favor religion in various contexts. As used here, by contrast, the term has a more specific meaning, one that describes the government's power to accommodate not religion, but *religious freedom*. More specifically, it describes the extent to which the Establishment Clause, informed by the Free Exercise Clause, permits the government to grant special protection to the exercise of religion by exempting religious conduct from legal burdens that would otherwise be applicable. This special protection might appear to advance and endorse religion— and to do so deliberately—in violation of the *Lemon* and endorsement tests. As a result, one might think of accommodation, like tradition, as an implicit exception to the Supreme Court's usual doctrinal tests. In reality, however, when accommodation is permitted, there is no benefit to religion that is constitutionally cognizable under the Establishment Clause. The point is subtle but important: it is religious freedom, not religion as such, that the government is advancing and endorsing. Thus, it is better to think of accommodation as religion-specific governmental action that facilitates and prefers the exercise of religion, but that does so in a manner that legitimately satisfies the Court's conventional Establishment Clause doctrine.

The Religion Clauses do not work at cross-purposes. At the very least, therefore, the concept of accommodation means that the government does not violate the Establishment Clause when it takes action that is constitutionally required by the Free Exercise Clause. Under current doctrine, the Free Exercise Clause generally does not protect religious conduct from nondiscriminatory burdens. Accordingly, it generally does not require religion-specific remedial

---

[58] For a more elaborate and somewhat different argument concerning the role of tradition under the Establishment Clause, *see* Conkle, *supra* note 24, at 1183–87.

action that would even arguably implicate the Establishment Clause. Prior to *Employment Division v. Smith*,[59] by contrast, the Free Exercise Clause sometimes required the government to exempt religious conduct from substantial burdens, even when the burdens resulted from nondiscriminatory, generally applicable laws. One could argue that these constitutionally required exemptions—for religious conduct and religious conduct alone—constituted benefits to religion in violation of the Establishment Clause. Reading the Religion Clauses together, however, the Supreme Court properly rejected that argument, finding that the removal of a free exercise burden does not amount to an Establishment Clause benefit. Even today, this reasoning still applies to the limited extent that the Free Exercise Clause continues to provide protection from nondiscriminatory burdens and therefore requires preferential treatment for religious conduct.[60]

Even when the accommodation of religious conduct is not required by the Free Exercise Clause, it is permissible, within limits, in the discretion of the government. In *Smith*, the Court broadly rejected the notion of constitutionally required accommodation. As we saw in Chapter 5, this restrictive interpretation of the Free Exercise Clause elevates the value of formal religious equality and gives only limited weight to other constitutional values. Even as the Court in *Smith* resisted vigorous judicial enforcement of the Free Exercise Clause, however, it emphasized that values reflected in the Bill of Rights, including the Free Exercise Clause, are not "banished from the political process."[61] It thus suggested that legislatures are free to protect religious voluntarism and other free exercise values—not as a matter of constitutional compulsion, but as a matter of legislative policy. In particular, the Court reaffirmed the permissibility of "nondiscriminatory religious-practice exemption[s]" from otherwise general laws, and it noted with approval, for example, that "a number of States have made an exception to their drug laws for sacramental peyote use."[62] Quite clearly, the Court did not regard the Establishment Clause as a barrier to such exemptions.

The Court in *Smith* spoke of state-law exemptions created by state legislative action, but the concept of permissible

---

[59]   494 U.S. 872 (1990).

[60]   *Cf. Hosanna-Tabor Evangelical Lutheran Church & Sch. v. EEOC*, 132 S. Ct. 694, 706 (2012) (holding that the Free Exercise Clause grants religious organizations a "ministerial exception" to otherwise applicable employment discrimination laws and that the Establishment Clause in this setting not only permits this result but confirms and supports it).

[61]   *Smith*, 494 U.S. at 890.

[62]   *Id.*

accommodation also applies to local lawmaking and to federal-law exemptions adopted by Congress. It likewise extends to state-law exemptions arising from state constitutional law. This is important because, as discussed in Chapter 6, the courts of some states, interpreting state constitutional provisions protecting the free exercise of religion, have rejected the rule of *Smith*. Instead, they have adhered to an approach along the lines of federal constitutional doctrine prior to *Smith* or have crafted distinctive doctrines of their own. Whatever their particular approach, state courts, utilizing state constitutional law, sometimes provide religion-based exemptions from state laws that are otherwise nondiscriminatory and generally applicable.

Although state constitutional law can be a significant source of permissible accommodation, the primary source is legislative action. Resting mainly in the hands of legislatures, permissible accommodation is hardly a perfect vehicle for protecting free exercise values—especially if legislatures confine themselves to specific statutory accommodations, as opposed to more general religious freedom statutes.[63] In the first place, legislatures do not have the benefit of case-by-case adjudication, which permits courts to consider and resolve particular issues as they arise. At the time it enacts a law—for example, a law prohibiting the use of peyote—a legislature might not be aware that the law will affect religious conduct in some future application—for example, in the context of a Native American religious ceremony. Obviously, if the legislature does not anticipate such a case, it will not consider the possibility of a religion-based exemption. Second, to the extent that legislatures do consider exemptions, they might well reject them, especially if the exemptions would protect religious practices that are unpopular or unconventional. As the Supreme Court conceded in *Smith*, "leaving accommodation to the political process" places minority religious practices "at a relative disadvantage,"[64] a prospect that threatens the value of substantive religious equality.

1. Establishment Clause Limits on Permissible Accommodation

Whatever its weaknesses, permissible accommodation is the only available vehicle for honoring free exercise values that the Court no longer protects as a matter of constitutional right. More specifically, permissible accommodation can provide religion-based exemptions that protect religious conduct from nondiscriminatory burdens—burdens that, after *Smith*, are largely immune from the

---

[63] As discussed below, more general religious freedom statutes, such as the Religious Freedom Restoration Act, have certain advantages.

[64] *Smith*, 494 U.S. at 890.

Free Exercise Clause itself. It is critical, therefore, to determine the legitimate scope of permissible accommodation and, in particular, to determine the limits that the Establishment Clause imposes in this context. As we will see, these limits can be unclear or contested in specific instances. Even so, we can identify four basic conditions that legislative action (or state constitutional interpretation) must meet in order to qualify as permissible accommodation and therefore avoid Establishment Clause invalidation.

First, an accommodation is not permissible if it violates *Lemon's* prohibition on the excessive institutional entanglement of religion and government. More precisely, even if the government is attempting to protect the exercise of religion, it cannot adopt a religion-based exception to an otherwise applicable law if the exception amounts to a purposeful delegation of governmental power to a religious organization or group. In *Larkin v. Grendel's Den, Inc.,*[65] for example, the Supreme Court invalidated a Massachusetts law that granted churches the power to veto liquor licenses for nearby restaurants. Likewise, in *Board of Education of Kiryas Joel Village School District v. Grumet,*[66] the Court ruled that New York had violated the Establishment Clause when it created a special public school district that was drawn in a manner that confined the district, and therefore its governance, to the members of a discrete community of Hasidic Jews.

Second, a religion-based exemption, to qualify as permissible accommodation, must be designed to provide relief from what would otherwise be a substantial burden on the exercise of religion, typically a burden arising from the application of a law or from other governmental action.[67] As explained in Chapter 5, a substantial burden is a direct or indirect burden that dissuades or discourages the exercise of religion by exerting substantial coercive pressure on religious decisionmaking. In the context of permissible accommodation, the legislature (or state court interpreting the state's constitution) may have some leeway in assessing the substantiality of a burden, permitting it to address burdens that the Supreme Court might not regard as sufficiently substantial to be constitutionally cognizable under the Free Exercise Clause itself. But the burden must at least be one that the legislature (or state court) could reasonably characterize as substantial.[68] Otherwise, a

---

[65]   459 U.S. 116 (1982).

[66]   512 U.S. 687 (1994).

[67]   As discussed below, there is some room for permissible accommodation even in the context of burdens that are imposed by private actors rather than government.

[68]   Cf. *Corporation of the Presiding Bishop v. Amos,* 483 U.S. 327, 335–36 (1987) (suggesting that permissible accommodation legitimately can address "significant" burdens).

religion-based exemption would be promoting religion, not religious freedom.

This requirement that permissible accommodation be designed to relieve a substantial burden helps explain the Supreme Court's competing results in two Establishment Clause cases, both decided in the late 1980s. In *Texas Monthly, Inc. v. Bullock*,[69] the Court invalidated a sales tax exemption for the sale of religious literature by religious organizations. Although the Court could not agree on an opinion, a majority of the Justices concluded that this religion-based exemption violated the Establishment Clause. As part of its reasoning, the plurality opinion emphasized that the exemption was not designed to protect religious scruples or religious decisionmaking. Rather, the burden of the sales tax, at least for most religious organizations, was simply financial. The tax exemption therefore was not redressing a substantial burden on religious exercise, and it did not qualify as permissible accommodation.[70] Conversely, in *Corporation of the Presiding Bishop v. Amos*,[71] the Court approved, as permissible accommodation, a religion-based exemption in Title VII of the Civil Rights Act of 1964. As discussed in Chapter 6, the Act generally prohibits religious discrimination in employment, but it exempts religious organizations so that they can make religion-based employment decisions, even for jobs without specifically religious duties.[72] According to the Court, Congress permissibly concluded that without the exemption, the Act's prohibition would have substantially burdened the exercise of religion. In particular, it would have impaired the ability of religious organizations to define and carry out their religious missions by preventing them from making and implementing religious decisions in selecting organizational personnel. Unlike the exemption rejected in *Texas Monthly*, the exemption approved in *Amos* was designed to protect religiously informed conduct, that is, conduct that reflected decisions of religious conscience or religious doctrine.

---

[69]   489 U.S. 1 (1989).

[70]   A sales tax exemption extending more broadly, to religious and nonreligious literature alike, would be a different matter. Under the reasoning of the plurality in *Texas Monthly*, the broader exemption still would fall outside the zone of permissible accommodation, because it would not be redressing a substantial burden on religious exercise. But the benefit to religion might now be seen as nondiscriminatory, and it might therefore be approved under the basic standards of *Lemon* and the endorsement test. *Cf. Walz v. Tax Comm'n*, 397 U.S. 664 (1970) (approving a scheme of property tax exemptions that extended to religious organizations along with other nonprofit organizations).

[71]   483 U.S. 327 (1987).

[72]   *See* 42 U.S.C. § 2000e–1(a).

A third requirement for permissible accommodation, as the Court suggested in *Smith*, is that the religion-based exemption must be "nondiscriminatory."[73] This requirement does not prevent the government from preferring the exercise of religion over nonreligious conduct. As the Court wrote in *Amos*, "Where, as here, government acts with the proper purpose of lifting a regulation that burdens the exercise of religion, we see no reason to require that the exemption come packaged with benefits to secular entities."[74] Rather, the requirement of "nondiscriminatory" accommodation merely precludes discrimination between or among religions. This ban on sectarian discrimination, however, raises questions of its own. One important question relates to the critical issue of definition that the Supreme Court has yet to resolve: what qualifies as a religion for the purpose of defining religious exercise? If religion is given a broad definition for this purpose, one that includes deeply held moral beliefs of various sorts, it might be improperly "sectarian" to discriminate among "religions" by limiting an exemption to *conventional* religions. Under this sort of reasoning, for example, it might be unconstitutional to grant an exemption from compulsory military service to those who conscientiously object for reasons that are conventionally religious, but to deny the same treatment to others whose moral values lead them to the same ethical position.[75]

However religion is defined, moreover, different religions have different tenets and practices, meaning that an exemption designed to protect one form of religious exercise may help one religion but not another. An exemption for the religious use of peyote, for example, protects members of the Native American Church in their sacramental practice, but it does nothing to protect the Amish or Orthodox Jews from legal requirements that might impede their particular forms of religious exercise. Yet differential treatment in this general sense does not constitute improper sectarian discrimination; if it did, permissible accommodation for specific religious practices would be nearly impossible. Rather, the forbidden sectarian discrimination is present only when an exemption is not extended to all religions that face the same or comparable situations. The ban on sectarian discrimination certainly requires, for example, that the government extend an

---

[73] *Employment Div. v. Smith*, 494 U.S. 872, 890 (1990).

[74] *Amos*, 483 U.S. at 338.

[75] In *United States v. Seeger*, 380 U.S. 163 (1965), and *Welsh v. United States*, 398 U.S. 333 (1970), the Supreme Court avoided this constitutional issue by interpreting a statutory religious-objector provision expansively, permitting it to extend to objectors who were not conventionally religious. These cases are addressed in Chapter 4's discussion of the problem of defining religion.

exemption for the religious use of peyote to all religions that use peyote in a manner comparable to the Native American Church.[76] Beyond this obvious point, however, the determination of sectarian discrimination is more difficult, and it requires the exercise of judgment. The governing principle appears to be this: accommodating one religious practice but not another is improperly sectarian if, but only if, the distinction cannot reasonably be justified on the basis of the government's secular interests. For example, if the government exempts religious users of peyote from its drug laws, must it also exempt those who use marijuana or heroin for religious reasons? Perhaps, but probably not. The issue is whether the government's secular interests can reasonably justify its decision to exempt for peyote but not for the other drugs.

The question of reasonable justification itself requires a comparison of the two competing situations under an inquiry analogous to the "strict scrutiny" that governed constitutional claims for exemptions prior to *Smith*. As Justice Blackmun wrote in his unsuccessful defense of that constitutional regime, "Though the State must treat all religions equally, and not favor one over another, this obligation is fulfilled by the uniform application of the 'compelling interest' test to all free exercise claims, not by reaching uniform results as to all claims."[77] As to permissible accommodation, it seems that a modified version of Blackmun's argument remains valid: the government can grant one exemption but not another that is arguably similar as long as there is a distinction that is *reasonable* in terms of the relative strength of the government's secular interests and the relative harm to those interests that a religious exemption would cause. For example, granting a religious exemption for the use of marijuana or heroin, for which there are significant illegal markets and extensive nonreligious demand, might threaten the government's anti-drug campaign in a way that a peyote exemption might not.[78] In other

---

[76] If the government grants an exemption to a specific religious group, creating the risk of sectarian discrimination, it may be required to provide or authorize exemptions for other, similarly situated religious groups at the same time, rather than simply await the other groups' requests for their own exemptions. *Cf. Board of Educ. of Kiryas Joel Village Sch. Dist. v. Grumet*, 512 U.S. 687, 702–07 (1994) (invalidating the creation of a special public school district for a community of Hasidic Jews, based in part on a concern that other religious (and nonreligious) groups would not be treated in like fashion).

[77] *Employment Div. v. Smith*, 494 U.S. 872, 918 (1990) (Blackmun, J., dissenting) (emphasis omitted).

[78] *See id.* at 916–19. Conversely, some religious uses of otherwise illegal drugs may be no more harmful to the government's secular interests than the religious use of peyote. If so, then to exempt the religious use of peyote but not the other religious uses would implicate the prohibition on sectarian discrimination. *Cf. Gonzales v. O Centro Espírita Beneficente União do Vegetal*, 546 U.S. 418 (2006) (granting an exemption under the Religious Freedom Restoration Act for a sacramental tea

settings as well, it may be entirely reasonable, and therefore constitutionally permissible under the Establishment Clause, to limit religious exemptions to groups whose practices do not undermine the government's secular interests.[79]

The fourth and final condition for permissible accommodation is that the religion-based exemption cannot impose undue burdens or costs on third parties, parties who do not share the religious belief or follow the religious practice in question. In other words, an exemption must be crafted in a manner that considers not only the religious freedom of those who are being accommodated but also the interests of third parties who might be adversely affected by the exemption. If it fails to do so, the exemption may go beyond the permissible promotion of religious freedom. Instead, it may have the impermissible effect of promoting or endorsing the religion itself, as compared to competing religious and irreligious beliefs, including especially those of the affected third parties.

In its 1985 decision in *Estate of Thornton v. Caldor, Inc.*,[80] the Supreme Court cited this concern in concluding that a Connecticut statute violated the Establishment Clause. Unlike the typical accommodation statute, the Connecticut law was designed to address private rather than governmental burdens on the exercise of religion. In particular, it applied to private employers, prohibiting them from requiring Sabbath-observing employees to work on their stated day of Sabbath. Declaring the law unconstitutional under the second prong of the *Lemon* test, the Court emphasized that the statute provided "Sabbath observers with an absolute and unqualified right not to work on whatever day they designate as their Sabbath."[81] It took "no account of the convenience or interests of the employer or those of other employees who do not observe a Sabbath," requiring them to "adjust their affairs to the command of the State whenever the statute is invoked by an employee."[82] Because of its "unyielding weighting in favor of Sabbath observers

---

containing a substance banned under the Controlled Subtances Act, in part because the requested exemption was comparable in relevant respects to an existing regulatory exemption for the religious use of peyote).

[79] *See Cutler v. U.S. Dept. of Health & Human Services*, 797 F.3d 1173, 1183, 1181 (D.C. Cir. 2015) (ruling that the Affordable Care Act, which exempts the members of certain religious groups from the Act's requirement that individuals maintain health insurance, is not impermissibly sectarian and therefore does not violate the Establishment Clause because there is "an objective, non-sectarian basis" for extending the exemption only to religions that maintain "an established, alternative support network that ensures individuals will not later seek to avail themselves of the federal benefits for which they did not contribute").

[80] 472 U.S. 703 (1985).

[81] *Id.* at 709.

[82] *Id.*

over all other interests," the Court concluded, the statute went too far, having "a primary effect that impermissibly advance[d] a particular religious practice."[83]

The Court invalidated the Connecticut statute because it was categorical, taking no account whatsoever of the competing interests of employers and other employees. The Court did not rule that statutory accommodations cannot burden third parties in any way. Nor did it preclude accommodations that are addressed to privately imposed burdens on the exercise of religion.[84] Indeed, in a concurring opinion, Justice O'Connor distinguished and defended the "reasonable accommodation" provision of Title VII of the Civil Rights Act of 1964. As noted in Chapter 6, this provision requires employers, including private employers, to "reasonably accommodate" their employees' religious observances and practices if this can be done "without undue hardship on the conduct of the employer's business."[85] Unlike the Connecticut Sabbath law, this provision balances the accommodation claim of a religious employee against the employer's competing interests, including its interest in maintaining a workplace that deals fairly with all employees. Invoking the endorsement test, Justice O'Connor explained that an objective observer would view the Connecticut law as an endorsement of a particular religious belief and practice. Conversely, she argued, an objective observer would see the more flexible and balanced Title VII provision, within the context of Title VII generally, as a legitimate means for protecting religious employees from improper and unjustified employment discrimination.[86]

Quite clearly, accommodations sometimes are permissible even if they impose burdens or costs on third parties. Just two years after *Caldor*, for example, the Supreme Court decided *Amos*. As already discussed, *Amos* approved the statutory exemption that Title VII provides for religious organizations, permitting them to make religion-based employment decisions that favor their own members, even for nonreligious jobs. The Court's unanimous ruling found the accommodation permissible even though it plainly imposes a

---

[83] *Id.* at 710.

[84] Privately imposed burdens on the exercise of religion plainly do not implicate the Free Exercise Clause, which is directed to governmental action. But such burdens can nonetheless impair religious freedom, arguably presenting an appropriate case, within limits, for legislative accommodation.

[85] 42 U.S.C. § 2000e(j).

[86] *Caldor*, 472 U.S. at 711–12 (O'Connor, J., concurring). Justice O'Connor also noted another distinguishing factor. The Title VII provision applies to various religious practices, whereas the Connecticut law singled out a particular religious practice, Sabbath observance, for distinctive protection, thus suggesting sectarian favoritism. *See id.*

significant burden on both the livelihood and the religious freedom of third parties—the applicants and employees who face employment discrimination because they choose not to conform to the employer's religion. As Justice Brennan explained in his separate opinion, the exemption "necessarily has the effect of burdening the religious liberty of prospective and current employees," putting them "to the choice of either conforming to certain religious tenets or losing a job opportunity, a promotion, or . . . employment itself."[87] But the free exercise interest of religious organizations—"an interest in autonomy in ordering their internal affairs"[88] and in defining their own religious communities—was sufficiently important to override the burden on third parties, permitting the Court to approve "a categorical exemption" in this setting because it "appropriately balances these competing concerns."[89]

More generally, it seems that determining whether burdens on third parties are excessive or disproportionate, rendering an accommodation impermissible, requires a contextualized consideration of the interests on both sides. The question depends in part on the character and degree of the third-party burdens that the accommodation imposes. As *Amos* suggests, however, it may also depend on whether those burdens are sufficiently counterbalanced and outweighed by the free exercise interest that is being advanced. This sort of balancing, of course, requires the exercise of judgment. The proper result may vary from one context to the next, and, in any given context, there may be disagreement and debate about what the proper result should be.

In any event, the Supreme Court continues to insist that the Establishment Clause precludes accommodations that impose undue burdens or costs on third parties. In its 2005 decision in *Cutter v. Wilkinson*,[90] for instance, the Court, citing *Caldor*, unanimously reaffirmed that "courts must take adequate account of the burdens a requested accommodation may impose on nonbeneficiaries."[91] The Court explained that "an accommodation must be measured so that it does not override other significant interests," which should be considered "in an appropriately

---

[87] *Corporation of the Presiding Bishop v. Amos*, 483 U.S. 327, 340 (1987) (Brennan, J., concurring in the judgment).

[88] *Id.* at 341.

[89] *Id.* at 345, 346.

[90] 544 U.S. 709 (2005).

[91] *Id.* at 720 (citing *Caldor*, 472 U.S. 703).

balanced way."[92] But the precise scope of this restriction remains unsettled and contested.

2. RFRA, RLUIPA, and Comparable State Statutes

So far, we have discussed specific statutory accommodations, that is, accommodations in the form of specific exemptions from particular laws. Congress exempts religious employers from particular provisions of Title VII, for instance, or states exempt the sacramental use of peyote from their criminal drug laws. As discussed in Chapter 6, however, the Supreme Court's restrictive interpretation of the Free Exercise Clause has given rise to accommodation statutes of a different and quite remarkable sort. They include the Religious Freedom Restoration Act of 1993 (RFRA),[93] the Religious Land Use and Institutionalized Persons Act of 2000 (RLUIPA),[94] and comparable state statutes. These statutes demand strict scrutiny for substantial burdens on the exercise of religion in a wide variety of governmental contexts. Because the statutes extend to nondiscriminatory burdens, they effectively authorize statutory religious exemptions, but they do so generally, not specifically. Thus, courts are required to apply the statutory strict scrutiny and to grant relief—typically in the form of religion-based exemptions—whenever they find that substantial burdens cannot be justified. Although hardly a substitute for constitutional protection under the Free Exercise Clause, these broadly written statutes suggest that "leaving accommodation to the political process"[95] need not disadvantage minority religions. Because they proceed generally, moreover, these statutes also overcome the problem of legislative anticipation; that is, they do not require speculative legislative judgments about the potential application of particular statutes to religious conduct.

In the previous chapter, we noted that RFRA and RLUIPA raise potential constitutional questions apart from the Establishment Clause, questions relating to separation of powers and federalism. We also noted, however, that lower courts have rejected constitutional challenges raising these issues, and the Supreme Court has strongly suggested that it agrees with these rulings. The remaining constitutional question—to be addressed here—is whether RFRA, RLUIPA, and their state-law analogues violate the Establishment Clause. The answer is almost certainly no, because the statutes rather clearly qualify as permissible

---

[92] *Id.* at 722.

[93] 42 U.S.C. §§ 2000bb to 2000bb–4.

[94] 42 U.S.C. §§ 2000cc to 2000cc–5.

[95] *Employment Div. v. Smith*, 494 U.S. 872, 890 (1990).

accommodation.[96] Justice Stevens once argued otherwise, contending that RFRA—and by implication any comparable statute—violates the Establishment Clause by favoring religious exercise over nonreligious conduct.[97] But this argument appears to ignore the Supreme Court's permissible accommodation doctrine.

More specifically, these statutes satisfy each of the four Establishment Clause conditions that we have identified. First, they do not delegate governmental power to a religious organization or group. Second, by their explicit terms, they are designed to redress substantial burdens on the exercise of religion.[98] Third, they are broadly nonsectarian, extending to religious exercise of all sorts. And fourth, they do not require the granting of religion-based exemptions that would impose undue burdens or costs on third parties.

To be sure, the third and fourth conditions could be violated if the statutes were interpreted in particular ways. For instance, there would be a problem of sectarian discrimination if the Supreme Court were to define the exercise of religion broadly for constitutional purposes and if the statutes, by contrast, were confined to practices that were conventionally religious. Under this scenario, the statutes indeed would violate the Establishment Clause because they would prefer some "religions" over others. This constitutional problem could readily be avoided, however, by interpreting the statutes to follow the constitutional definition, so that the statutes themselves would extend to all religious exercise within the meaning of the Constitution, whether that exercise was conventionally religious or not. Likewise, it would violate the Establishment Clause to read RFRA, RLUIPA, or a comparable state statute to demand a religion-based exemption that would impose undue burdens or costs on third parties. Here again, however, this problem can easily be avoided by interpreting the statutes to conform to the Establishment Clause. In particular, courts can and should find that the government satisfies strict scrutiny in these circumstances, meaning that the requested exemption should be denied. Indeed, the government has a compelling interest not only in protecting third parties from undue burdens or costs, but also in avoiding a violation of the

---

[96] The same is true for state constitutional doctrine that follows a comparable approach.

[97] *See City of Boerne v. Flores,* 521 U.S. 507, 536–37 (1997) (Stevens, J., concurring).

[98] Most state RFRAs copy the federal statute by redressing "substantial burdens." A state RFRA providing relief from burdens that are not "substantial" would present a closer question.

Establishment Clause. In short, the statutes should not be read to demand what would be an unconstitutional exemption.

In its 2005 decision in *Cutter v. Wilkinson*,[99] the Supreme Court (including Justice Stevens, who silently joined the opinion) unanimously rejected an Establishment Clause challenge to that portion of RLUIPA that authorizes religious exemption claims by institutionalized persons, typically prisoners. The Court noted that because of their confinement, institutionalized persons can face not only substantial but "exceptional" governmentally imposed burdens on their religious exercise, clearly justifying permissible accommodation.[100] It also emphasized that the protection of RLUIPA extends to any and all religions, without sectarian discrimination, and it implied that the statute could and should be construed to avoid any Establishment Clause issues that might arise in particular applications. In particular, as noted earlier, the Supreme Court stated that "courts must take adequate account of the burdens a requested accommodation may impose on nonbeneficiaries"[101] and that "an accommodation must be measured so that it does not override other significant interests."[102] Although some of the Court's reasoning was specific to the institutionalized-persons context, *Cutter* strongly suggests that the Establishment Clause likewise does not invalidate the remainder of RLUIPA, nor does it imperil RFRA or its state-law counterparts.[103]

To say that these statutes do not violate the Establishment Clause is not to say that the Establishment Clause plays no role in their proper interpretation. Much to the contrary, as *Cutter* makes clear, these statutes should be interpreted and applied in a manner that complies with the Establishment Clause limits that we have identified. Indeed, to state an obvious but important point: the statutes are constitutional only if they are interpreted and applied in conformity with the Constitution. There is no disagreement on this general point. But the precise meaning of the Establishment Clause limits on permissible accommodation is subject to debate. As a result, even if the Justices agree that these constitutional limits should and must inform the interpretation of RFRA and similar statutes, that does not mean that they will agree on the particular

---

[99] 544 U.S. 709 (2005).

[100] *Id.* at 720; *see id.* at 720–21.

[101] *Id.* at 720 (citing *Estate of Thornton v. Caldor, Inc.*, 472 U.S. 703 (1985)).

[102] *Id.* at 722.

[103] As discussed in Chapter 6, the Supreme Court has applied RFRA in the federal realm without questioning its constitutional validity. *See Gonzales v. O Centro Espírita Beneficente União do Vegetal*, 546 U.S. 418 (2006); *Burwell v. Hobby Lobby Stores, Inc.*, 134 S. Ct. 2751 (2014).

meaning of these limits, nor, therefore, on the implications of these limits for statutory interpretation.

A prominent case in point is the Supreme Court's five-to-four decision in *Burwell v. Hobby Lobby Stores, Inc.*[104] As discussed in previous chapters, the majority interpreted RFRA to exempt Hobby Lobby and certain other closely held corporations from providing their employees with insurance coverage for various contraceptives, as otherwise required by the Affordable Care Act (ACA). Speaking for the four dissenters, Justice Ginsburg argued that the exemption should have been rejected, in part because, in her view, the government had satisfied RFRA's strict scrutiny by providing a compelling justification for denying the exemption. In so interpreting the statute, Ginsburg relied in part on what we have described as the fourth Establishment Clause limit on permissible accommodation, and she cited *Caldor* and *Cutter* as support for her position. Noting that "the government's license to grant religion-based exemptions from generally applicable laws is constrained by the Establishment Clause"[105] and that accommodations "must not significantly impinge on the interests of third parties,"[106] she contended that a religion-based exemption must be denied "when the accommodation would be harmful to others—here, the very persons the contraceptive coverage requirement was designed to protect."[107] Elaborating elsewhere in her opinion, she explained that the requested exemption was improper because it "would override significant interests of the corporations' employees and covered dependents, . . . deny[ing] legions of women who do not hold their employers' beliefs access to contraceptive coverage that the ACA would otherwise secure."[108] For Ginsburg, it was not enough that the coverage might be provided by other means; rather, it must be provided "through the existing employer-based system of health insurance 'so that [employees] face minimal logistical and administrative obstacles.' "[109]

The majority, also citing *Cutter*, accepted as "certainly true" the proposition that "in applying RFRA 'courts must take adequate account of the burdens a requested accommodation may impose on nonbeneficiaries,' "[110] and it observed that this consideration "will often inform the analysis of the Government's compelling interest

---

[104] 134 S. Ct. 2751 (2014).

[105] *Id.* at 2802 n.25 (Ginsburg, J., dissenting) (citing *Cutter*, 544 U.S. at 720–22).

[106] *Id.* at 2790; *see id.* at 2790 n.8 (citing *Caldor*, 472 U.S. 703, and *Cutter*, 544 U.S. at 720, 722).

[107] *Id.* at 2801.

[108] *Id.* at 2790.

[109] *Id.* at 2802 (citing 78 Fed. Reg. 39888 (July 2, 2013)).

[110] *Id.* at 2781 n.37 (majority opinion) (quoting *Cutter*, 544 U.S. at 720).

and the availability of a least restrictive means of advancing that interest."[111] But the majority did not agree that the requested exemption should be denied on this basis, concluding instead that the exemption "need not result in any detrimental effect on any third party."[112] As explained in Chapter 6, the majority relied heavily on the ability of the government to extend a regulatory accommodation that was already in place for religious nonprofit organizations, an accommodation that exempted objecting organizations from providing the contested coverage but that required their insurance companies (or third-party administrators, if they were self-insured) to offer the same coverage separately. Disagreeing with Justice Ginsburg, the majority concluded that extending the same treatment to the objecting corporations would not seriously impair the interests of their employees, who "would continue to 'face minimal logistical and administrative obstacles,' because their employers' insurers would be responsible for providing information and coverage."[113] As a result, "[t]he effect . . . on the women employed by Hobby Lobby and the other companies involved in these cases would be precisely zero."[114]

The issue of third-party harms also is implicated in ongoing litigation concerning the ACA's contraceptive mandate, now pending in the Supreme Court. In the pending cases,[115] as discussed in previous chapters, religious nonprofit organizations have challenged the very accommodation provision on which the majority relied in *Hobby Lobby*. The organizations contend that the accommodation itself violates RFRA and that they should be entirely exempted from the contraceptive coverage requirement.[116] Relying on RFRA to void the regulatory accommodation, however, might leave the government with no equally effective means of providing the organizations' employees with ready access to the contested insurance coverage, thus presenting a stronger case than

---

[111] *Id.*

[112] *Id.*

[113] *Id.* at 2782 (citations omitted).

[114] *Id.* at 2760; *cf. id.* at 2787 (Kennedy, J., concurring) (religious exercise cannot "unduly restrict other persons, such as employees, in protecting their own interests, interests the law deems compelling," but in the current case "the means to reconcile those two priorities are at hand in the existing accommodation").

[115] The Court has granted review in seven cases, which it has consolidated. The cases probably will be decided under the name *Zubik v. Burwell*, which was the first of these cases to be filed in the Supreme Court. *See Zubik v. Burwell*, 136 S. Ct. 444 (2015), *granting cert. to Geneva College v. Secretary U.S. Dep't of Health & Human Services*, 778 F.3d 422 (3rd Cir. 2015).

[116] As discussed in Chapters 5 and 6, the organizations claim that the accommodation substantially burdens their religious exercise because it operates in a manner that leaves them complicit in providing the insurance coverage to which they object.

in *Hobby Lobby* for arguing that the requested exemption would impose undue burdens or costs on third parties.[117] This Establishment Clause concern could influence the Court's interpretation of RFRA in these cases, potentially persuading the Court that the RFRA claims should be rejected.

Similar questions are presented by religious objections to antidiscrimination laws, including laws prohibiting discrimination based on sexual orientation. As discussed in Chapter 6, for example, some wedding vendors, including photographers, florists, and bakers, have declined on religious grounds to provide services for same-sex weddings. If a wedding vendor invokes a state RFRA in response to an antidiscrimination claim, should the vendor be granted an exemption from the law, or would the exemption impose an undue burden or cost on the same-sex couple? Does it matter whether the same-sex couple could readily obtain the same service from another vendor? Or would the couple still suffer undue harm based simply on the indignity of the discrimination, a dignitary harm that is difficult to quantify but that courts are likely to regard as quite substantial? Here again, the disputed question is what counts as an undue burden or cost on third parties, implicating the fourth Establishment Clause limit on permissible accommodation. If that limit would be violated, the requested exemption should be denied as a matter of statutory interpretation, typically by finding strict scrutiny satisfied. Indeed, as explained in the last chapter, this is the result that courts are likely to reach in resolving wedding-vendor controversies. Discrimination by a religious organization, by contrast, might be protected under a state RFRA (or, if applicable, the federal RFRA) if the organization is acting to define its religious community and to preserve its internal religious character and identity. As Justice Brennan explained in *Amos*, this interest is such an important component of religious freedom that it sometimes overrides the competing interests of third parties.[118]

In summary, RFRA, RLUIPA, and their state-law analogues almost certainly constitute permissible accommodation and therefore do not violate the Establishment Clause.[119] This

---

[117] The challengers have argued that the organizations' employees need not be affected adversely, suggesting, for example, that the government could permit them to obtain the contested coverage through the government's existing healthcare exchanges.

[118] *See Corporation of the Presiding Bishop v. Amos*, 483 U.S. 327, 340–46 (1987) (Brennan, J., concurring in the judgment).

[119] For a competing argument, see IRA C. LUPU & ROBERT W. TUTTLE, SECULAR GOVERNMENT, RELIGIOUS PEOPLE 27, 197–201, 226–48 (2014) (suggesting that RFRA and other general regimes of accommodation are problematic, if not unconstitutional, because they are difficult to administer on the basis of principled, secular reasoning, and because they may provide unjustified favoritism of religious conduct).

conclusion, however, assumes that the statutes are properly interpreted and applied in a manner that complies with the Establishment Clause limits that we have identified. One hotly contested limit is the Establishment Clause prohibition on religious exemptions that impose undue burdens or costs on third parties. This prohibition is not disputed as a matter of principle, but its application depends upon a value-laden process of judicial balancing and the exercise of judgment. It is hardly surprising that such an inquiry leads to disagreements and controversy in particular cases, such as those arising under the ACA and antidiscrimination laws.

IV. The Dominant Doctrinal Position of the Lemon and Endorsement Tests

Accommodation is important both as a general concept and as a specialized field of Establishment Clause inquiry. It is doctrinally exceptional in a fundamental sense, however, because accommodation is permitted on the ground that it provides no benefit to religion that is constitutionally cognizable under the Establishment Clause. Instead, when accommodation meets the conditions we have identified, the governmental action is properly seen as advancing religious freedom, not religion as such. Outside the context of accommodation, by contrast, virtually any assistance to religion can be seen as a cognizable benefit, and the critical question is whether the benefit is impermissible. In answering this question, the Supreme Court has employed the three general tests discussed earlier—*Lemon*, endorsement, and coercion— supplemented by an implicit exception for traditional governmental practices. The exception based on tradition is narrow. It generally extends only to governmental practices that favor religion in a manner that is traditional, nonsectarian, and symbolic rather than tangible or coercive. The coercion test likewise has limited doctrinal importance. It plays a role in confining the tradition exception, but it is largely superfluous in the broader run of Establishment Clause cases. There, the *Lemon* and endorsement tests continue to govern. Because those tests are more restrictive than the coercion test, the coercion test does little more than identify an especially troublesome subset of constitutional violations.

In most Establishment Clause cases, then, the critical inquiry is whether governmental benefits to religion are impermissible, and the controlling general doctrine is that of the *Lemon* and endorsement tests. As noted earlier, these tests have been vigorously challenged by various Justices, but the Supreme Court continues to use them, albeit less often than in the past. And even when the Court has not applied these tests, neither has it renounced them. In its most recent Establishment Clause decision, for example, the Court in *Town of Greece v. Galloway*[120] rejected a challenge to legislative prayer without applying *Lemon* or the endorsement test. Instead, reaffirming its earlier decision in *Marsh v. Chambers*,[121] the Court noted that "*Marsh* found those tests unnecessary because history supported the conclusion that legislative invocations are compatible with the Establishment Clause."[122] Although the Court found the tests inapposite in the context at hand, however, it did not reject them for application in other settings.[123] It could do so in the future, but at least for now, the *Lemon* and endorsement tests continue to govern most Establishment Clause cases, and lower courts continue to apply them as a matter of controlling doctrine.[124]

The *Lemon* and endorsement tests are not identical, but their elements overlap substantially. Indeed, the two tests can be combined into a single, more unitary inquiry. Under this analysis, governmental action runs afoul of the Establishment Clause if it violates any of three constitutional prohibitions. First, the government cannot act with the purpose of advancing or endorsing religion (either one religion or religion generally); instead, it must have a secular purpose for its action. Whether phrased in terms of advancement or endorsement, this first prohibition protects the value of formal religious equality by preventing the government from purposefully discriminating in favor of religion (either one religion or religion generally) through the award of deliberately discriminatory benefits. Second, even if the government has a secular purpose, its action cannot have the primary effect of advancing or endorsing religion (either one religion or religion generally). As discussed earlier, this second prohibition takes on a

---

[120] 134 S. Ct. 1811 (2014).

[121] 463 U.S. 783 (1983).

[122] *Town of Greece*, 134 S. Ct. at 1818.

[123] *But cf. Elmbrook Sch. Dist. v. Doe*, 134 S. Ct. 2283, 2284 (2014) (Scalia, J., dissenting from denial of certiorari) (arguing, but only for himself and Justice Thomas, that "*Town of Greece* abandoned the antiquated 'endorsement test' " and, presumably, the *Lemon* test as well).

[124] *See, e.g., Jewish People for the Betterment of Westhampton Beach v. Village of Westhampton Beach*, 778 F.3d 390, 395 (2d Cir. 2015) ("Although 'much criticized,' the *Lemon* test still governs cases alleging violations of the Establishment Clause."); *Smith v. Jefferson Co. Bd. of Sch. Comm'rs*, 788 F.3d 580, 589, 588 (6th Cir. 2015) (concluding that "*Town of Greece* gives no indication that the Court intended to completely displace" prior doctrine and that it has no impact on the *Lemon* and endorsement tests in cases "that cannot be resolved by resorting to historical practices"); *but cf. id.* at 602, 601 (Batchelder, J., concurring in part and concurring in the result) (arguing that "*Town of Greece* is apparently a major doctrinal shift"—a "sea change" heralding a new general test based on history and coercion—but agreeing that "unless and until the Supreme Court explicitly holds that it has abandoned the *Lemon*/endorsement test, the lower courts are bound to continue applying that test in contexts where the Court has previously employed it").

somewhat different meaning—less quantitative and concrete, more qualitative and symbolic—when it is phrased in terms of endorsement rather than advancement. Under either phrasing, however, the second prohibition can reach benefits to religion that are not deliberately discriminatory. As a result, this prohibition goes beyond formal equality and serves other constitutional values. Third, the governmental action cannot create an excessive governmental entanglement with religion. This third prohibition, which now is sometimes viewed as part of the second, addresses institutional separation and suggests a concern for structural constitutional values.

In summary, contemporary Establishment Clause doctrine is dominated by the *Lemon* and endorsement tests, with coercion, tradition, and accommodation playing significant but subsidiary roles. Taken as a whole, these tests and considerations provide useful doctrinal guidelines. To more fully understand this doctrine, however, we need to know how the Supreme Court has elaborated and applied these general standards. We have already examined the concept of accommodation at this more particular level. In the next chapter, we will explore the Court's decisionmaking in several other areas of Establishment Clause concern: religion and the public schools; religious symbolism in other public contexts; and public aid to religious schools, organizations, and individuals.

Chapter 8

THE ESTABLISHMENT CLAUSE IN PARTICULAR SETTINGS

As explained in the last chapter, the Supreme Court has developed various general tools for deciding Establishment Clause cases. Despite criticism, the *Lemon* and endorsement tests continue to dominate the doctrinal landscape.[1] Accommodation is permissible, within limits, because it satisfies these tests by promoting religious freedom, rather than religion. Tradition, by contrast, has generated an implicit exception to the Court's general tests. The Court also has introduced a competing test, the coercion test. Yet because the Court has not repudiated the *Lemon* and endorsement tests, the coercion test mainly serves two subsidiary roles: limiting the scope of the tradition exception, and identifying constitutionally illicit promotions or endorsements of religion that are especially offensive to the Establishment Clause.

The general tests and concepts that we have identified reflect and inform the constitutional values that underlie the Establishment Clause. The Supreme Court formulates and implements these general tests and concepts, however, only in the course of resolving specific constitutional questions. And its resolution of these questions, in turn, helps clarify the meaning of the Court's general doctrinal tools as well as the significance and relative weight of the constitutional values that are at work.

In the modern period, most Establishment Clause cases have arisen in three settings: religion and the public schools; religious expression and symbolism in other public contexts; and public aid to religious schools, organizations, and individuals.[2] In this chapter, we will examine each of these settings in turn, thus enhancing our understanding of the Establishment Clause and of the values it embodies.

---

[1] The *Lemon* test derives from *Lemon v. Kurtzman*, 403 U.S. 602, 612–13 (1971). Citations supporting the endorsement test and the Court's other general tests and concepts can be found in Chapter 7.

[2] Another significant group of cases deals with accommodation. We have already discussed this area in detail, in Chapter 7, examining accommodation both as a general concept and as a distinctive and complex field of Establishment Clause decisionmaking.

I. Religion and the Public Schools

A. Prayer and Religious Instruction

In a long line of cases dating from 1948 to the present, the Supreme Court has invalidated school-sponsored prayer and religious instruction in the public schools, even when student participation is designated as voluntary. Apart from the aberrational case of *Zorach v. Clauson*,[3] the Court has consistently reasoned that the public schools cannot purposefully favor either specific religions or religion in general. The Court's decisions, including those decided before the *Lemon* and endorsement tests were formulated, rest on what is now the first prong of those tests. This prong forbids the government, including the public schools, from acting with the purpose of advancing or endorsing either one religion over others or religion over irreligion. Any such purposeful advancement or endorsement confers benefits on religion that are deliberately discriminatory and therefore impermissible. Since the government is not acting to remove a substantial burden on the exercise of religion, arguments of accommodation are unavailing. Arguments based on tradition are likewise unpersuasive. Even if a public school practice promotes prayer or religious instruction in a manner that is both traditional and nonsectarian, and even if participation is formally voluntary, the risk of coercion in the public school context is sufficient to rule out the implicit exception.[4]

The Court's decisionmaking in this context reflects the constitutional value of religious equality, which includes equality not only between and among religions, but also between religion and irreligion. Because the Court's decisions are directed to purposeful governmental discrimination, they can be fully explained in terms of formal equality. Even so, formal religious equality in this context also tends to promote substantive religious equality— not only for students, but also for parents, who have an interest in inculcating the religious or irreligious values of their choice. For simplicity, the discussion that follows will speak only of students, but the analysis clearly implicates the interests of parents as well.

The actions that are constitutionally forbidden—school-sponsored prayer and religious instruction—are actions that would impair substantive religious equality by their unequal impact on students of differing religions or of no religion at all. The impact on

---

[3]   343 U.S. 306 (1952).

[4]   The Pledge of Allegiance, which involves neither a prayer nor religious instruction, might be a different matter. As discussed in Chapter 7, the implicit exception might permit school-sponsored recitations of the Pledge, complete with its "under God" language, as long as students are not directly or substantially coerced to actively join the recitations.

dissenting students could be considerable, and it could significantly impair other constitutional values. Certainly, the religious identity of the dissenting students would be threatened, and they would likely feel exclusion, affront, and alienation. Given the requirement of compulsory attendance and the impressionability of children, moreover, there also would be a substantial risk to religious voluntarism. In other words, the schools' promotion of religion might have its intended effect, inducing children to adopt religious beliefs and practices that they otherwise would not. At the very least, there would be "subtle coercive pressure" of the sort identified in *Lee v. Weisman*,[5] as discussed in Chapter 7. By precluding schools from acting in this fashion, the Court's doctrine in this area may also serve structural constitutional values, promoting a religiously inclusive political community even as it allows religion to thrive and compete in the private domain, free from the potentially debasing and corrosive effects of governmental involvement.

The Supreme Court's initial encounter with religion and the public schools was in 1948, only a year after *Everson v. Board of Education*.[6] In *Everson*, the Court had declared that the Establishment Clause forbids the government from aiding either one religion or religion in general. In *Illinois ex rel. McCollum v. Board of Education*,[7] the Court relied on this principle to invalidate a public school program that provided religious instruction through a "released-time" arrangement. Under the program, weekly classes in religious instruction, taught by privately employed religious teachers representing various faiths, were conducted in the school building during regular school hours. The classes were offered only to students whose parents had requested that they attend; students not attending continued their secular studies. The Court noted the challengers' argument that the program was voluntary in name only, and it also noted the fact of compulsory school attendance. But the Court did not base its decision on coercion. Instead, the Court ruled that the program of religious instruction was unconstitutional because it singled out religion for special, advantageous treatment. By adopting and implementing this program, the public school had purposefully promoted religion over irreligion in violation of what would later become the first prong of the *Lemon* and endorsement tests.

Four years later, by contrast, the Court in *Zorach v. Clauson*[8] upheld a very similar program of religious released-time. In *Zorach*,

---

5   505 U.S. 577, 592 (1992).

6   330 U.S. 1 (1947).

7   333 U.S. 203 (1948).

8   343 U.S. 306 (1952).

as in *McCollum*, the challenged program offered weekly religious instruction by privately employed religious teachers of various faiths, with the classes taught during regular school hours to students whose parents requested that they attend, and with nonparticipating students continuing their secular studies. Unlike in *McCollum*, however, the religious classes in *Zorach* were conducted off the premises of the public schools, at religious centers to which the participating students retreated. For the Court in *Zorach*, this made all the difference, because now the public schools were doing "no more than accommodat[ing] their schedules to a program of outside religious instruction."[9]

In reality, the Court's attempt to distinguish *McCollum* was tenuous. Yes, the on-the-premises program in *McCollum* may have favored religion to a greater degree than the off-the-premises program in *Zorach*. Both before and after *Zorach*, however, the Court has consistently ruled that the public schools cannot to *any* degree promote religion over irreligion by purposefully favoring the former over the latter. Yet purposeful favoritism is precisely what happens in a religious released-time program, regardless of where the religious instruction takes place. The public schools give special treatment to religion, and to religion alone, in an attempt to facilitate and promote religious instruction. This preferential treatment confers a discriminatory benefit on religion, and it violates what is now the first prong of the *Lemon* and endorsement tests.

In defending its decision in *Zorach*, the Court invoked the concept of accommodation.[10] But the accommodation argument is weak, certainly in light of more recent decisions that have clarified the meaning and limits of permissible accommodation. As explained in Chapter 7, the concept of accommodation permits religion-based governmental action only if it is designed to provide relief from what would otherwise be a substantial burden on the exercise of religion—a direct or indirect burden that dissuades or discourages the exercise of religion by exerting substantial coercive pressure on religious decisionmaking. In the circumstances presented by *Zorach*, it is difficult to find such a burden. Compulsory attendance at a public school, where students must focus on secular subjects, restricts the time available for religious instruction, but students remain free to pursue such instruction during the many hours when school is not in session. As a result, it is difficult to argue that the

---

[9]   *Id.* at 315.

[10]   "When the state encourages religious instruction or cooperates with religious authorities by adjusting the schedule of public events to sectarian needs," the Court stated, it "respects the religious nature of our people and accommodates the public service to their spiritual needs." *Id.* at 313–14.

public schools are either prohibiting religious conduct or placing religious students on the horns of a dilemma in their religious decisionmaking. Religious released-time programs, whether of the *Zorach* or of the *McCollum* variety, seem designed less to remove a burden on religious exercise than to confer an affirmative benefit on religion. As such, they are not strong candidates for an accommodation analysis.

Tenuous at the time the case was decided, the reasoning of *Zorach* is even more dubious today. Despite numerous decisions undermining its premises, however, *Zorach* has not been overruled, and off-the-premises released-time programs remain valid as a matter of prevailing constitutional law. Thus, *Zorach* stands—but as a decidedly aberrational decision.

In the years since *Zorach*, the Supreme Court has decided a number of Establishment Clause challenges to school-sponsored prayer and devotional exercises in the public schools. Unlike in *Zorach*, the Court in these cases has consistently honored what is now the first prong of the *Lemon* and endorsement tests. Accordingly, the Court has repeatedly invalidated laws and policies promoting school-sponsored prayer or devotion, even if nonsectarian and formally voluntary, on the ground that the government, including the public schools, cannot purposefully advance or endorse religion over irreligion.

The Supreme Court first addressed the classic form of school-sponsored prayer and devotion: spoken exercises in the classroom. In 1962, in *Engel v. Vitale*,[11] the Court struck down a program that called for teachers to lead their students in a daily, state-prescribed prayer. The prayer was brief and nondenominational,[12] and objecting students were permitted to opt out, but these factors did not save the program from invalidation. A year later, in *School District of Abington Township v. Schempp*,[13] the Court extended *Engel* to public school policies that did not involve a state-prescribed prayer, but that instead required a reading of Bible verses to non-objecting students and their collective recitation of the Lord's Prayer. Although the Court's opinion in *Schempp* foreshadowed what later became the first and second prongs of the

---

[11]   370 U.S. 421 (1962).

[12]   Crafted by a governmental agency, New York's State Board of Regents, the prayer read as follows: "Almighty God, we acknowledge our dependence upon Thee, and we beg Thy blessings upon us, our parents, our teachers and our Country." *Id.* at 422.

[13]   374 U.S. 203 (1963).

Lemon test,[14] its decision in this case, as in *Engel*, rested easily on the first prong alone. Whether or not the state actually composes a prayer or devotional reading, to call for its recitation in the classroom is undeniably an action that purposefully advances religion over irreligion, conferring a discriminatory benefit that is constitutionally impermissible.

Justice Stewart, the sole dissenter in *Engel* and *Schempp*, suggested that school-sponsored religious exercises generally should be upheld in the absence of demonstrable coercion.[15] In his dissenting opinion in *Schempp*, he advanced an accommodation argument, contending that the challenged school policies furthered free exercise values.[16] As in *Zorach* and for similar reasons, however, it is difficult to see the challenged policies in either *Engel* or *Schempp* as attempts to remove what would otherwise be governmentally imposed, substantial burdens on the exercise of religion. In the absence of the school-sponsored exercises, the public schools would not be promoting religion during the school day, but, given the limited hours of compulsory attendance, neither would the schools be prohibiting religious students from engaging in religious conduct nor placing them on the horns of a dilemma in their religious decisionmaking.[17] Despite Justice Stewart's argument, it seems clear that the challenged policies of school-sponsored prayer and devotion went well beyond a permissible promotion of religious freedom. Instead, they advanced and endorsed religion.[18]

Some two decades later, in its 1985 decision in *Wallace v. Jaffree*,[19] the Supreme Court ruled that even policies that call for moments of silence in public school classrooms can violate the Establishment Clause, but only if the policies are purposefully crafted to promote the use of these moments for silent *prayer*. In *Wallace*, the Court addressed a 1981 Alabama statute that authorized a period of classroom silence "for meditation or

---

[14] "The test may be stated as follows: . . . [T]o withstand the strictures of the Establishment Clause there must be a secular legislative purpose and a primary effect that neither advances nor inhibits religion." *Id.* at 222.

[15] *See Engel*, 370 U.S. at 445 (Stewart, J., dissenting); *Schempp*, 374 U.S. at 316–20 (Stewart, J., dissenting).

[16] *See Schempp*, 374 U.S. at 311–13 (Stewart, J., dissenting).

[17] Contrast the view of Justice Stewart: "[A] compulsory state educational system so structures a child's life that if religious exercises are held to be an impermissible activity in schools, religion is placed at an artificial and state-created disadvantage." *Id.* at 313.

[18] In *Stone v. Graham*, 449 U.S. 39 (1980) (per curiam), the Supreme Court extended the reasoning of *Engel* and *Schempp* to a state law that required public schools to post the Ten Commandments in their classrooms. The Court found the law unconstitutional because it had no secular purpose and therefore violated the first prong of the *Lemon* test.

[19] 472 U.S. 38 (1985).

voluntary prayer." Significantly, pre-existing Alabama law had already authorized a period of silence "for meditation," and the stark legislative history of the 1981 enactment confirmed that it was "entirely motivated by a purpose to advance religion" by "convey[ing] a message of State endorsement and promotion of prayer."[20] Accordingly, the Court concluded that the 1981 legislative action was unconstitutional under the first prong of the *Lemon* and endorsement tests. Conversely, the Court's opinion suggested that a moment-of-silence law not mentioning prayer would be constitutionally permissible. Taking into account the views of the five Justices who wrote concurring and dissenting opinions,[21] moreover, it appears that the Court likewise would have approved a law that did mention prayer as one permissible use for a moment of silence—as long as the law's language and history did not reveal the impermissible purpose of favoring and endorsing silent prayer over other forms of quiet reflection. Lower courts have read *Wallace* accordingly.[22]

In more recent cases, the Supreme Court has invalidated school-sponsored prayer outside the classroom setting. In its 1992 decision in *Lee v. Weisman*,[23] the Court held that it was unconstitutional for a public school to sponsor a clergy-led, nonsectarian prayer at a graduation ceremony. As explained in the last chapter, the Court found illicit coercion, but only by defining coercion very broadly. A more straightforward explanation for the decision, as four Justices suggested, was that—quite apart from coercion—the challenged practice was invalid because it purposefully advanced and endorsed religion.[24] Eight years later, in *Santa Fe Independent School District v. Doe*,[25] the Court invalidated a school board policy that called for student votes to determine

---

[20] *Id.* at 56, 59. The Court cited candid statements from the legislative sponsor of the 1981 law and noted that the Alabama legislature went on in 1982 to authorize a prescribed spoken prayer that was clearly unconstitutional. *See id.* at 40, 56–61.

[21] *See id.* at 62–67 (Powell, J., concurring); *id.* at 67–84 (O'Connor, J., concurring in the judgment); *id.* at 84–90 (Burger, C.J., dissenting); *id.* at 90–91 (White, J., dissenting); *id.* at 91–114 (Rehnquist, J., dissenting).

[22] *See, e.g., Sherman ex rel. Sherman v. Koch*, 623 F.3d 501 (7th Cir. 2010) (upholding an Illinois statute requiring "a brief period of silence . . . for silent prayer or for silent reflection"); *Brown v. Gilmore*, 258 F.3d 265 (4th Cir. 2001) (upholding a Virginia statute requiring a "minute of silence" for students to "meditate, pray, or engage in any other silent activity").

[23] 505 U.S. 577 (1992).

[24] *See id.* at 609 (Blackmun, J., joined by Stevens and O'Connor, JJ., concurring) ("[O]ur cases have prohibited government endorsement of religion, its sponsorship, and active involvement in religion, whether or not citizens were coerced to conform."); *id.* at 627 (Souter, J., joined by Stevens and O'Connor, JJ., concurring) ("[T]he State may not favor or endorse either religion generally over nonreligion or one religion over others.").

[25] 530 U.S. 290 (2000).

whether there would be student-led "invocations" or "messages" before high school football games, in part "to solemnize" the games. A six-Justice majority found that the policy violated the Establishment Clause, largely because its transparent purpose, as revealed by the policy's text and context, was to preserve and promote the school district's longstanding practice of school-sanctioned prayers at the games. As in *Weisman*, the Court in *Santa Fe* found indirect and subtle coercion even in the absence of compulsory attendance. But the Court in *Santa Fe* also relied explicitly on the *Lemon* and endorsement tests. Under those tests and under the reasoning of the Court's other school prayer decisions, public school practices and policies of the sort confronted in *Weisman* and *Santa Fe* are clearly invalid. In each case, there is governmental action that purposefully advances and endorses religion over irreligion, and that is enough to render it unconstitutional.[26]

It is important to emphasize that prayer and religious instruction are not themselves unconstitutional, even if they occur on the premises of public schools. What is unconstitutional is governmental sponsorship or promotion of these activities, either by law or through the policies or practices of public school boards, officials, or teachers. The government, including the public schools, cannot purposefully advance or endorse religion over irreligion. Students and other private actors, by contrast, are perfectly free to advance or endorse religion themselves, even in the context of the public schools. Indeed, they are constitutionally protected in this activity, primarily on the basis of free speech principles, as discussed in Chapter 5.

Freedom of speech, first and foremost, means that students can engage in personal prayer and other religious expression, even during the school day, subject only to the same regulations that apply to other sorts of student speech. Public schools cannot target the personal religious expression of students for special disadvantage, and even content-neutral regulations must be constitutionally reasonable. Students certainly are free, for example, to engage in silent prayer during a quiet time in class or nondisruptive spoken prayer in the hallway or the lunchroom. (As

---

[26] A more difficult question was confronted in a 2012 lower court decision that did not reach the Supreme Court: whether public high schools, for nonreligious reasons, can hold their graduation ceremonies in a church. The U.S. Court of Appeals for the Seventh Circuit found the practice unconstitutional, at least in the case at hand, because it had the effect of endorsing religion in violation of the second prong of the *Lemon*/endorsement inquiry and also was indirectly coercive in the sense discussed in *Weisman* and *Santa Fe*. See *Doe ex rel. Doe v. Elmbrook Sch. Dist.*, 687 F.3d 840 (7th Cir. 2012) (en banc), *cert. denied*, 134 S. Ct. 2283 (2014).

the saying goes, as long as there are math tests, there will be prayer in the public schools!)

According to the Supreme Court's equal access doctrine, moreover, freedom of speech gives private religious groups the right to use public school buildings, after hours, on the same basis as other private groups. This doctrine applies to noncurricular student groups,[27] and it also applies to community groups. In its 1993 decision in *Lamb's Chapel v. Center Moriches Union Free School District*,[28] for example, the Court ruled that a public school district, having opened its facilities for after-hours use by a variety of community groups, could not exclude a religious group that wanted to present a film series promoting Christian family values.

In a 2001 decision, the Court extended the equal access doctrine even to after-school religious meetings for elementary students. In *Good News Club v. Milford Central School*,[29] a Christian organization requested permission to conduct meetings for elementary school students immediately after school, meetings at which the children would sing songs, hear Bible lessons, memorize scripture, and pray. School policy permitted privately sponsored after-school meetings for various purposes, including morals and character education for children, but it prohibited the use of school facilities for religious purposes. Citing this prohibition as well as the Establishment Clause, the school denied the organization's request. The Supreme Court ruled that the school's policy, as applied to the proposed meetings, amounted to impermissible viewpoint discrimination and therefore violated freedom of speech. Contrary to the school's argument, moreover, the Court found that the policy was not redeemed by the Establishment Clause. The Court reasoned that although the Clause forbids public schools from advancing or endorsing religion, this does not occur when schools merely provide the sort of nondiscriminatory access that the Christian organization was seeking—possible misperceptions to the contrary notwithstanding. (Later in the

---

[27] In *Widmar v. Vincent*, 454 U.S. 263 (1981), the Supreme Court ruled that state universities were required to give equal access to student groups that wished to use university facilities for religious worship and religious discussion. Congress then extended the policy of *Widmar* to public secondary schools by statute, through the Equal Access Act of 1984, 20 U.S.C. §§ 4071–4074, and the Supreme Court later upheld the Act against an Establishment Clause challenge. *See Board of Educ. of Westside Community Schools v. Mergens*, 496 U.S. 226 (1990). In *Good News Club v. Milford Central School*, 533 U.S. 98 (2001), which is further discussed in the next paragraph of the text, the Court ruled that freedom of speech demands that the requirement of equal access be extended to public elementary schools as well. At least after *Good News Club*, it seems that the Equal Access Act does little or nothing more than the First Amendment itself requires as a matter of freedom of speech.

[28] 508 U.S. 384 (1993).

[29] 533 U.S. 98 (2001).

chapter, we will more fully address the Establishment Clause analysis of public aid to religious organizations, including aid in the form of equal access to governmental property or other nondiscriminatory benefits.)

B.   Evolution and Creationism

At least since the notorious *Scopes* case of the 1920s,[30] there has been tremendous controversy concerning the topic of human origins and how it should be taught in the public schools. The Supreme Court has declared that the Establishment Clause imposes significant limitations in this context. In essence, the Court has treated creationism as a matter of religious instruction, bringing into play the same sort of reasoning that the Court has applied to school-sponsored prayer and religious instruction generally. Thus, in its 1968 decision in *Epperson v. Arkansas*[31] and its 1987 decision in *Edwards v. Aguillard*,[32] the Court invalidated laws that were designed to prohibit the teaching of evolution or to promote the teaching of creationism. The Court found that the challenged laws were intended to protect and further a religious understanding of human origins. As such, they had the purpose of advancing and endorsing religion over irreligion, thereby conferring benefits on religion that were deliberately discriminatory and constitutionally impermissible.

In *Epperson*, the Court invalidated an Arkansas law that had been enacted in 1928, in the aftermath of the *Scopes* case. Like the Tennessee law at issue in *Scopes*, the Arkansas law prohibited public school teachers from teaching "the theory or doctrine that mankind ascended or descended from a lower order of animals." Focusing on the history of the law, the Court concluded that "fundamentalist sectarian conviction was and is the law's reason for existence"[33] and that the law prohibited the teaching of human evolution "for the sole reason that it is deemed to conflict with a particular religious doctrine; that is, with a particular interpretation of the Book of Genesis by a particular religious group."[34] As a result, the law violated what is now the first prong of the *Lemon* test. It had the purpose of advancing religion, and, indeed, a particular religion, in this case by protecting the religion from competing views. Relying on other grounds, Justice Black concurred in the Court's result, but he questioned the religious

---

[30]   *See Scopes v. State*, 289 S.W. 363 (Tenn. 1927).

[31]   393 U.S. 97 (1968).

[32]   482 U.S. 578 (1987).

[33]   *Epperson*, 393 U.S. at 108.

[34]   *Id.* at 103.

neutrality of the Court's reasoning, noting that the teaching of evolution could "infringe[ ] the religious freedom of those who consider evolution an anti-religious doctrine."[35]

Going a step beyond its ruling in *Epperson,* the Court in *Edwards* invalidated a Louisiana "Balanced Treatment for Creation-Science and Evolution-Science Act." The Louisiana statute did not preclude the teaching of evolution, at least not categorically. Rather, it declared that any public school that elected to teach evolution was required to teach "creation science" as well. The state claimed that creation science reflected legitimate scientific opinion that had been improperly repressed, and it contended that the statute permitted students to confront the competing evidence and decide the matter for themselves. Over a vigorous dissent by Justice Scalia,[36] however, the Court rejected the state's arguments, calling the statute the "Creationism Act" and concluding that the legislature's secular defense of the law was a "sham."[37] The Court noted that public school teachers are free to teach genuinely scientific evidence about human origins, even if this evidence might undermine or place in question the prevailing theory of evolution, and it suggested that a legislature would be free to require that the public schools include this type of scientific critique. Based on the content of the Louisiana statute and its legislative history, however, the Court found that it was not designed to promote the teaching of diverse scientific theories. Rather, the legislature's "primary" and "preeminent" purpose was to advance and endorse a particular religious understanding of creation, an understanding that appeared to be drawn from a literal reading of Genesis.[38] Accordingly, this statute, like the one in *Epperson,* violated the first prong of the *Lemon* and endorsement tests.[39]

The Supreme Court has not addressed the concept of "intelligent design," but, in a 2005 ruling, a federal district court concluded that it, too, should be treated as a religious understanding of creation that cannot be advanced or endorsed by public schools. The theory of intelligent design, or ID, is not linked in any overt or obvious way to a Biblical account of creation. Rather, on purportedly scientific grounds, it contends in essence that life in its various forms is so complex that it cannot be fully explained by

---

[35] *Id.* at 113 (Black, J., concurring in the result).

[36] *See Edwards,* 482 U.S. at 610–40 (Scalia, J., dissenting).

[37] *Id.* at 580, 586–87 (majority opinion).

[38] *Id.* at 593 ("Because the primary purpose of the Creationism Act is to advance a particular religious belief, the Act endorses religion in violation of the First Amendment."); *id.* at 590 ("[W]e need not be blind in this case to the legislature's preeminent religious purpose in enacting this statute.").

[39] *See id.* at 585–95; *see also id.* at 597–604 (Powell, J., concurring).

the process of evolution. Instead, the complexity of life suggests an intelligent design and therefore an intelligent designer. In *Kitzmiller v. Dover Area School District*,[40] the court invalidated a school board policy calling for students to be made aware of this theory. In particular, they were to be read a statement declaring that "Intelligent Design is an explanation of the origin of life that differs from Darwin's view," and they were to be referred to a book presenting this viewpoint. The court found that intelligent design, in reality, is a religious rather than a scientific perspective—simply a newly refined version of religious creationism. And the school board's purpose, it concluded, was to promote this religious perspective. According to the court, the policy was designed "to advance creationism, an inherently religious view, both by introducing it directly under the label ID and by disparaging the scientific theory of evolution."[41] The board had asserted secular objectives—improving science education and critical thinking skills. But in the court's view, these asserted purposes were a "sham" and "a pretext for the Board's real purpose, which was to promote religion in the public school classroom, in violation of the Establishment Clause."[42]

Justice Black's separate opinion in *Epperson*, invoking the religious freedom of those who reject evolution, raises the possibility of a free exercise objection to the study of evolution in the public schools, at least as a required subject. Although our focus here is on the Establishment Clause, the free exercise issue deserves comment. Under contemporary Free Exercise Clause doctrine, as discussed in Chapter 5, a claim for constitutional relief from the compulsory study of evolution might be viable, but it would be difficult to maintain. In the first place, the challenger would have to show that studying evolution would impose a substantial burden on the exercise of religion by exerting substantial coercive pressure on the student's religious understanding of creation. Even if the challenger could make this showing, that alone would not be enough to trigger heightened constitutional scrutiny under the doctrine of *Employment Division v. Smith*,[43] because the burden would be nondiscriminatory, a product of the school's general curriculum. One possible route around *Smith* would be a hybrid-claim argument, citing the right of parents to control the education of their children and attempting to rely upon and extend *Wisconsin v.*

---

[40]   400 F. Supp. 2d 707 (M.D. Pa. 2005).

[41]   *Id.* at 747.

[42]   *Id.* at 762, 763. The court rested its Establishment Clause ruling not only on the purpose prong of *Lemon* but also the effect prong, as well as the endorsement test. *See id.* at 714–64.

[43]   494 U.S. 872 (1990).

Yoder,[44] which the Court in *Smith* claimed not to disturb. If this argument succeeded, the challenger would achieve strict constitutional scrutiny, but that still would not guarantee a religious exemption from the curricular requirement. The remaining question would be whether the compulsory study of evolution, as an important aspect of contemporary science, serves a compelling interest that does not permit a religious exemption.[45]

C.   Teaching About Religion

Under the Supreme Court's Establishment Clause cases, public schools are forbidden from promoting religion through school-sponsored prayer or religious instruction, including instruction that advances a religious understanding of creation. There is a critical distinction, however, between the public schools' promotional teaching *of* religion, which is constitutionally forbidden, and their objective teaching *about* religion, which is not. The public schools cannot purposefully advance or endorse religion (either one religion or religion generally) by promoting a religious perspective as true or sound. Conversely, schools are free to present and describe religion, including competing religious understandings, as part of a secular program of education.

The Supreme Court first embraced this distinction in its 1963 decision in *School District of Abington Township v. Schempp*.[46] The Court in *Schempp* invalidated public school policies that called for the devotional reading of Bible verses and the recitation of the Lord's Prayer, but it emphasized that its ruling did not extend to the "study of the Bible or of religion, when presented objectively as part of a secular program of education."[47] The Court stated that "the Bible is worthy of study for its literary and historic qualities" and that "it might well be said that one's education is not complete without a study of comparative religion or the history of religion and its relationship to the advancement of civilization."[48] In later cases, the Court has preserved and reaffirmed the distinction introduced in *Schempp*, suggesting, for example, that public schools

---

[44]   406 U.S. 205 (1972).

[45]   For a pre-*Smith* lower court decision addressing and rejecting a Free Exercise Clause claim analogous to that described in this paragraph, see *Mozert v. Hawkins County Bd. of Educ.*, 827 F.2d 1058 (6th Cir. 1987). Beyond invoking the Free Exercise Clause, a challenger might claim a religious exemption under a state-law Religious Freedom Restoration Act or under state constitutional law, as discussed in Chapter 6. These alternative sources of religious freedom might permit the challenger to bypass the doctrine of *Smith*, but the substantial burden and strict scrutiny inquiries might still make it difficult for the challenger to prevail.

[46]   374 U.S. 203 (1963).

[47]   *Id.* at 225.

[48]   *Id.*

can discuss the Ten Commandments "in an appropriate study of history, civilization, ethics, comparative religion, or the like."[49] Following the same reasoning, public schools likewise would be free to discuss and explain religious understandings of creation, assuming that the schools maintained their required objectivity.

Needless to say, there is a fine line between the neutral and objective teaching *about* religion and the partisan or promotional teaching *of* religion. The question necessarily turns on the specific content and context of the teaching, including the age of the students. Some public schools and public school teachers might be inclined to test the limits of permissible teaching, or they might deliberately cross the line from objectivity to religious partisanship. Conversely, other schools and teachers might steer away from any mention of religion, perhaps wishing to avoid any risk of Establishment Clause challenges or perhaps wishing simply to avoid controversy. As the Supreme Court itself suggested in *Schempp*, however, a student's education is incomplete without an understanding of religion and its historical and contemporary significance. Despite the difficulties, it seems that teaching about religion is sound educational policy. In any event, such teaching is constitutionally permissible.

II. Religious Expression and Symbolism Outside the Public School Context

The Supreme Court has decided a large number of Establishment Clause cases alleging impermissible benefits to religion outside the public school context. Many of them involve the inclusion of religious beneficiaries (including private religious schools or their students or parents) in public programs of financial aid or other tangible support. We will consider those cases later in the chapter. In this section, by contrast, the alleged benefits to religion are primarily and fundamentally symbolic. The challenged governmental actions provide no significant tangible support to religion and typically present no serious claim of coercion.[50] Examples include references to God or religion in official declarations, such as our national motto, along with the use of religious expression or symbolism in governmentally sponsored public displays, including holiday displays as well as permanent monuments. Legislative prayer is a distinctive variant of governmentally sponsored religious expression, which we will discuss separately.

---

[49] *Stone v. Graham*, 449 U.S. 39, 42 (1980).

[50] As discussed below, the Supreme Court considered but rejected a claim of illicit coercion in its legislative prayer ruling in *Town of Greece v. Galloway*, 134 S. Ct. 1811 (2014).

A. Governmental Declarations and Displays

As in its public school cases, the Supreme Court generally has addressed Establishment Clause challenges to governmentally sponsored religious expression or symbolism in non-school settings by using the *Lemon* and endorsement tests. In these cases, as in the public school cases, arguments of accommodation are unavailing, because the government is not acting to remove a substantial burden on the exercise of religion. In this non-school context, however, the challenged religious expression or symbolism typically presents little or no risk of meaningful coercion, not even indirect and subtle coercion of the sort discussed in *Lee v. Weisman*.[51] Therefore, if the governmental practice is highly traditional, it may fall within the Court's implicit, tradition-based exception to the *Lemon* and endorsement tests. This implicit exception honors the value of tradition, which serves as a counterweight to other constitutional values. Accordingly, as discussed in Chapter 7, the Supreme Court has suggested that the Establishment Clause does not forbid traditional governmental practices that are nonsectarian and essentially symbolic, even though they appear to advance and endorse religion in violation of the Court's usual Establishment Clause tests. As we emphasized in that earlier discussion, the contours of this implicit exception are quite uncertain, but the exception appears to sanction such practices as presidential Thanksgiving proclamations; the Supreme Court's opening cry, "God Save the United States and this Honorable Court"; our national motto, "In God We Trust"; and the "under God" language in the Pledge of Allegiance.[52]

Whatever its precise contours, the tradition-based exception has a limited scope. Unless the government's action is supported by a deep and longstanding American tradition, even nonsectarian and purely symbolic governmental action remains subject to the three-pronged analysis of the *Lemon* and endorsement tests. The Supreme Court accordingly has applied these tests in a series of cases addressing public displays containing religious expression or symbolism. The Court has upheld some displays and rejected others.

---

[51] 505 U.S. 577 (1992).

[52] *See, e.g., Lynch v. Donnelly*, 465 U.S. 668, 674–78 (1984). As explained in Chapter 7, the weight of tradition might support the "under God" reference in the Pledge of Allegiance even for school-sponsored recitations in the public school setting, this despite the risk of indirect and subtle coercion, as long as students are not directly or substantially coerced to actively join the recitations. *See Elk Grove Unified School District v. Newdow*, 542 U.S. 1, 25–33 (2004) (Rehnquist, C.J., concurring in the judgment); *id.* at 33–45 (O'Connor, J., concurring in the judgment).

The third prong of the analysis, concerning entanglement, has not been a major focal point in these cases.[53] The first prong would seem highly relevant, but, unlike in the public school context, it has not always played a determinative role here. Instead, the Court sometimes has concluded, or else has assumed, that the government's purpose in including religious expression or symbolism in a public display is not to advance or endorse religion, but instead is merely to acknowledge or recognize some aspect of religion that makes it relevant to the display. For example, a city might include a Christian nativity scene in a Christmas display to acknowledge or recognize the religious origins of Christmas. Under the first prong of the *Lemon* and endorsement tests, the government cannot act with the purpose of promoting religion, but it is free to address religion—in effect, to teach about religion, even outside the public school context—in a neutral and objective manner. Needless to say, the government's claim that it has included religious expression or symbolism to serve this objective, non-promotional purpose may be highly contentious. In any event, a judicial evaluation of the government's purpose may be difficult, and it therefore is not surprising that the Court sometimes has passed over the first prong and focused its attention on the second.

Under the second prong of the *Lemon* and endorsement tests, governmental action, whatever its purpose, violates the Establishment Clause if it has the primary effect of advancing or endorsing religion. Because the context here is symbolic by nature, the Court has focused especially on the endorsement reformulation of the second prong, which, indeed, was first suggested by Justice O'Connor in a holiday display case, *Lynch v. Donnelly*.[54] Under this analysis, the question is whether a "reasonable observer" or an "objective observer," properly informed of the relevant history and context of the public display in question, would perceive a message of governmental endorsement of religion (either one religion or religion generally). This inquiry addresses the symbolic effect of the government's action, focusing on its objective or apparent meaning, not its intended purpose. Even so, if a reasonable, objective observer would conclude that the government is endorsing religion, it is likely that this is precisely the government's intention. Indeed, in its 2005 decision in *McCreary County v. ACLU*,[55] a Ten

---

[53] As noted in the last chapter and as discussed further below, the third prong has been merged into the second in the financial aid context, with the Court considering entanglement as a part of its inquiry into effect. *See Agostini v. Felton,* 521 U.S. 203, 232–33 (1997). It is not clear whether this doctrinal development extends beyond the financial aid context.

[54] 465 U.S. 668 (1984); *see id.* at 687–94 (O'Connor, J., concurring).

[55] 545 U.S. 844 (2005).

Commandments case to which we will return shortly, the Supreme Court largely equated the purpose and effect prongs in this context, declaring that public displays should be found to rest on the impermissible purpose of advancing religion if a reasonable, objective observer would so conclude.[56] With or without the explicit linkage invoked in *McCreary*, it seems that the second prong of the analysis is being used to police violations of the first, even as the Court avoids the treacherous evidentiary problems that a more direct evaluation of purpose would entail.

As *McCreary* makes clear, the Court's decisionmaking in this context can serve to prevent the purposeful endorsement of religion. But *McCreary's* focus on the reasonable, objective observer, coupled with the Court's reliance upon the impermissible effect of endorsement in other cases, suggests that the inquiry here is not designed merely to preclude formal or deliberate discrimination. Instead, the governing analysis reflects a concern for the symbolic impact of the government's action, especially on dissenters, who may be affronted and alienated if the government appears to be endorsing religious beliefs they do not share. Thus, the Court's doctrine in this setting promotes not merely formal religious equality, but also substantive equality. It gives special weight to the value of respecting the religious identity of dissenting citizens, and, relatedly, it serves the structural value of promoting a religiously inclusive political community.

The Court's analysis—whether under the endorsement variant of the second prong or under *McCreary's* inquiry into objective purpose—requires sensitive judgments about the objective meaning of particular public displays, taking into account the specific history and setting of each display and the particular expression or symbolism that it includes. In the Court's 1984 decision in *Lynch*, for instance, the Justices upheld the use of a nativity scene in a municipal Christmas display that also included a Santa Claus house, reindeer, and other secular symbols. Although the majority opinion invoked and emphasized the original *Lemon* test, Justice O'Connor argued in her concurrence that the nativity scene, in context, did not have the effect of communicating a message of governmental endorsement of religion or, more specifically, Christianity. To O'Connor, the breadth of the city's overall display suggested a different and permissible governmental message—one

---

[56] *See id.* at 861–63; *cf.* B. Jessie Hill, *Anatomy of the Reasonable Observer*, 79 BROOKLYN L. REV. 1407, 1453 (2014) (properly understood, the endorsement inquiry addresses the "social meaning" of a display "in its present physical and social context," attempting to discern the "reconstructed intent of a hypothetical government speaker," not "the subjective intent of any particular individual or even composite speaker").

that simply celebrated Christmas, a public and heavily secularized holiday, by giving recognition to its various traditional symbols. An objective observer, she concluded, would not believe that the government included the nativity scene to endorse its religious content.[57]

Five years later, in *County of Allegheny v. ACLU*,[58] the Court itself adopted the endorsement reformulation of the second prong in its evaluation of two separate holiday displays. Shifting majorities held that a county-sponsored nativity scene was unconstitutional, but that it was permissible for a city to display a Chanukah menorah alongside a Christmas tree and a sign saluting liberty. Unlike the nativity scene in *Lynch*, this one was not part of a broader display that included secular symbols. Instead, it stood essentially alone in a prominent location within the county courthouse, and it included a banner proclaiming "Gloria in Excelsis Deo!" ("Glory to God in the Highest!"). Focusing on the objective meaning of the display, the Court found that in context, the nativity scene conveyed an impermissible message of governmental endorsement.[59] Conversely, Justices Blackmun and O'Connor, casting the deciding votes concerning the menorah, concluded that its inclusion in the city's display conveyed a message that did not endorse Judaism or religion in general. Instead, when viewed with the other elements of the display, the menorah was part of an overall message that celebrated the secular dimensions of the winter holiday season (Justice Blackmun's position)[60] or that promoted pluralism and freedom of belief (the view of Justice O'Connor).[61]

In its 2005 decision in *McCreary* and in a companion case, *Van Orden v. Perry*,[62] the Supreme Court addressed public displays of the Ten Commandments.[63] Four Justices urged a new and more relaxed approach to "passive" religious symbolism outside the public school context,[64] but their view did not command a majority.

---

[57] *See Lynch*, 465 U.S. at 691–94 (O'Connor, J., concurring).

[58] 492 U.S. 573 (1989).

[59] *See id.* at 598–602.

[60] *See id.* at 613–21 (opinion of Blackmun, J.).

[61] *See id.* at 632–37 (O'Connor, J., concurring in part and concurring in the judgment). Four Justices joined Justices Blackmun and O'Connor to create a 6-Justice majority for upholding the menorah display. These four Justices would have permitted the nativity scene as well, but they were in dissent on that issue. *See id.* at 655–79 (Kennedy, J., concurring in the judgment in part and dissenting in part).

[62] 545 U.S. 677 (2005).

[63] *See generally* Jesse H. Choper, *The Story of the Ten Commandments Cases: Van Orden v. Perry and McCreary County v. ACLU, in* FIRST AMENDMENT STORIES 513 (Richard W. Garnett & Andrew Koppelman eds., 2012).

[64] *See Van Orden*, 545 U.S. at 686–92 (plurality opinion).

Instead, a divided Supreme Court again offered a pair of mixed decisions, with the Court's competing results resting on the context-specific approach of *Lynch* and *Allegheny*, now linked to the inquiry into purpose.

In *McCreary*, a five-Justice majority invalidated recently erected courthouse displays of framed copies of the Ten Commandments. The Commandments were surrounded by the Magna Carta, the Declaration of Independence, the Bill of Rights, and other historical documents, but the current arrangements had been preceded by earlier, more limited displays that clearly were designed to promote the religious content of the Commandments. According to the Court, a reasonable, objective observer would conclude from the sequence of events that the current displays were intended to further the same, predominantly religious purpose as the displays they had replaced.[65]

In *Van Orden*, by contrast, a different five-Justice majority upheld the constitutionality of a longstanding, forty-year-old display of the Ten Commandments on the outdoor grounds of the Texas State Capitol, where the Commandments stood as one monument among many in a large, park-like setting. Switching sides as he cast the deciding vote, Justice Breyer reasoned in his controlling opinion that unlike the displays in *McCreary*, the Texas monument, in its particular historical context and physical setting, conveyed a predominately secular message—a message about the Ten Commandments' historical significance and their importance to secular morality. Breyer claimed to rely on "legal judgment" in *Van Orden*, rather than *Lemon* or the endorsement test as such, but his "fact-intensive" analysis was largely consistent with the endorsement reformulation of the second prong, as well as *McCreary*'s inquiry into objective purpose.[66]

The Supreme Court's context-specific approach extends to holiday and other public displays, including not only displays that are clearly sponsored by the government, but also private displays on governmental property. The private endorsement of religion of course is not unconstitutional, but if a private religious display is on

---

[65] *See McCreary*, 545 U.S. at 867–74.

[66] *Van Orden*, 545 U.S. at 700 (Breyer, J., concurring in the judgment); *see id.* at 698–706. A more recent case involving a Ten Commandments monument, *Pleasant Grove City v. Summum*, 555 U.S. 460 (2009), did not present an Establishment Clause issue. Instead, as discussed in Chapter 5, the challenger claimed a free speech right to erect a competing religious monument, but the Court found that the Ten Commandments monument was government speech and that there was no free speech right to equal access. If there had been an Establishment Clause challenge in *Summum*, it might well have been rejected on the authority of *Van Orden*, given the factual similarities between the two cases. *See Summum*, 555 U.S. at 483 (Scalia, J., concurring).

governmental property, contextual considerations could suggest the improper appearance of governmental endorsement. If the property is a public forum open equally to religious and nonreligious displays, an Establishment Clause violation is highly unlikely. In its 1995 decision in *Capitol Square Review and Advisory Board v. Pinette*,[67] for example, the Supreme Court ruled that the Establishment Clause did not preclude a privately sponsored Latin cross, accompanied by a sign disclaiming governmental sponsorship, from being accorded equal access to a traditional public forum. Even so, five Justices, speaking through separate opinions, affirmed the need for a context-specific inquiry under the endorsement reformulation of the second prong.[68] In so doing, they specifically rejected the position of a four-Justice plurality opinion, which argued that private religious speech can never be restricted in a public forum in order to avoid an Establishment Clause violation predicated on perceived governmental endorsement.[69]

Needless to say, governmental sponsorship of a Latin cross, the preeminent symbol of Christianity, normally would violate the Establishment Clause. But this might not be true in every case. For instance, if a Latin cross serves as a war memorial, would a reasonable observer still regard its message as religious in general and Christian in particular? Or might the reasonable observer find the message predominantly secular, in which case governmental sponsorship might be constitutionally permissible? The Supreme Court obliquely addressed this issue, but did not resolve it, in its complicated and fractured decision in *Salazar v. Buono*.[70] Speaking for three Justices, Justice Kennedy suggested that "a Latin cross is not merely a reaffirmation of Christian beliefs [but also] is a symbol

---

[67] 515 U.S. 753 (1995).

[68] *See id.* at 772–83 (O'Connor, J., joined by Souter and Breyer, JJ., concurring in part and concurring in the judgment); *id.* at 783–96 (Souter, J., joined by O'Connor and Breyer, JJ., concurring in part and concurring in the judgment); *id.* at 797–816 (Stevens, J., dissenting); *id.* at 817–18 (Ginsburg, J., dissenting).

[69] *See id.* at 763–70 (plurality opinion).

[70] 559 U.S. 700 (2010). The case involved a Latin cross that served as a World War I memorial on federal land in the Mojave National Preserve. The cross was originally erected in 1934 by members of a private group, the Veterans of Foreign Wars (VFW). The district court found an Establishment Clause violation and issued an injunction that forbade the government from permitting the cross to be displayed. By the time the litigation reached the Supreme Court, however, the district court's original Establishment Clause ruling was not at issue. Instead, the question was whether a congressionally mandated transfer of the cross site to private ownership, with the government conveying the land to the VFW, would violate or undermine the existing injunction, as the district court and court of appeals had concluded. The Supreme Court's five-four decision reversed and remanded, but two of the five Justices in the majority did not reach the merits, finding instead that the challenger lacked standing to pursue the relief being sought. *See id.* at 729–35 (Scalia, J., joined by Thomas, J., concurring in the judgment).

often used to honor and respect those whose heroic acts, noble contributions, and patient striving help secure an honored place in history for this Nation and its people."[71] Justice Stevens, by contrast, expressed a different view, also on behalf of three Justices. "Making a plain, unadorned Latin cross a war memorial," he argued, "does not make the cross secular. It makes the war memorial sectarian."[72] Addressing an analogous issue in the immediate aftermath of *Salazar*, the U.S. Court of Appeals for the Tenth Circuit ruled that roadside memorial crosses for fallen Utah state troopers violated the Establishment Clause because a reasonable observer would conclude that the state was endorsing Christianity.[73] But four of nine judges, urging rehearing en banc, contended that the court's decision was mistaken because "the memorial crosses at issue conveyed a message of memorialization, not endorsement."[74]

B. Legislative Prayer

The Supreme Court has approved the constitutionality of legislative prayer without applying the *Lemon* or endorsement tests, ruling instead that the practice is permissible on the basis of tradition. Legislative prayer is supported by a long historical tradition, dating back to the First Congress, and it normally is not coercive. The Court's implicit, tradition-based exception to its usual doctrinal tests, however, typically requires that a practice be not only traditional and non-coercive, but also nonsectarian. "In God We Trust," for example, meets this condition; "In Jesus We Trust" would not, and such a national motto would plainly be unconstitutional. As explained in Chapter 7, however, the practice of legislative prayer combines governmental sponsorship with

---

[71] *Id.* at 721 (plurality opinion of Kennedy, J., joined by Roberts, C.J., and Alito, J.).

[72] *Id.* at 747 (Stevens, J., joined by Ginsburg and Sotomayor, JJ., dissenting).

[73] *See American Atheists, Inc. v. Davenport*, 637 F.3d 1095, 1119–24 (10th Cir. 2010) (amended opinion). The court so ruled despite Justice Kennedy's conspicuous observation in *Salazar* that "[a] cross by the side of a public highway marking, for instance, the place where a state trooper perished need not be taken as a statement of governmental support for sectarian beliefs." *Salazar*, 559 U.S. at 718–19 (plurality opinion).

[74] *American Atheists, Inc. v. Davenport*, 637 F.3d at 1102 (Kelly, J., dissenting from denial of rehearing en banc). The Supreme Court denied certiorari over the vigorous dissent of Justice Thomas, who argued that the Court should use the case to reconsider the *Lemon* and endorsement tests. *See Utah Highway Patrol Ass'n v. American Atheists, Inc.*, 132 S. Ct. 12, 12–23 (2011) (Thomas, J., dissenting from denial of certiorari). *Cf. American Atheists, Inc. v. Port Authority of N.Y. & N.J.*, 760 F.3d 227 (2d Cir. 2014) (rejecting an Establishment Clause challenge to the National September 11 Museum's display of "the Cross at Ground Zero," a steel column and cross-beam recovered from the wreckage of the World Trade Center and taking the form of a Latin cross, with the court finding that a reasonable observer would not perceive a governmental endorsement of religion or Christianity).

individual religious speech, that of the prayer-giver. It thus implicates the value of religious free speech as well as tradition, and these two values, taken together, have led the Court to approve legislative prayer without requiring that prayers be nonsectarian. The Justices have decided two legislative prayer cases, addressing and approving different variations of this practice.

In *Marsh v. Chambers*,[75] decided in 1983, the Supreme Court approved the practice of legislative prayer by publicly paid chaplains, not only in Congress but in state legislatures as well. The case focused on the Nebraska legislature, which employed a chaplain to offer prayers at the beginning of each legislative session. In upholding the Nebraska practice, the Court noted that it was very similar to the longstanding practice of Congress and of most other states. It did not matter that the Nebraska legislature had employed the same chaplain, a Presbyterian minister, for more than fifteen years, nor that his prayers were "in the Judeo-Christian tradition."[76] Whether the Court meant to permit specifically sectarian prayers—prayers referring to Christ, for example—was not entirely clear for several decades, until 2014, when the Court issued its second legislative prayer decision, *Town of Greece v. Galloway*.[77]

Rejecting contrary dicta in *County of Allegheny*,[78] *Town of Greece* declared that *Marsh* was not confined to nonsectarian prayer.[79] The Court noted that *Marsh* relied upon the tradition of legislative prayer and that this tradition includes prayers that are Christian or otherwise sectarian. Moreover, a requirement that prayers be nonsectarian would improperly "force the legislatures that sponsor prayers and the courts that are asked to decide these cases to act as supervisors and censors of religious speech."[80] The Court suggested that prayers should be "solemn and respectful in tone, . . . invit[ing] lawmakers to reflect upon shared ideals and common ends."[81] But to avoid the hovering specter of censorship, the Court indicated that an Establishment Clause challenge based on content would be viable only if there were a pattern, over time, of

---

[75] 463 U.S. 783 (1983).

[76] *Id.* at 793.

[77] 134 S. Ct. 1811 (2014).

[78] *See County of Allegheny v. ACLU*, 492 U.S. 573, 603 (1989) (suggesting that the prayers in *Marsh* were approved only "because the particular chaplain had 'removed all references to Christ' ") (quoting *Marsh*, 463 U.S. at 793 n.14).

[79] *See Town of Greece*, 134 S. Ct. at 1821 (rejecting the dicta from *County of Allegheny* as "irreconcilable with the facts of *Marsh* and with its holding and reasoning").

[80] *Id.* at 1822.

[81] *Id.* at 1823.

rather extreme religious rhetoric—more precisely, "[i]f the course and practice over time shows that the invocations denigrate nonbelievers or religious minorities, threaten damnation, or preach conversion."[82]

Unlike *Marsh*, *Town of Greece* presented a challenge to the practice of legislative prayer in a local governmental body. Like similar bodies across the country, the town board of Greece, New York, exercised not only lawmaking power but also certain administrative functions. Moreover, unlike in the legislative sessions of Congress and state legislatures, citizens participated directly in the board's meetings, commenting on proposed laws and sometimes presenting individual petitions, for instance, seeking business licenses or zoning variances. Despite these differences, the Court ruled that the tradition of legislative prayer extended to local bodies such as the board. It also rejected the argument that citizens attending the meetings, especially citizens presenting petitions to the board, would inevitably feel pressure to participate in the prayer—for example, by bowing their heads—at least in the form of subtle coercive pressure of the sort identified in *Lee v. Weisman*.[83] On this point, Justice Kennedy spoke for a controlling plurality,[84] noting that "board members and constituents are 'free to enter and leave with little comment and for any number of reasons' "[85] and that, if they choose to remain, their mere presence is not likely to be understood as participation in or agreement with the prayer. Unlike in *Weisman*, here the objectors were mature adults, and putting them in this situation did not amount to impermissible coercion. Justice Kennedy did not entirely rule out the possibility that there could be unconstitutional coercion in a local governmental body such as the board. But this would occur, he suggested, only if "the pattern and practice" of a local body showed that legislative prayer was being used "to coerce or intimidate others," for example, "if town board members directed the public to participate in the prayers, singled out dissidents for opprobrium, or indicated that their decisions might be influenced by a person's acquiescence in the

---

[82] *Id.* "Prayer that reflects beliefs specific to only some creeds," the Court continued, "can still serve to solemnize the occasion, so long as the practice over time is not 'exploited to proselytize or advance any one, or to disparage any other, faith or belief.' " *Id.* (quoting *Marsh*, 463 U.S. at 794–95).

[83] 505 U.S. 577 (1992).

[84] In this part of his opinion, Justice Kennedy spoke for himself, Chief Justice Roberts, and Justice Alito. *See Town of Greece*, 134 S. Ct. at 1824–28 (plurality opinion). Justices Thomas and Scalia also rejected the coercion argument, but they would have ruled that the Establishment Clause only forbids actual legal coercion, not subtle coercion of the *Lee v. Weisman* variety. *See id.* at 1837–38 (Thomas, J., joined by Scalia, J., concurring in part and concurring in the judgment).

[85] *Id.* at 1827 (plurality opinion) (quoting *Weisman*, 505 U.S. at 597).

prayer opportunity."[86] This language suggests that challenges based on coercion are no more likely to succeed than challenges based on the content of the prayers.

Town of Greece differed from Marsh in another respect as well. The town did not employ a paid chaplain. Instead, prayers before the town board were given by volunteer "chaplains of the month," who were invited to offer the monthly prayers on a rotating basis. For a number of years, nearly all of the prayer-givers had been Christian ministers, and most of the prayers had been explicitly Christian, with the ministers invoking distinctively Christian concepts or offering their prayers in the name of Jesus. As already noted, the Court ruled that legislative prayer is not unconstitutional simply because prayers are Christian or otherwise sectarian, and it accordingly found the content of the prayers unproblematic. It likewise concluded that the predominance of Christian ministers did not render the practice unconstitutional. The Court suggested that a rotational system of volunteer prayer-givers requires a nondiscriminatory selection process, but it found this condition satisfied. The town mainly invited local clergy, and nearly all of the town's congregations were Christian, but "[t]he town at no point excluded or denied an opportunity to a would-be prayer giver," and "[i]ts leaders maintained that a minister or layperson of any persuasion, including an atheist, could give the invocation."[87] According to the Court, this policy of formal nondiscrimination was fully sufficient. In other words, it was enough that the town did not purposefully or deliberately discriminate in favor of Christian prayer-givers and that it therefore honored the value of formal equality between and among competing religions.[88] It was not required to promote religious balance—arguably a form of substantive religious equality—by seeking out non-Christians, perhaps from outside town. In the Court's view, demanding that type of affirmative outreach would have required the town to decide what religions should be represented, and to what extent, "a form of government entanglement with religion that is far more troublesome than the current approach."[89]

Taking Marsh and Town of Greece together, it seems that a lawmaking body has at least two permissible options in selecting its prayer-giver(s). It can employ a legislative chaplain, in which case,

---

[86] Id. at 1826.

[87] Id. at 1816 (majority opinion).

[88] Despite the possibility of atheist prayer-givers, it seems clear that the practice of legislative prayer, by its very nature, deliberately prefers religion over irreligion and therefore violates that component of formal religious equality.

[89] Town of Greece, 134 S. Ct. at 1824.

as in *Marsh*, it is free to select a person from a particular religious faith or denomination. In the alternative, it can use a rotational system of volunteers, as in *Town of Greece*. If it uses that option, the lawmaking body is constrained, to a degree, by the principle of formal religious equality: it must utilize a nondiscriminatory selection process, that is, a process that does not formally or deliberately discriminate in favor of Christians or any other religious denomination or group.[90] But it need not seek out a diverse array of volunteers.[91]

Town of Greece was a five-four decision. The four dissenting Justices accepted *Marsh*, but they found improper sectarian favoritism in the case at hand, with the Town of Greece favoring Christianity in violation of the core Establishment Clause prohibition on sectarian discrimination. Writing for the dissenters, Justice Kagan found the overwhelmingly Christian content of the prayers—"the month in, month out sectarianism"[92]—especially troubling in the intimate and participatory setting of the town board meetings. In this setting, she observed, dissenting citizens might feel pressure to join or acquiesce in the prayers, and, in any event, they likely would experience a deep sense of religion-based exclusion. Calling for a fact-sensitive, totality-of-the-circumstances approach, Kagan would have required local bodies such as the board to make efforts to avoid predominantly Christian prayers.[93] For instance, they could take active steps to invite non-Christian prayer-givers. In the alternative, or in addition, they could encourage prayer-givers to offer inclusive prayers by providing them with advisory guidelines, a practice that is followed by Congress and many state legislatures.

Under the controlling doctrine of the majority, by contrast, legislative prayer is largely immune from constitutional challenge. Sectarian content is not problematic, nor is the sort of subtle coercive pressure that inevitably surrounds this practice. Challenges to rotational systems might be viable, but only if the selection process is deliberately skewed to favor one or more

---

[90] The precise character of this nondiscrimination requirement remains to be seen. For example, although the record in *Town of Greece* suggested that laypersons and atheists were eligible to give prayers, it is not clear that their exclusion would have made the policy impermissibly discriminatory.

[91] Although not yet addressed by the Supreme Court, a lawmaking body probably has a third permissible option for selecting prayer-givers: simply asking its own elected members to offer the prayers, perhaps on a rotating basis.

[92] *Town of Greece*, 134 S. Ct. at 1852 (Kagan, J., dissenting).

[93] *See also id.* at 1841 (Breyer, J., dissenting) (joining Kagan's dissenting opinion and observing that in this "fact-sensitive" case, as in *Van Orden*, he saw " 'no test-related substitute for the exercise of legal judgment' ") (quoting *Van Orden v. Perry*, 545 U.S. 677, 700 (2005) (Breyer, J., concurring in the judgment)).

particular religions over others. In short, the judiciary has a very limited role to play, with the Supreme Court being content to promote the constitutional values of tradition, religious free speech, and (to a degree) formal religious equality. Conversely, legislative bodies are free to promote other constitutional values—even though they are not required to do so—by taking steps along the lines suggested by Justice Kagan. In so doing, they might advance a more substantive understanding of religious equality, one that more fully respects the religious identity of dissenting citizens and that, relatedly, promotes a religiously inclusive political community.

III. Public Aid to Religious Schools, Organizations, and Individuals

We turn now to our final group of Establishment Clause cases. These cases, like the religious expression and symbolism cases we have just discussed, involve claims of impermissible benefits to religion outside the public school context. Here, however, the benefits to religion are not primarily symbolic. Instead, they take the form of significant financial aid or other tangible support to religious beneficiaries, including religious schools, organizations, and individuals. Neither accommodation nor tradition is pertinent in this context. The governmental action does not qualify as accommodation because it is not designed to remove a substantial burden on the exercise of religion. Likewise, although some forms of tangible support might be traditional, the governmental action is not merely or essentially symbolic, and it therefore falls outside the tradition-based exception. No inquiry into coercion is required, and the coercion test therefore does not play a significant role in the analysis. With these other concepts and tests thus out of the picture, the Supreme Court's decisionmaking in this area has been governed by the basic Establishment Clause standards of the *Lemon* and endorsement tests.

Virtually without exception, the first requirement of constitutionality, that of secular purpose, has been readily satisfied in the public aid context. This requirement of formal equality forbids the government from acting with the purpose of advancing or endorsing religion (either one religion or religion generally) through the conferral of deliberately discriminatory benefits. But the challenged governmental actions in this area typically do not involve formal or deliberate discrimination. Rather, they are general programs of aid that include both religious and nonreligious beneficiaries, without distinction. As a result, the Court's decisions have hinged on the remaining portions of the analysis, addressing effect and entanglement.

The third prong of the analysis, precluding excessive entanglement between religion and government, sometimes has been an issue, especially when a program of aid requires close governmental supervision. In the bulk of the cases, however, the debate has centered on the second prong, which bars governmental action that has the primary effect of advancing or endorsing religion (either one religion or religion generally). Indeed, since 1997, the Court in the public aid context has formally weakened the doctrinal significance of entanglement by folding the third prong into the second and by treating entanglement as simply one aspect of the effect inquiry.[94]

In its 1971 opinion in *Lemon*, the Court declared that the second prong precludes programs of aid that have the "principal or primary effect" of advancing religion.[95] Supplemented to some degree by the endorsement reformulation, this general standard continues to be affirmed.[96] As stated, however, the standard is exceedingly vague, and it raises a variety of questions, including two that are basic. First, does the second prong preclude benefits to religion under a formally nondiscriminatory aid program if, in actual operation, the program has a discriminatory *effect* that favors religious beneficiaries? Second, does it preclude some benefits to religion even under programs that are *entirely* nondiscriminatory, not only formally but also in effect?

Depending on the answers to these basic questions and other, subsidiary ones, the Court's interpretation and enforcement of the Establishment Clause in this context might serve a variety of constitutional values, both individual and structural. Religious voluntarism might be threatened by benefit programs that induce individuals to modify their religious beliefs or practices in order to qualify. Relatedly, at a more structural level, the extension of benefits to religious beneficiaries, with conditions attached, might compromise the vitality of religion and the autonomy of religious institutions. At the same time, an aid program that includes religious beneficiaries—even if the program is formally nondiscriminatory—might appear to endorse religion in a manner that disrespects the religious identity of dissenting citizens. Indeed, dissenting citizens might find it especially offensive that they are being forced to support, through their taxes, programs that have the effect of aiding religious beliefs and practices that are not their own.

---

[94] *See Agostini v. Felton*, 521 U.S. 203, 232–33 (1997).

[95] *Lemon v. Kurtzman*, 403 U.S. 602, 612 (1971).

[96] *See, e.g., Agostini*, 521 U.S. at 222–23, 235; *Zelman v. Simmons-Harris*, 536 U.S. 639, 648–49, 654–55 (2002).

These feelings of offense and alienation in turn might undermine the religious inclusiveness of the political community.

Although all of these constitutional values are implicated in the public aid context, the value that has been the most influential, especially in recent cases, is that of religious equality. Understood in a strictly formal sense, this value would sanction any program of aid that is formally nondiscriminatory. Standing alone, therefore, it would suggest that the first prong of the analysis should be determinative, and that the second prong (and with it the remaining content of the third) should be jettisoned altogether. Understood in a more substantive sense, by contrast, the value of religious equality looks beyond the form or purpose of the governmental action. It honors religious equality, but with a focus on the actual impact of governmental action on religious and irreligious citizens and organizations. So understood, the value of religious equality would not sanction a formally nondiscriminatory program if, despite its form, it nonetheless had a discriminatory effect.

Everson v. Board of Education,[97] decided in 1947, was the Supreme Court's first modern case addressing the question of public aid. In *Everson*, the Court used strongly separationist language, but it nonetheless upheld a formally nondiscriminatory program of bus-fare reimbursement that extended to parents whose children were being transported to Roman Catholic schools. After *Everson*, the Court did not return to the public aid context for twenty years, but, since then, it has decided a large number of cases.

In the 1970s and 1980s, the Supreme Court approved some public aid programs, but it invalidated others. The Court's doctrine was muddled and depended on fine distinctions. Even so, it appeared to reflect a concern for religious equality in its substantive sense, as well as other constitutional values, both individual and structural. Indeed, in its invalidation of various programs, the Court sometimes appeared to adopt a strong and categorical interpretation of its separationist language in *Everson*, which had declared that the government cannot "pass laws which aid one religion [or] all religions" and that "[n]o tax in any amount, large or small, can be levied to support any religious activities or institutions, whatever they may be called, or whatever form they may adopt to teach or practice religion."[98] This interpretation suggested separationist responses to the two basic questions regarding the second prong of the *Lemon* test. First, it suggested

---

[97]   330 U.S. 1 (1947).
[98]   *Id.* at 15–16.

that a formally nondiscriminatory aid program would be constitutionally problematic if it had a discriminatory effect that favored religion. Second, it implied—albeit more ambiguously—that public aid simply could not be extended to religious beneficiaries, not even if the program of aid was entirely nondiscriminatory, both in purpose and in effect.

More recently, by contrast, the Supreme Court's decisionmaking has shifted substantially, making its doctrine more coherent and simple, and at the same time far less separationist. The Court has emphasized formal equality more than substantive, and it has minimized the independent role of other constitutional values. The Court has suggested that formal equality itself tends to promote substantive equality and other constitutional values in this context, and that, in any event, increased doctrinal clarity is important. Indicating a retreat from more separationist responses to the two basic questions under the second prong, the Court has made it clear that formally nondiscriminatory programs of aid generally will be upheld—even if they extend to religious beneficiaries and even if they might appear, in practical effect, to discriminate in their favor. Nonetheless, the Court has not abandoned the second prong of the analysis altogether, and it continues to recognize some constitutional limits even on formally nondiscriminatory programs.

A. The Doctrinal Approach of the 1970s and 1980s

Beginning with *Lemon v. Kurtzman* itself[99] and continuing through a series of cases in the 1970s and 1980s, the Supreme Court suggested that it would analyze public aid programs with an eye to various considerations, generally under the rubric of the second prong of the *Lemon* test. Almost all of these cases involved aid to religious schools or their students or parents. The Court's decisions rested on sometimes doubtful distinctions, and its decisionmaking criteria were decidedly ambiguous. Even so, at least five sorts of considerations appeared to be playing significant roles.

First, the Supreme Court addressed the manner in which the aid was provided. The Court was more likely to invalidate aid that was provided directly to the religious schools, and it was less likely to invalidate aid that was targeted initially to individual students or parents and that reached the religious schools only indirectly, as a result of individual choice. A program that directly reimbursed

---

[99] *Lemon v. Kurtzman*, 403 U.S. 602 (1971). The Supreme Court decided one public aid case between *Everson* and *Lemon*. In *Board of Education v. Allen*, 392 U.S. 236 (1968), the Court ruled that the Establishment Clause did not bar a state from lending secular textbooks, free of charge, to students at religious as well as other private and public schools.

religious schools for educational expenses, for example, was more likely to be invalidated than a program of educational tax deductions that extended to parents who chose to educate their children at such schools.[100] As we will see later, this emphasis on the manner of aid—direct or indirect—has become a critical factor in contemporary doctrine. In the 1970s and 1980s, it was an important factor, but it did not appear to be as crucial as it plainly is today.

Second, the Court suggested that the quantity or percentage of aid reaching religious beneficiaries was a relevant consideration in evaluating the effect of a public aid program. Substantial benefits, or benefits that mainly assisted religious schools, were more likely to be invalidated.[101]

Third, the Court was more likely to invalidate programs of aid that were designed to benefit elementary or secondary education, as opposed to higher education. Although most religious colleges and universities have strong secular components, the Court described elementary and secondary religious schools as "pervasively sectarian"[102]—religious through and through.[103] At the same time, the younger age of the students made them more susceptible to the religious training and instruction that they received. For these reasons, the Court believed that public aid reaching religious beneficiaries in the context of elementary or secondary education was more likely to be used—and used successfully—to advance religion, suggesting a constitutionally impermissible effect. Conversely, the Court was more likely to uphold aid programs that were directed to higher education, even if religious colleges and universities were included.[104]

Fourth, the Court considered the substance of the aid being provided, with the question being whether this particular type of

---

[100] *Compare Lemon*, 403 U.S. at 621 (invalidating a program of direct reimbursement, based in part on this constitutional "defect"), *with Mueller v. Allen*, 463 U.S. 388, 399 (1983) (approving a program of indirect funding through educational tax deductions and emphasizing, as one factor among others, that the aid did not involve "the direct transmission of assistance from the State to the schools themselves").

[101] *See, e.g., Committee for Public Educ. & Religious Liberty v. Nyquist*, 413 U.S. 756 (1973).

[102] *See, e.g., School Dist. of Grand Rapids v. Ball*, 473 U.S. 373, 379, 384 & n.6 (1985).

[103] *See id.* at 384 ("At the religious schools here—as at the sectarian schools that have been the subject of our past cases—'the secular education those schools provide goes hand in hand with the religious mission that is the only reason for the schools' existence.' ") (quoting *Lemon*, 403 U. S. at 657 (opinion of Brennan, J.)).

[104] *See Tilton v. Richardson*, 403 U.S. 672 (1971); *Hunt v. McNair*, 413 U.S. 734 (1973); *Roemer v. Board of Public Works*, 426 U.S. 736 (1976).

aid might itself be used to inculcate religion, again suggesting an improper effect. For example, providing instructional materials and equipment for use in religious schools was more problematic than providing textbooks on purely secular subjects, because the instructional materials and equipment could more readily be used for religious as well as secular education.[105] Aid that was clearly and effectively segregated to secular activities was more likely to be approved.

Fifth, the Court considered the extent to which a particular program of aid might require continuing governmental involvement and monitoring. Using what was then the separate third prong of the *Lemon* test, the Court reasoned that this kind of continuing relationship might create a constitutionally impermissible entanglement of religion and government.

Two 1985 cases provide examples of the Supreme Court's reasoning in this period, and they also illustrate the Court's sometimes separationist decisionmaking. In *School District of Grand Rapids v. Ball*[106] and *Aguilar v. Felton*,[107] a deeply divided Court ruled that the Establishment Clause barred publicly paid teachers from providing secular, remedial education on the premises of primary and secondary religious schools. The challenged programs extended to religious and nonreligious schools alike, and the Court found that they had the purpose of supporting secular education, thereby satisfying the first prong of *Lemon*. Utilizing some of the considerations just outlined, however, the Court concluded that the programs could not survive the remainder of the analysis.

In *Grand Rapids*, the Supreme Court found that the challenged programs had the primary effect of advancing religion and therefore violated the second prong of *Lemon*. The Court reasoned that the programs impermissibly advanced the "sectarian enterprise" of the religious schools because the aid was "direct and substantial."[108] Addressing the substance of the aid, the Court observed that the publicly funded teachers might knowingly or unwittingly "conform

---

[105] *Compare Board of Educ. v. Allen*, 392 U.S. 236 (1968) (approving aid in the form of secular textbooks), *with Meek v. Pittenger*, 421 U.S. 349 (1975), and *Wolman v. Walter*, 433 U.S. 229 (1977) (rejecting aid in the form of instructional materials and equipment). This specific distinction has since been expressly rejected, with *Meek* and *Wolman* being overruled on this point. *See Mitchell v. Helms*, 530 U.S. 793, 808, 835 (2000) (plurality opinion); *id.* at 837 (O'Connor, J., concurring in the judgment).

[106] 473 U.S. 373 (1985).

[107] 473 U.S. 402 (1985).

[108] *See Grand Rapids*, 473 U.S. at 393–96.

their instruction to the environment in which they teach,"[109] thereby furthering the schools' religious mission. In part as a result, the Court also concluded that the impressionable children attending the schools might perceive a "symbolic union of church and state" reflecting an improper governmental endorsement of religion.[110]

In *Aguilar*, the challenged program was designed to mitigate the Establishment Clause vices that the Court identified in *Grand Rapids*. In particular, it included a system of governmental monitoring to ensure that the remedial classes, and therefore the aid, would remain entirely secular, both in reality and in perception. That very system of monitoring, however, led the Court to find an excessive governmental entanglement with religion, this in violation of *Lemon*'s third prong. "[T]hough a comprehensive system of supervision might conceivably prevent teachers from having the primary effect of advancing religion," the Court observed, "such a system would inevitably lead to an unconstitutional administrative entanglement between church and state."[111]

Then-Justice Rehnquist's dissenting opinion in *Aguilar* lamented the "Catch-22" that he believed the Court had created.[112] His position has since prevailed, and *Grand Rapids* and *Aguilar* have been overruled.[113] Indeed, in hindsight, *Grand Rapids* and *Aguilar* represent the end of a doctrinal era. They are the last Supreme Court decisions to follow the complex and sometimes separationist approach of the 1970s and 1980s. Today, an approach along those lines is advanced only in dissenting opinions. It is worth noting, however, that these dissenting opinions are often joined by as many as four Justices,[114] suggesting that this view still commands considerable support and that—with modest changes in the Court's membership—something like the approach of the 1970s and 1980s could conceivably return in the future.

---

[109] *Id.* at 388.

[110] *See id.* at 389–92; *see also id.* at 397 ("The symbolic union of church and state inherent in the provision of secular, state-provided instruction in the religious school buildings threatens to convey a message of state support for religion to students and to the general public.").

[111] *Aguilar*, 473 U.S. at 410.

[112] *Id.* at 420–21 (Rehnquist, J., dissenting).

[113] *See Agostini v. Felton*, 521 U.S. 203, 235–36 (1997) (overruling *Aguilar* in full and *Grand Rapids* in part).

[114] *See, e.g., id.* at 240–54 (Souter, J., joined by Stevens and Ginsburg, JJ., and in part by Breyer, J., dissenting); *Mitchell v. Helms*, 530 U.S. 793, 867–913 (2000) (Souter, J., joined by Stevens and Ginsburg, JJ., dissenting); *Zelman v. Simmons-Harris*, 536 U.S. 639, 686–717 (2002) (Souter, J., joined by Stevens, Ginsburg, and Breyer, JJ., dissenting); *id.* at 717–29 (Breyer, J., joined by Stevens and Souter, JJ., dissenting).

B. Contemporary Doctrine Regarding Indirect Aid[115]

The contemporary Supreme Court has replaced the multifaceted approach of the 1970s and 1980s with a two-track doctrine for public aid cases, with the Court selecting one track or the other based upon the manner in which the aid is provided. Thus, the Court sharply distinguishes between direct aid, which flows directly from the government to religious schools or organizations, and indirect aid, which flows initially to individuals and which reaches religious schools or organizations only because the individual recipients, as a matter of private choice, elect to use it there.[116] As discussed earlier, the distinction between direct and indirect aid was a significant consideration under the doctrinal approach of the 1970s and 1980s. Over time, the importance of this distinction became increasingly apparent, but its overriding significance—in dividing cases into two separate doctrinal tracks—became clear only in 2002, when the Supreme Court decided *Zelman v. Simmons-Harris*.[117]

In *Zelman*, the Court rejected an Establishment Clause challenge to a school voucher program that provided substantial tuition support for low-income parents, who could use the support at religious as well as nonreligious schools. The program was formally nondiscriminatory, but over ninety percent of the vouchers were being used at religious schools. The program's purpose was concededly secular, and the Court concluded that the program likewise passed scrutiny under the effect prong. Of broader doctrinal consequence, the Court made it clear that indirect aid, as in *Zelman*, is subject to a different Establishment Clause analysis than direct aid. As we will see shortly, the Court's contemporary doctrine concerning direct aid is considerably more permissive than it was in the past, but direct aid remains subject to certain restrictions that apply even to formally nondiscriminatory programs. By contrast, the Court in *Zelman* suggested that a formally nondiscriminatory program of indirect aid is virtually immune from Establishment Clause invalidation, even if the final

---

[115] For a more elaborate discussion, including an analysis of Chief Justice Rehnquist's instrumental role in the development of this doctrine, see Daniel O. Conkle, *Indirect Funding and the Establishment Clause: Rehnquist's Triumphant Vision of Neutrality and Private Choice, in* THE REHNQUIST LEGACY 54 (Craig M. Bradley ed., 2006).

[116] The discussion that follows adheres to the stated distinction between direct and indirect aid. It is important to recognize, however, that there are other possible meanings of "direct" and "indirect" and that the Supreme Court itself sometimes uses these terms in a different or more general way.

[117] 536 U.S. 639 (2002).

destination of the aid would suggest a strongly discriminatory effect.

Focusing on the second prong of the *Lemon* test and interpreting earlier cases to rest on similar reasoning, the Supreme Court declared in *Zelman* that "our decisions have drawn a consistent distinction between government programs that provide aid directly to religious schools and programs of true private choice, in which government aid reaches religious schools only as a result of the genuine and independent choices of private individuals."[118] As long as a program of indirect aid is formally nondiscriminatory and is "a program of true private choice" that is not "skewed" to create incentives favoring the selection of religious schools, the program "is not readily subject to challenge under the Establishment Clause."[119] Indeed, the Court emphasized that it had never invalidated such a program, and it implied that it never would. The Court suggested that programs of private choice honor the value of religious voluntarism and that, in the absence of an improper skewing that favors or disfavors religious choices, formal equality in this context promotes substantive equality as well. The Court further argued that there is no improper appearance of *governmental* endorsement of religion even if individuals disproportionately direct their benefits to religious destinations. If not, then one might likewise conclude that these programs of private choice neither disrespect the religious identity of citizens nor undermine the religious inclusiveness of the political community.

With the benefit of hindsight, we can see the two-track approach—and the Supreme Court's consistent approval of formally nondiscriminatory programs of indirect aid—in three earlier decisions that the Court cited and relied upon in *Zelman*. This series of cases stretches back to *Mueller v. Allen*,[120] which was decided in 1983, two years before *Grand Rapids* and *Aguilar* sounded the last hurrah for the doctrinal approach of the 1970s and 1980s. Given the multifaceted doctrine that prevailed at that time, the Court's reasoning in *Mueller* was more complex than the Court in *Zelman* was willing to admit. Even so, the Court in *Mueller* did rely heavily on the theme of private choice. In so doing, the Court approved a program of educational tax deductions for the parents of children attending religious as well as nonreligious schools, even though, as in *Zelman*, more than ninety percent of the aid in fact accrued to the benefit of individuals choosing religious schools.

---

[118] *Id.* at 649 (citations omitted).

[119] *Id.* at 653, 650, 652; *see id.* at 649–53.

[120] 463 U.S. 388 (1983).

In *Zelman*, the Supreme Court also cited its 1986 decision in *Witters v. Washington Department of Services for the Blind*[121] and its 1993 decision in *Zobrest v. Catalina Foothills School District*.[122] In *Witters*, the Court addressed a vocational scholarship program that provided tuition assistance to the visually impaired, and it ruled that the Establishment Clause did not forbid the extension of this aid to a blind student who had chosen to attend a religious college in preparation for a religious career. In like fashion, the Court in *Zobrest* ruled that a federal program providing sign-language interpreters for deaf children could be extended to a student who was attending a religious high school.

Unlike in *Mueller*, the aid programs in *Witters* and *Zobrest* did not have the effect of disproportionately favoring religious institutions, not even indirectly, but the Court in *Zelman* made it clear that that feature of the programs was not essential to their constitutionality. "The constitutionality of a neutral educational aid program," the Court wrote, "simply does not turn on whether and why, in a particular area, at a particular time, most private schools are run by religious organizations, or most recipients choose to use the aid at a religious school."[123] More generally, when this track of the Court's doctrine is in play, the ultimate destination of the aid is beside the point, and there is no need whatever to segregate the aid to ultimate uses that are secular in nature. Likewise, the other factors that the Court invoked under the multifaceted doctrine of the 1970s and 1980s appear to be irrelevant. Thus, if the aid is provided indirectly, it apparently does not matter whether it is substantial or whether it is designed to benefit elementary or secondary education, as opposed to higher education. It also appears that the indirect manner of funding is likely to defeat any claim of excessive governmental entanglement with religion.

In the wake of *Zelman*, formally nondiscriminatory programs of indirect aid are almost certain to be upheld—not only in the context of education but also in the provision of social services, such as poverty relief or drug counseling. Thus, *Zelman* strongly supports the constitutionality of including religious organizations in federal and state "charitable choice" or "faith-based initiative" programs to the extent that they rely on indirect funding.[124] In other words, these programs are almost certainly constitutional to the extent

---

[121] 474 U.S. 481 (1986).

[122] 509 U.S. 1 (1993).

[123] *Zelman*, 536 U.S. at 658.

[124] *See generally* Ira C. Lupu & Robert W. Tuttle, *The Faith-Based Initiative and the Constitution*, 55 DEPAUL L. REV. 1 (2005) (providing a comprehensive account and analysis of the federal faith-based initiative, especially as promoted by President George W. Bush).

that they authorize social-service vouchers that recipients can use at the provider of their choice, whether or not the provider is a religious organization, as long as the recipients have a genuine choice and there is no improper skewing.[125]

One question left unresolved by *Zelman* is whether the government even retains the *option* of excluding religious schools or organizations from otherwise general programs of indirect funding for privately provided education or social services. Notably, many state constitutions contain specific prohibitions on public aid to religion or religious entities, and these provisions have been invoked against voucher and similar programs of indirect funding. Some state courts have rejected these state constitutional challenges.[126] Others, by contrast, noting that *Zelman* is not controlling on state constitutional questions, have ruled that their state constitutions go beyond the Establishment Clause, imposing barriers on indirect funding that require the exclusion of religious schools and organizations.[127] But does this exclusion—even if grounded on state constitutional law—itself violate the First Amendment? If so, of course, the state constitutional provisions would have to give way.

The strongest First Amendment argument in this setting derives not from the Establishment Clause but from the Free Exercise Clause. By excluding religious schools or organizations from voucher or similar programs and thereby precluding individuals from choosing religious options, the government arguably is imposing a substantial and discriminatory burden on religious decisionmaking, triggering strict scrutiny and probable invalidation under the Free Exercise Clause. The Supreme Court's 2004 decision in *Locke v. Davey*,[128] however, tends to undermine this argument, because the Court in that case approved a discriminatory denial of indirect funding, there in the form of college scholarships. Even so, as explained in Chapter 5, the scope of the Court's decision is uncertain. In *Locke*, the Court rejected a free exercise challenge to a state's decision—based on a state constitutional provision—to deny scholarship funding to students who were majoring in devotional theology, typically in preparation

---

[125] *Cf. Freedom From Religion Found'n, Inc. v. McCallum*, 324 F.3d 880 (7th Cir. 2003) (upholding, as permissible indirect funding, a program that extended funding not only to various secular halfway houses but also to one that incorporated Christianity into its treatment program, with funds being provided to particular halfway houses on the basis of the individual decisions of criminal offenders, who were free to choose the halfway house in which they wished to reside).

[126] *See, e.g., Meredith v. Pence*, 984 N.E.2d 1213 (Ind. 2013).

[127] *See, e.g., Taxpayers for Public Educ. v. Douglas Co. Sch. Dist.*, 351 P.3d 461 (Colo. 2015).

[128] 540 U.S. 712 (2004).

for careers in the ministry. Given the context and the Court's reasoning, *Locke* might be confined to the discriminatory denial of funding for the devotional religious work and training of clergy and other religious professionals. Conversely, and perhaps more likely, it might permit the government to exclude religious beneficiaries in other indirect funding contexts as well.[129] If so, then restrictive state constitutional provisions, barring the extension of indirect funding to religious schools and organizations, do not violate the Free Exercise Clause.[130] More generally, under a broad reading of *Locke*, combined with the Court's Establishment Clause ruling in *Zelman*, Congress and the states have considerable discretion. Under *Zelman*, they are free to include religious beneficiaries in their indirect funding programs. And under *Locke* (if read broadly), they are equally free to exclude them.

We may soon learn more about the scope and meaning of *Locke*, the Supreme Court having granted review in a case raising analogous issues but arising in the context of direct as opposed to indirect aid. In the pending case, *Trinity Lutheran Church v. Pauley*,[131] the U.S. Court of Appeals for the Eighth Circuit rejected free exercise and other federal constitutional challenges to a decision by the State of Missouri to deny funding to a church for resurfacing its preschool playground with rubber from recycled tires. The church would have qualified for the funding under an otherwise nondiscriminatory program of grants, but the state cited a provision in the Missouri Constitution barring the provision of

---

[129] Lower courts have read *Locke* to permit the exclusion of religious schools from voucher programs for elementary and secondary education. *See, e.g., Eulitt v. Maine*, 386 F.3d 344 (1st Cir. 2004); *Bush v. Holmes*, 886 So. 2d 340 (Fla. Dist. Ct. App. 2004) (en banc), *aff'd on other grounds*, 919 So. 2d 392 (Fla. 2006); *Taxpayers for Public Educ.*, 351 P.3d 461. By contrast, in *Colorado Christian Univ. v. Weaver*, 534 F.3d 1245 (10th Cir. 2008), the court distinguished *Locke* in the course of invalidating a state-sponsored college scholarship program that excluded all students attending "pervasively sectarian" religious colleges.

[130] Some of the state constitutional provisions at issue, barring aid to "sectarian" schools or organizations, may be subject to a distinctive objection under the Free Exercise Clause. These provisions are sometimes called "Blaine amendments" due to their relationship—in content, historical timing, and perhaps political motivation—to similar provisions in the failed federal Blaine Amendment, which, as discussed in Chapter 2, was considered by Congress in 1875 and 1876. The distinctive free exercise argument is that these state constitutional provisions (or at least some of them), like the failed federal amendment, were driven by constitutionally illicit animus and discrimination against Roman Catholics and the Roman Catholic Church. *See, e.g., Taxpayers for Public Educ.*, 351 P.3d at 483–86 (Eid, J., concurring in part and dissenting in part). *Cf. Mitchell v. Helms*, 530 U.S. 793, 828 (2000) (plurality opinion) ("[T]he [federal] Blaine Amendment, which would have amended the Constitution to bar any aid to sectarian institutions[,] . . . arose at a time of pervasive hostility to the Catholic Church and to Catholics in general, and it was an open secret that 'sectarian' was code for 'Catholic.' ").

[131] 788 F.3d 779 (8th Cir. 2015), *cert. granted*, 2016 WL 205949 (U.S. Jan. 15, 2016) (No. 15-577).

public money, "directly or indirectly, in aid of any church, sect, or denomination of religion." The Supreme Court's interpretation of the Free Exercise Clause in this case could have broad implications for the validity of state constitutional restrictions on the extension of public aid—direct or indirect—to religion or to religious entities. The Court also could use this case to revisit or clarify its Establishment Clause doctrine concerning direct aid, the topic to which we turn next. The Court's decision is expected in 2016.

C. Contemporary Doctrine Regarding Direct Aid

What, then, of direct aid, that is, public aid that flows directly to religious schools or organizations? As *Zelman's* two-track analysis suggests, direct aid is subject to Establishment Clause restrictions that do not apply to indirect aid. Indeed, under the doctrine of the 1970s and 1980s, the Supreme Court was generally inclined to invalidate direct aid, at least when the benefitted institutions were not merely religiously affiliated but "pervasively sectarian"—a designation that the Court extended not only to churches, synagogues, and mosques, but also to primary and secondary religious schools. As in the context of indirect aid, however, the Supreme Court has moved away from its earlier doctrine, and the Court today is quite permissive even concerning direct aid. Contemporary doctrine is consistent with certain precedents from the 1970s and 1980s, but it is frankly inconsistent with others, and the Court has explicitly overruled a number of prior decisions. More generally, the Court now embraces a more lenient approach, one that emphasizes formal religious equality and that allows the Court to uphold most programs that are formally nondiscriminatory. Nonetheless, the Court's approach to direct aid is more complex than its approach to indirect aid, and formally nondiscriminatory programs remain subject to certain constitutional limitations.

The dominant features of the Supreme Court's contemporary doctrine concerning direct aid are marked by the Court's 1997 decision in *Agostini v. Felton*[132] and by its 2000 decision in *Mitchell v. Helms.*[133] In *Agostini,* the Supreme Court addressed the very same program of aid that it had considered twelve years earlier in *Aguilar v. Felton.*[134] Overruling *Aguilar* and the Court's companion ruling in *School District of Grand Rapids v. Ball,*[135] the Court declared in *Agostini* that the Establishment Clause does not forbid

---

[132] 521 U.S. 203 (1997).

[133] 530 U.S. 793 (2000).

[134] 473 U.S. 402 (1985).

[135] 473 U.S. 373 (1985). *See Agostini,* 521 U.S. at 235–36 (overruling *Aguilar* in full and *Grand Rapids* in part).

publicly paid teachers from providing secular, remedial education on the premises of primary and secondary religious schools. As noted in our earlier discussion of *Aguilar* and *Grand Rapids*, the challenged aid extended to religious and nonreligious schools alike, and the purpose of the program—supporting secular education for those with special educational needs—readily satisfied the first prong of *Lemon*. Rejecting the contrary reasoning of its 1985 decisions, the Court in *Agostini* concluded that the aid program also survived the remainder of the *Lemon* analysis, now modified to relax the entanglement inquiry by merging it into the effect prong. In *Mitchell*, the Supreme Court likewise approved a program of aid that provided federally funded computers and other instructional equipment and materials to primary and secondary schools, religious as well as nonreligious, with the amount of aid dependent on the number of students at each school. As in *Agostini*, a secular purpose was clearly present, and the Court also found the effect prong satisfied, even though this conclusion required it to overrule two additional precedents from the earlier doctrinal era.[136]

Agostini and *Mitchell* make it clear that even in the context of direct aid, programs that are formally nondiscriminatory are likely to be upheld. When "aid is allocated on the basis of neutral, secular criteria that neither favor nor disfavor religion, and is made available to both religious and secular beneficiaries on a nondiscriminatory basis," the Court wrote in *Agostini*, "the aid is less likely to have the effect of advancing religion."[137] As with comparable programs of indirect aid, the Court reasoned, such programs do not "give aid recipients any incentive to modify their religious beliefs or practices" in order to qualify.[138] Here again, it seems that the Court believes that formal religious equality tends to promote substantive equality and religious voluntarism as well. Under the Court's reasoning, moreover, formally nondiscriminatory programs of aid do not have the effect of endorsing religion. Rather, they fully and equally respect the religious identity of all citizens, and, as a result, they do nothing to weaken the religious inclusiveness of the political community.

One might extend this reasoning to sanction all programs of aid that are formally nondiscriminatory. A four-Justice plurality appeared to be moving in that direction in *Mitchell*,[139] and the

---

[136] In *Mitchell*, the Court overruled its contrary holdings in *Meek v. Pittenger*, 421 U.S. 349 (1975), and *Wolman v. Walter*, 433 U.S. 229 (1977). *See Mitchell*, 530 U.S. at 808, 835 (plurality opinion); *id.* at 837 (O'Connor, J., concurring in the judgment).

[137] *Agostini*, 521 U.S. at 231.

[138] *Id.* at 232.

[139] *See Mitchell*, 530 U.S. at 801–36 (plurality opinion).

plurality's view could find majority support in the future. At present, however, direct aid, even if formally nondiscriminatory, is subject to certain additional restrictions. Although the Court has not fully explained its reasoning, these additional restrictions might reflect structural constitutional values, both political and religious—protecting the government from potentially divisive religious involvement and protecting religion and the autonomy of religious organizations from the government's potentially unhelpful financial "help," which typically comes with strings attached. These structural values might support the separationist limits that the Court has continued to affirm even in the context of formally nondiscriminatory programs.

There appear to be four surviving Establishment Clause limits on formally nondiscriminatory programs of direct aid. These limits can be seen as remnants of the doctrinal approach of the 1970s and 1980s.

First, a program of direct aid cannot involve an unduly excessive entanglement between the government and religious organizations. Even after *Agostini* and *Mitchell*, for example, the government presumably cannot provide direct aid in a manner that includes a delegation of governmental power to religious organizations.[140] Under the Supreme Court's recent decisions, however, the entanglement limitation apparently is confined to rather extreme institutional entanglement. Routine administrative cooperation and governmental monitoring are no longer regarded as problematic.[141]

Second, the Court has suggested that the amount of direct aid to religious schools or organizations—at least if "pervasively sectarian"[142]—cannot be too substantial. In *Agostini*, for example, the Court emphasized that the publicly funded remedial education was "supplemental to the regular curricula" and therefore did not " 'reliev[e] sectarian schools of costs they otherwise would have borne in educating their students.' "[143]

Third, the Court has indicated that the substance of direct aid must be secular. More precisely, the aid must be segregated and

---

[140] *Cf. Larkin v. Grendel's Den, Inc.*, 459 U.S. 116 (1982) (holding that the government cannot grant churches, along with schools, the power to veto liquor licenses for nearby restaurants).

[141] *See Agostini*, 521 U.S. at 232–34.

[142] In *Mitchell*, a four-Justice plurality argued that whether a religious organization is "pervasively sectarian" should not matter, not even in the context of direct aid, but this opinion did not command majority support. *See Mitchell*, 530 U.S. at 826–29 (plurality opinion).

[143] *Agostini*, 521 U.S. at 228 (citation omitted).

confined to secular uses and cannot be diverted by its recipients to religious purposes. This point was emphasized by Justice O'Connor in her controlling opinion in *Mitchell*, in which she and Justice Breyer concurred only in the judgment, thereby limiting the reach of the Court's holding. Thus, Justices O'Connor and Breyer joined the plurality in concluding that the government can provide computers and other instructional equipment to religious schools, but they insisted that the schools cannot be allowed to use the equipment for religious purposes and that the government must establish adequate safeguards against this improper use.[144]

Fourth, the Court has suggested—albeit with ambiguity—that direct money payments (as opposed to in-kind support) to "pervasively sectarian" religious schools and organizations might be problematic even if the payments are restricted to secular uses. In *Agostini*, for instance, the Court noted that under the program it upheld, "No [government] funds ever reach the coffers of religious schools."[145] Conversely, the Court has been quite willing to approve direct money payments to religious organizations that are not pervasively sectarian—including religiously affiliated colleges, universities, hospitals, and charities—as long as the grants are in fact restricted to secular uses.[146] Under this analysis, "charitable choice" or "faith-based initiative" programs calling for direct money grants can permissibly extend to religiously affiliated social-service

---

[144] *See Mitchell*, 530 U.S. at 840–44, 857–67 (O'Connor, J., joined by Breyer, J., concurring in the judgment). Even the plurality in *Mitchell* would have recognized a limit on the substance of direct aid, but it would have required only that the content of the aid be secular at the time the government provides it. The plurality would not have precluded religious uses of the aid after it reached the hands of religious organizations. Accordingly, the plurality reasoned that it was permissible for the government to provide religious schools with computers and other instructional equipment—a secular form of aid—even if the schools thereafter used the equipment for religious purposes. Conversely, the plurality indicated that it would preclude the government from providing the schools with Bibles or other religious materials as such. *See id.* at 820–25, 831–35 (plurality opinion).

[145] *Agostini*, 521 U.S. at 228. *But cf. Committee for Public Educ. & Religious Liberty v. Regan*, 444 U.S. 646 (1980) (upholding direct cash reimbursement from state funds to religious schools for certain state-required testing and reporting activities); *Mitchell*, 530 U.S. at 818–20 & n.8 (plurality opinion) (noting that direct money payments raise special concerns, but questioning whether those concerns are enough to justify a distinctive Establishment Clause limitation); *American Atheists, Inc. v. City of Detroit Downtown Dev. Auth.*, 567 F.3d 278 (6th Cir. 2009) (upholding direct cash reimbursement grants from city to churches under downtown development program that provided funds for refurbishing downtown building exteriors and parking lots).

[146] *See, e.g., Roemer v. Board of Public Works*, 426 U.S. 736 (1976); *Bowen v. Kendrick*, 487 U.S. 589 (1988); *cf. id.* at 624–25 (Kennedy, J., concurring) (arguing that grant money should be permitted to flow even to pervasively sectarian organizations as long as the money is not used to further religion); *see generally Mitchell*, 530 U.S. at 826–29 (plurality opinion) (contending that the Court should abandon the distinction between pervasively sectarian and other religious organizations).

providers, but arguably not to providers that are pervasively sectarian.[147]

Given the trend favoring formal religious equality as the dominant constitutional value in this area and the Supreme Court's resulting inclination to approve formally nondiscriminatory programs of aid, it is not clear that these four Establishment Clause limits will continue to be recognized.[148] Indeed, even as they stand, most of the limitations are not categorical, and the Court is likely to construe them in a relatively permissive fashion. Thus, the Court could readily uphold a challenged program by finding, for example, that any entanglement is not excessive or that the aid to religious organizations is not unduly substantial.

The most categorical of the four limitations is the requirement that direct aid must be segregated and confined to secular uses and cannot be diverted by its recipients to religious purposes. If the plurality opinion in *Mitchell* were to become a majority view, however, this requirement would largely disappear.[149] Moreover, even as it stands, this limitation is subject to two significant and longstanding exceptions.

The first exception is direct aid in the form of tax exemptions. Thus, the Supreme Court has upheld the extension of tax exemptions to churches, synagogues, mosques, and other religious organizations, pervasively sectarian or otherwise, as part of a formally nondiscriminatory program of exemptions for nonprofit organizations in general. The financial benefit of this tax-exempt status is in no way segregated and confined to secular activities. Instead, it extends without limitation to the distinctively religious activities, including worship, of the churches and other religious organizations that qualify. Nonetheless, in its 1970 decision in *Walz*

---

[147] Discretionary grant programs, calling for governmental officials to allocate public money selectively on the basis of case-by-case evaluations, may give rise to special Establishment Clause concerns unless the government's discretion is carefully confined by clearly stated secular criteria. Otherwise, the awarding of grants to pervasively sectarian organizations might suggest purposeful religious discrimination in the grant-making process or, at least, the appearance of improper religious favoritism or endorsement. Indeed, these concerns might arise even if the discretionary awards provided not money, but in-kind support.

[148] The limitation on direct money payments to pervasively sectarian organizations is especially fragile, and, indeed, it may or may not be recognized as a matter of current law. Notably, existing charitable choice and faith-based initiative programs generally do not adhere to any such limitation. Instead, they permit direct money grants regardless of the religious or pervasively sectarian character of the grantee, as long as the funds are confined to secular uses. The Supreme Court may address this issue in the pending case of *Trinity Lutheran Church v. Pauley*, 788 F.3d 779 (8th Cir. 2015), *cert. granted*, 2016 WL 205949 (U.S. Jan. 15, 2016) (No. 15-577), involving a potential grant to a church for resurfacing its preschool playground.

[149] *See supra* note 144 and accompanying text.

v. Tax Commission,[150] the Court found that this type of direct and unsegregated aid is constitutionally permissible, in part because it is highly traditional[151] and in part because the aid is negative, not affirmative. The tax exemption simply leaves the religious organizations untaxed, along with other nonprofit organizations.[152] For reasons discussed in Chapter 7, this type of aid cannot be said to redress a substantial burden on religious exercise and therefore cannot be defended as a matter of permissible accommodation. But tax exemptions can be seen to limit the entanglement between religion and government, thereby promoting the structural values that are associated with institutional separation.

The second exception is direct aid in the form of access to public property for the purpose of engaging in religious speech. We already have discussed various aspects of the Supreme Court's equal access doctrine, both earlier in this chapter and in Chapter 5. To recapitulate, the Supreme Court has ruled in a series of cases that the Establishment Clause generally does not preclude the government from providing religious speakers with the same access to public property that it affords to other private speakers. In these cases, the Court has not only rejected the government's Establishment Clause argument for denying access, but it has further concluded that when the government has created a forum for a broad range of private expression, freedom of speech affirmatively demands that the religious speakers be given the equal access that they seek. Applying this reasoning, the Court has permitted—and required—the government to provide this formally nondiscriminatory aid to religious groups without in any way segregating and confining the aid to secular activities. Thus, the religious groups are provided with access to public property that they can use for prayer, religious discussion, evangelism, and other distinctively religious activities.

This series of cases began in 1981 with the Supreme Court's decision in *Widmar v. Vincent*,[153] which permitted—and required—a state university to allow student religious groups to use the university's meeting rooms on the same basis as other student groups. Since *Widmar*, the Court has extended this analysis to the

---

[150] 397 U.S. 664 (1970).

[151] This is not to suggest that tax exemptions, which provide tangible as opposed to merely symbolic support, could fit within the Court's implicit, tradition-based exception to its usual Establishment Clause doctrine.

[152] Contrast *Texas Monthly, Inc. v. Bullock*, 489 U.S. 1 (1989), which we discussed in Chapter 7. In *Texas Monthly*, the Court invalidated a sales tax exemption that was not general and nondiscriminatory, but that instead was limited to the sale of religious literature by religious organizations.

[153] 454 U.S. 263 (1981).

after-hours use of public school buildings by private religious groups, including those wishing to conduct after-school religious meetings for elementary students.[154] Notably, the Court also has ruled that formally nondiscriminatory access is sometimes permitted—and required—for public "property" in the form of aid beyond the provision of physical space. Thus, in its 1995 decision in *Rosenberger v. Rector and Visitors of the University of Virginia,*[155] the Court held that the University of Virginia could not deny "student activities" financial support to a student religious group seeking payment for the cost of printing its Christian publication.

Rosenberger is a precedent of limited reach. The Court emphasized that the funding was broadly available to a diverse array of student groups, thereby creating a "metaphysical" forum for private expression.[156] It also noted, for example, that the funding was derived from student fees, not general tax money; that the university had disassociated itself from the student speech in question; that the university would be paying the third-party printer and would not be providing public money directly to the "coffers" of the religious group itself; and that the group was not a church or similar "religious institution" as such.[157] More generally, a majority of the Court has insisted that even with respect to physical space, equal access for religious speech is not permitted, not even in a public forum, if the context—for example, close proximity to the seat of government and the absence of an appropriate disclaimer of official sponsorship—would create the appearance of governmental endorsement.[158]

Although the Court's equal access doctrine itself is subject to limitations,[159] it represents an important exception to the Establishment Clause requirement that direct aid be segregated

---

[154] *See Lamb's Chapel v. Center Moriches Union Free Sch. Dist.*, 508 U.S. 384 (1993); *Good News Club v. Milford Cent. Sch.*, 533 U.S. 98 (2001); *see also Board of Educ. of Westside Community Schools v. Mergens*, 496 U.S. 226 (1990) (rejecting an Establishment Clause attack on the Equal Access Act of 1984, 20 U.S.C. §§ 4071–4074, which provides statutory equal access rights for noncurricular student groups at public secondary schools).

[155] 515 U.S. 819 (1995).

[156] *Id.* at 830. *Cf. Locke v. Davey*, 540 U.S. 712, 720 n.3 (2004) (holding that *Rosenberger* did not extend to a state-sponsored college scholarship program because the program was not designed to encourage a variety of private views and therefore was "not a forum for speech").

[157] *See Rosenberger*, 515 U.S. at 828–46.

[158] As noted earlier in this chapter, five Justices expressed this view in their separate opinions in *Capitol Square Review & Advisory Bd. v. Pinette*, 515 U.S. 753 (1995). *See supra* note 68 and accompanying text.

[159] For further elaboration, see Chapter 5, including the discussion of *Pleasant Grove City v. Summum*, 555 U.S. 460 (2009), and *Christian Legal Society v. Martinez*, 561 U.S. 661 (2010).

and confined to secular uses. This exception honors the general free speech principle of viewpoint neutrality. More specifically, it protects religious speech from discriminatory treatment, thus serving the value of religious free speech, a value that counterbalances the Establishment Clause values that might otherwise support the segregation requirement.

IV. Constitutional Values and the Establishment Clause

As the last chapter and this one reveal, the Supreme Court's Establishment Clause decisionmaking is quite complex. At the level of general doctrine, the Court simultaneously recognizes three basic tests: the *Lemon* test, the endorsement test, and a coercion test. Beyond that, it considers two additional general factors or concepts: tradition and accommodation. At a more specific level, the Court's doctrine includes separate strands, with differing points of analysis and emphasis, for religion and the public schools, religious expression and symbolism in other contexts, and public aid to religious schools, organizations, and individuals. Both the Court's general doctrine and its particular decisions serve a variety of constitutional values, both individual and structural in nature. Indeed, one can find support for each of the constitutional values that we initially addressed in Chapter 3. Thus, in various and complicated ways, the Court's doctrine and decisions can be said to protect religious voluntarism, religious identity, and religious equality; to promote a religiously inclusive political community and to protect the government from improper religious involvement; to protect religion and the autonomy of religious institutions; to preserve traditional governmental practices; and to protect religious free speech.

This complex picture, however, may be somewhat misleading. The Court's doctrine and decisions are indeed complex, but they also include common themes. Thus, the *Lemon* and endorsement tests, working together, provide the Court's general approach except when the discrete areas of tradition or accommodation are implicated. Under these tests, at least as they are understood today, the government generally is forbidden from conferring discriminatory benefits on religion, but it generally is free to extend nondiscriminatory benefits to religious beneficiaries, including religious organizations. More specifically, the conferral of benefits on religion typically is unconstitutional if, but only if, the government is formally or deliberately discriminating in religion's favor. Relatedly, the dominant constitutional value under the Establishment Clause is that of religious equality, understood in a formal sense. Substantive religious equality and other constitutional values certainly have not disappeared from view, but their role in most settings is secondary, with the Court generally assuming that formal equality will tend to promote these other values as well.

Chapter 9

CONCLUDING OBSERVATIONS

We began in Chapter 1 by highlighting the broad range of questions that arise from the seemingly simple command of the First Amendment's Religion Clauses: "Congress shall make no law respecting an establishment of religion, or prohibiting the free exercise thereof." In Chapter 2, we discussed the intellectual origins of American religious liberty in the arguments of philosopher John Locke and considered how those and similar arguments influenced developments in America, especially in Virginia. We then turned to the First Amendment, examining the original understanding of the Religion Clauses and also of the Fourteenth Amendment provisions that have been used to extend the Religion Clauses to the states. We concluded that the original understanding cannot support the Supreme Court's contemporary constitutional doctrine, which instead reflects a value-laden process of creative interpretation. Through this process of creative interpretation, the Court has identified and protected a variety of constitutional values, including values that are embedded in our political and cultural history and values that have emerged and evolved over time.

In an attempt to unearth these embedded and evolving values, Chapter 3 traced the historical development of American religious liberty from the founding to the present. Focusing on the contemporary period in the light of this history, we suggested that the Supreme Court's decisionmaking under the Religion Clauses has been influenced by at least six constitutional values or sets of values: religious voluntarism; respecting religious identity; religious equality; promoting a religiously inclusive political community and protecting government from improper religious involvement; protecting the autonomy and independence of religious institutions and of religion itself; and preserving traditional governmental practices. We also noted an additional First Amendment value, linked mainly to the Free Speech Clause, the value of religious liberty in the context of speech.

In Chapter 4, we addressed doctrinal fundamentals that are common to both the Free Exercise and Establishment Clauses. We discussed impermissible burdens and impermissible benefits, the general principle of nondiscrimination, the definition of religion, and the role of courts in addressing the content and sincerity of religious beliefs. Chapters 3 and 4, taken together, provided analytical building blocks, both in the form of constitutional values and in the form of general doctrinal principles. These chapters thus set the stage for the remainder of the book, in which we utilized these values and principles in explaining and evaluating the various facets of the Supreme Court's constitutional decisionmaking.

Chapter 5 examined religious free exercise and free speech under the First Amendment. We learned that freedom of belief is protected by the Free Exercise Clause, and that religious speech is protected by the Free Speech Clause, especially from laws that discriminate against it on the basis of content or viewpoint. As for religiously motivated conduct other than speech, the Free Exercise Clause likewise offers protection from discriminatory laws. In selective contexts, it offers additional protection as well, including protection for the institutional autonomy of religious organizations. In general, however, under the restrictive doctrine of *Employment Division v. Smith*,[1] religious claimants under the Free Exercise Clause are denied relief, even from substantial burdens on the exercise of religion, except when the government has deliberately targeted their religious conduct for discriminatory disadvantage.

The Supreme Court's restrictive approach to the Free Exercise Clause has given rise to important developments both legislatively and in state constitutional law, as discussed in Chapter 6. These developments include the Religious Freedom Restoration Act of 1993 (RFRA),[2] the Religious Land Use and Institutionalized Persons Act of 2000 (RLUIPA),[3] similar state statutes, and state constitutional rulings providing comparable protection. These alternative fonts of religious freedom, along with specific statutory accommodations in particular settings, often protect the exercise of religion even when the First Amendment does not. In particular, unlike *Smith*, they often demand religious exemptions from otherwise neutral laws of general applicability.

In Chapter 7, we turned back to the First Amendment and, in particular, to the Establishment Clause, exploring the general doctrinal tests and concepts that the Supreme Court has employed. We learned that the Court recognizes three general Establishment Clause tests—the *Lemon* test,[4] the endorsement test, and a coercion test—and that two other general factors or concepts—tradition and accommodation—also play influential roles. Tradition is important in certain settings, but the concept of accommodation has broader significance. In particular, it makes it clear that the government is

---

[1]   494 U.S. 872 (1990).

[2]   42 U.S.C. §§ 2000bb to 2000bb–4.

[3]   42 U.S.C. §§ 2000cc to 2000cc–5.

[4]   The *Lemon* test is derived from *Lemon v. Kurtzman*, 403 U.S. 602, 612–13 (1971).

free, within limits, to protect the free exercise of religion to a greater degree than the Free Exercise Clause requires. The concept of accommodation thus sanctions, as constitutionally permissible under the Establishment Clause, the legislative and state court developments discussed in Chapter 6. More generally, the *Lemon* and endorsement tests, despite criticism, continue to provide the dominant doctrinal framework for Establishment Clause cases.

In Chapter 8, we examined the operation of the *Lemon* and endorsement tests, as well as the impact of coercion and tradition, in several important Establishment Clause contexts. We reviewed the Supreme Court's general disapproval of school-sponsored prayer and religious instruction in the public schools and its more nuanced approach to religious expression and symbolism in other settings, where tradition sometimes has played a greater role. In addition, we examined the Court's increasingly relaxed approach to the inclusion of religious beneficiaries, including religious schools and organizations, in otherwise general programs of public aid. In both Chapter 7 and Chapter 8, we confronted an array of constitutional issues, examined the Supreme Court's diverse responses, and noted the relative influence of particular constitutional values in various contexts. In so doing, we discovered that the Court's Establishment Clause decisionmaking is complex and multifaceted, and that its relationship to constitutional values is both subtle and complicated.

Despite the complexity of the Supreme Court's constitutional doctrine, a common theme emerges from Chapters 4, 5, 7, and 8. In recent decades, under the Free Exercise and Establishment Clauses alike, the Court has emphasized the constitutional value of religious equality, and it increasingly has understood this value in formal rather than substantive terms. In Chapter 4, we introduced the basic proposition that formal or deliberate discrimination on the basis of religion is a critical touchstone under the Religion Clauses, regardless of whether the discrimination imposes a burden or confers a benefit. Chapter 5 elaborated this proposition in the context of the Free Exercise Clause, especially in discussing the doctrine of *Employment Division v. Smith*, according to which burdens on the exercise of religion generally are unconstitutional if, but only if, they are deliberately discriminatory. As Chapters 7 and 8 revealed, the Supreme Court's Establishment Clause doctrine is far too complicated to be captured in a single theme. Even so, the Court's decisionmaking under the Establishment Clause, like that under the Free Exercise Clause, is driven heavily by the value of formal religious equality. Thus, the Court generally invalidates deliberately discriminatory benefits to religion even as it generally upholds the inclusion of religious beneficiaries in formally nondiscriminatory programs of aid. In cases exemplifying this pattern, it has followed longstanding precedent in precluding the public schools from purposefully favoring religion,[5] and it has confirmed that the government likewise cannot purposefully promote religion through symbolic displays outside the public school context.[6] At the same time, relaxing prior doctrine, the Court increasingly has upheld formally nondiscriminatory programs of aid, both direct and indirect, that extend to religious recipients.[7]

The trend toward formal equality brings increasing coherence to the Supreme Court's constitutional decisionmaking under the Religion Clauses. But this trend is not cost-free. Formal religious equality often promotes substantive religious equality and other constitutional values, but sometimes it does not. A single-minded focus on formal equality, therefore, inevitably sacrifices other constitutional values by denying them independent consideration. This is certainly true under the Free Exercise Clause, where, under *Smith*, the government generally is free to impose nondiscriminatory burdens on the exercise of religion, no matter how substantial the burdens might be. The approach of *Smith* promotes doctrinal clarity, but it seriously impairs religious voluntarism, religious identity, and other constitutional values.

In the Establishment Clause context, by contrast, the Supreme Court's increasing emphasis on formal religious equality seems more benign, and perhaps it is. More specifically, the inclusion of religious organizations in formally nondiscriminatory programs of aid may, as the Court believes, further not only formal equality but other constitutional values as well. Even so, there are subtle but significant risks to religious liberty.[8] Notably, governmental programs of aid typically include conditions that the recipient organizations must honor. Under the school voucher program approved in *Zelman v. Simmons-Harris*,[9] for instance, participating schools were barred from discriminating on the basis of religion. This precluded religious schools from favoring members of their own religion—or even religious believers in general over atheists—in the admission of students and, apparently, also in the hiring of

---

[5]   *See Lee v. Weisman*, 505 U.S. 577 (1992); *Santa Fe Indep. Sch. Dist. v. Doe*, 530 U.S. 290 (2000).

[6]   *See McCreary County v. ACLU*, 545 U.S. 844 (2005).

[7]   *See, e.g., Agostini v. Felton*, 521 U.S. 203 (1997); *Mitchell v. Helms*, 530 U.S. 793 (2000); *Zelman v. Simmons-Harris*, 536 U.S. 639 (2002).

[8]   *See* Daniel O. Conkle, *The Path of American Religious Liberty: From the Original Theology to Formal Neutrality and an Uncertain Future*, 75 IND. L.J. 1, 21–24 (2000).

[9]   536 U.S. 639 (2002).

administrators and teachers.[10] Moreover, the strings attached to funding programs such as this can expand over time, even as the participating organizations become more and more dependent on the government's financial support. Although the financial support is a carrot, not a stick, it might nonetheless induce religious organizations to modify and weaken their religious practices and requirements in order to meet the government's demands. This prospect threatens important constitutional values: protecting religion from government and protecting the autonomy of religious institutions. Due to differences in theology and mission, moreover, the adverse impact might be greater for some religions than others, meaning that formal equality here might jeopardize substantive equality.[11]

The Supreme Court's elevation of formal religious equality to a central position reflects a particular understanding of evolving constitutional values. This understanding is driven by various philosophical, jurisprudential, and religious forces.[12] It is influenced, for example, by the general emphasis on nondiscrimination in today's constitutional and legal culture, a culture that supports a vibrant equal protection doctrine under the Fourteenth Amendment as well as nondiscrimination statutes of all sorts. The trend favoring formal equality is also a response to America's ever-increasing religious diversity, the bewildering array of potential claims under the Religion Clauses, and, as discussed in Chapter 4, the increasingly difficult problem of defining "religion" for the purpose of evaluating such claims. To the extent that the Court limits itself to formal equality and the principle of nondiscrimination, the Court need only determine whether "religion" has been targeted for formal or deliberate discrimination. This does not eliminate the definitional problem, but it does reduce its significance by narrowing and simplifying the constitutional doctrine to which it relates. More generally, and perhaps more importantly, a constitutional doctrine stressing formal equality and nondiscrimination supports contemporary policies of judicial restraint and federalism. Thus, it limits the role of the federal judiciary by emphasizing a relatively clear-cut, rule-based approach to constitutional questions even as it tends to encourage judicial

---

[10] *See id.* at 712–13 (Souter, J., dissenting). Likewise, by implication, this prohibition appeared to forbid religious schools from requiring students or teachers to participate in prayer or other religious exercises.

[11] For a discussion of these problems in the context of social service programs, see Daniel O. Conkle, *Religion, Politics, and the 2000 Presidential Election: A Selective Survey and Tentative Appraisal*, 77 IND. L.J. 247, 249–52 (2002).

[12] For elaboration beyond that offered here, see Conkle, *supra* note 8, at 25–36.

deference to majoritarian governmental policies, most of which are the product of state law.

Judicial restraint and federalism, of course, are constitutional values in their own right, values linked not so much to the Religion Clauses as to broader, structural considerations. As we have just noted, these values support the Supreme Court's emphasis on formal religious equality. At the same time, they also help explain some of the Court's departures from this trend. In particular, the Court sometimes has found that formal equality is constitutionally permissible but not constitutionally required.[13] In so doing, the Court has deferred to the majoritarian political process, finding that "there is room for play in the joints" between the Free Exercise and Establishment Clauses.[14]

Under *Employment Division v. Smith*, for example, formal equality generally is sufficient under the Free Exercise Clause, but the Establishment Clause doctrine of permissible accommodation gives Congress and the states considerable leeway to provide religion-based exemptions if they choose—either specifically or more generally, for instance, through statutes such as RFRA.[15] Likewise, in the context of public aid, formal equality—extending nondiscriminatory support to religious and nonreligious recipients alike—usually is enough to satisfy the Establishment Clause, but under *Locke v. Davey*'s interpretation of the Free Exercise Clause,[16] religion-based, discriminatory funding exclusions are sometimes permissible. As discussed in Chapter 7, the doctrine of permissible

---

[13] *See* Douglas Laycock, *Substantive Neutrality Revisited*, 110 W. VA. L. REV. 51, 60–64 (2007). Adapting Professor Laycock's phrasing to reflect the terminology we are using here, this approach can be described as "permissive formal [equality]— formal [equality] is permitted but some alternative is also permitted." *Id.* at 61. (Laycock uses the word "neutrality" instead of "equality.")

[14] *Locke v. Davey*, 540 U.S. 712, 718 (2004) (citation omitted); *Cutter v. Wilkinson*, 544 U.S. 709, 713, 719 (2005) (citations omitted).

[15] Within this zone of discretion, the legislature is free not only to grant or authorize religion-based exemptions but also to revoke them. Accordingly, if a legislature enacts a statute such as RFRA, it remains free to repeal it in full or in part, reverting to that extent to formal equality. In the aftermath of the Supreme Court's controversial interpretation of RFRA in *Burwell v. Hobby Lobby Stores, Inc.*, 134 S. Ct. 2751 (2014), for example, there was a congressional proposal—albeit unsuccessful—that would have overturned the Court's decision legislatively, thereby restricting the reach of RFRA. *See* H.R. 5051, 113th. Cong. (2014); S. 2578, 113th Cong. (2014). *See generally* Eugene Volokh, *A Common-Law Model for Religious Exemptions*, 46 UCLA L. REV. 1465 (1999) (explaining—and generally defending— the approach of RFRA and similar statutes, according to which courts are authorized to decide exemption claims but legislatures retain the ultimate authority to revise or reverse these judicial decisions).

[16] *See Locke*, 540 U.S. 712. The Supreme Court may clarify the meaning of *Locke* in *Trinity Lutheran Church v. Pauley*, 788 F.3d 779 (8th Cir. 2015), *cert. granted*, 2016 WL 205949 (U.S. Jan. 15, 2016) (No. 15-577), a pending case that is discussed in Chapter 8.

accommodation permits Congress and the states to promote religious voluntarism, substantive religious equality, and other free exercise values that the Supreme Court itself is not protecting under *Smith*. By contrast, as discussed in Chapter 5, *Locke v. Davey* permits the states, and presumably Congress, to discriminate against religion in a manner that seriously frustrates free exercise values. *Locke* thus suggests that the Court sometimes is willing to privilege judicial restraint and federalism over the values of the Religion Clauses, including even the formal equality that the Court itself has championed.

The Supreme Court's approval of legislative prayer—in Congress, state legislatures, and local lawmaking bodies—also privileges judicial restraint and federalism over religious equality, certainly in the sense of substantive equality and, at least to an extent, also in the sense of formal equality. According to *Marsh v. Chambers*[17] and *Town of Greece v. Galloway*,[18] legislative prayer, subject only to minimal constitutional constraints, does not violate the Establishment Clause even though the practice deliberately promotes religion over irreligion. Moreover, as *Town of Greece* makes clear, the practice may have the effect of promoting one religion over others, because prayer-givers are free to offer prayers that are specifically Christian or otherwise sectarian, even if such prayers predominate.[19] As explained in Chapters 7 and 8, the Court's deferential approach to legislative prayer honors tradition and freedom of religious speech, but it impairs religious equality and threatens other constitutional values, including religious voluntarism, respect for the religious identity of dissenting citizens, and the promotion of a religiously inclusive political community. Notably, however, legislative bodies are free to promote these other values if they wish, for instance, by seeking out prayer-givers from diverse religions and/or by encouraging, through advisory guidelines, the use of inclusive prayers. They also are free to dispense with prayer altogether or to substitute a moment of silence.[20] In other words, the Court's deferential position does not mandate a particular approach to legislative prayer, leaving the issue largely to the political process.

---

[17]   463 U.S. 783 (1983).

[18]   134 S. Ct. 1811 (2014).

[19] The Court in *Town of Greece* was content to suggest a requirement of formal—but not substantive—equality between and among religions in the selection of prayer-givers. *See id.* at 1824. As discussed in Chapter 8, moreover, this requirement of formal nondiscrimination is confined to legislative bodies using rotational systems of selection.

[20] Indeed, the town board in Greece, until changing its policy in 1999, had opened its meetings not with prayer but with a moment of silence. *See id.* at 1816.

244 *CONCLUDING OBSERVATIONS* Ch. 9

More generally, the Supreme Court's decisionmaking under the Religion Clauses, taken as a whole, tends to favor formal religious equality as well as deference to the political process, a stance that advances the values of judicial restraint and federalism.[21] With respect to the Establishment Clause, moreover, the Court may be poised to move even further in this direction. Thus, the plurality opinion in *Mitchell v. Helms*[22] could become a majority holding, further extending the permissible scope of nondiscriminatory public aid by permitting direct aid to religious organizations without the existing requirement that such aid be segregated and confined to secular uses and not be diverted by its recipients to religious purposes.[23] And the plurality opinion in *Van Orden v. Perry*,[24] if adopted by a majority, would permit the government (at least in many circumstances) to promote "passive" religious symbolism outside the public school setting, including displays of the Ten Commandments such as those invalidated in *McCreary County v. ACLU*.[25] Adopting the *Mitchell* plurality opinion would promote formal religious equality as well as deference to the political process. Adopting the plurality's view in *Van Orden*, by contrast, would honor deference to the political process but not formal religious equality, because it would permit the government (to some extent) to purposefully advance and endorse religion over irreligion.

---

[21] Beyond its substantive interpretations of the Religion Clauses, the Supreme Court can promote deference to the political process by vigorously enforcing the procedural prerequisites for federal court jurisdiction, including the requirement that challengers have proper standing to sue, especially in Establishment Clause cases. For recent decisions of this type, see *Elk Grove Unified Sch. Dist. v. Newdow*, 542 U.S. 1 (2004) (holding that a parent with limited and disputed custodial rights lacked "prudential standing" to challenge the "under God" language in public school recitations of the Pledge of Allegiance); *Hein v. Freedom from Religion Foundation, Inc.*, 551 U.S. 587 (2007) (rejecting taxpayer standing in an Establishment Clause challenge to executive branch expenditures funded by general as opposed to specific congressional appropriations); *Arizona Christian Sch. Tuition Org. v. Winn*, 131 S. Ct. 1436 (2011) (rejecting taxpayer standing in an Establishment Clause challenge to a tax credit program benefitting religious schools). *Cf. Salazar v. Buono*, 559 U.S. 700, 711 (2010) (plurality opinion) (finding standing to enforce an existing injunction without addressing the question of whether, absent the injunction, "offense at the presence of a religious symbol on federal land" would be sufficient).

[22] 530 U.S. 793 (2000).

[23] *See id.* at 801–36 (plurality opinion). The Court could revisit its direct funding doctrine in *Trinity Lutheran Church v. Pauley*, 788 F.3d 779 (8th Cir. 2015), *cert. granted*, 2016 WL 205949 (U.S. Jan. 15, 2016) (No. 15-577), a pending case that is discussed in Chapter 8.

[24] 545 U.S. 677 (2005).

[25] 545 U.S. 844 (2005). The *Van Orden* plurality suggested that the Court generally should approve "passive" religious symbolism, at least if the symbolism has secular as well as religious significance. *See Van Orden*, 545 U.S. at 686–92 (plurality opinion). And the same four Justices dissented in *McCreary*, making it appear that they would sanction virtually any Ten Commandments display (outside the public school setting). *See McCreary*, 545 U.S. at 900–12 (Scalia, J., joined by Rehnquist, C.J., and by Thomas and Kennedy, JJ., dissenting).

Indeed, the Supreme Court could repudiate the *Lemon* and endorsement tests altogether, giving Congress and the states a broader range of discretion across the full range of Establishment Clause cases.[26]

Although other constitutional values have not disappeared from view, the dominant values embraced by the Supreme Court— formal religious equality on the one hand, judicial restraint and federalism on the other—have eclipsed, to a degree, other and competing values that the Religion Clauses can be understood to promote. In the near-term future, the Court is unlikely to reverse course, and it may move further along the course it recently has charted. At the same time, as we have noted, the Court's approach gives considerable freedom to political actors, who can play a significant role in advancing their own understandings of religious liberty and of the constitutional values that it embodies.

Looking further into the future, the contours of religious liberty—both as enforced by the Supreme Court and as promoted in the political process—will almost certainly be affected, in some way, by ongoing changes in the American religious landscape. Three trends are worth noting. First, as we have already observed, religion in America has become radically diverse, and it is likely to become even more so in the decades that lie ahead. Second, and relatedly, contemporary religion is increasingly individualistic, with Americans crafting their own understandings of religion or spirituality, understandings that do not conform to the conventional beliefs and practices of any particular religious body or any particular religious faith. And third, secularization—long at work in Western Europe and elsewhere—now is making significant inroads in the United States. America remains far more religious than most Western countries. Even so, there are growing numbers of Americans who are frankly and openly secular, abandoning religious or spiritual outlooks or practices altogether, and there are others who have adopted increasingly secular perspectives even as they continue to claim a belief in God or continue to assert, at least nominally, a religious identification or affiliation.[27]

---

[26] The Court could replace the *Lemon* and endorsement tests with some version of a coercion test. Notably, however, such a development might not threaten the Court's public school precedents, because the Court might continue to follow the "indirect coercion" reasoning of *Lee v. Weisman*, 505 U.S. 577 (1992).

[27] For elaboration and documentation of these three trends (and a fourth, the modernization of religion, which can be seen as an aspect of secularization), see Daniel O. Conkle, *Religious Truth, Pluralism, and Secularization: The Shaking Foundations of American Religious Liberty*, 32 CARDOZO L. REV. 1755, 1767–73 (2011).

It is impossible to know exactly how these trends—diversification, individualization, and secularization—will influence constitutional law, legislation, and other legal and political developments. There is reason to believe, however, that these ongoing developments, over time, may have important implications for religious liberty and especially for the free exercise of religion. In particular, they may tend to undermine judicial and political support for the accommodation of free exercise through religion-based exemptions from otherwise applicable laws, for instance, under statutes such as RFRA.

In the first place, two pragmatic concerns—already supporting the restrictive constitutional doctrine of *Smith*—loom ever larger: the difficulty of defining what counts as the free exercise of "religion,"[28] and, relatedly, the social costs of extending presumptive protection to all manner of "religiously" motivated conduct. Second, and no less important, the changing character of the American religious landscape may mean that fewer and fewer Americans—that is, fewer and fewer citizens, political leaders, and judges—will support a vibrant understanding of religious freedom, one that regards religious voluntarism as sufficiently important to warrant protection even from nondiscriminatory laws. Devout traditional believers, whether they adhere to Christianity or other faiths, tend to support this view, often on the basis of deeply felt religious-moral commitments.[29] By contrast, the increasing number of Americans with individually crafted religious or spiritual beliefs may not. At the same time, secularists and secular-leaning Americans, another growing group, are even less likely to support special protection for religious practices.[30] Relatedly, RFRA and similar statutes are increasingly viewed (whether or not correctly) as politically conservative laws that may frustrate important politically progressive policies, such as the furtherance of women's reproductive freedom or the prevention of illicit discrimination. As a result, progressive secularists (and, for that matter, progressive

---

[28] *Cf.* WINNIFRED FALLERS SULLIVAN, THE IMPOSSIBILITY OF RELIGIOUS FREEDOM (2005) (suggesting that the law should no longer afford distinctive protection for religious freedom because it cannot coherently and impartially distinguish between religious and nonreligious claims).

[29] The teachings of Christianity and of various other religions can be understood to demand religious freedom as a matter of God-given human right, religious truth, or fundamental religious-moral principle. *See* Conkle, *supra* note 27, at 1763–67.

[30] Indeed, it may be difficult to defend special protection for religion on the basis of purely secular reasoning. *See, e.g.,* BRIAN LEITER, WHY TOLERATE RELIGION? (2012); *cf.* Steven D. Smith, *Discourse in the Dusk: The Twilight of Religious Freedom?,* 122 HARV. L. REV. 1869, 1884 (2009) (suggesting that under "the constraints of modern secular discourse . . . there simply is no good justification for treating religion as a special legal category").

religious believers as well) increasingly oppose these statutes, at least in particular applications and often more generally.

These various developments are putting into question the very idea that the exercise of religion should be accommodated when possible.[31] If current trends continue—and they show no signs of abating—the granting of religion-based exemptions may become less and less common over time. Laws such as RFRA may be narrowly construed, limited by amendment, or, eventually, perhaps repealed altogether.

For those committed to a vibrant understanding of religious liberty, one that includes the accommodation of free exercise through religion-based exemptions, the long-term future holds considerable peril.[32] But speculation about the future is exactly that, speculation and nothing more. The law generally moves slowly, not radically. As history continues to unfold, moreover, perhaps the trends and forces we have discussed will be resisted. Perhaps they will be counterbalanced by other, unforeseen developments. Perhaps a robust conception of religious freedom, in some form, will remain in place, even if it reflects a new calibration of constitutional values.

Wherever the future might lead, one thing is certain: the meaning of the Religion Clauses, and of American religious liberty generally, will continue to evolve over time, both in the courts and in the political process. Thus, the Supreme Court's constitutional doctrine will change in the future, as it has in the past. And to the extent that the Court's doctrine continues to give deference to political actors, they, too, will adopt new approaches to religious liberty. And these judicial and political developments, whatever path they might follow, will inevitably reflect some combination of embedded and evolving constitutional values.

---

[31] *See* Paul Horwitz, *The Hobby Lobby Moment*, 128 HARV. L. REV. 154, 155 (2014) ("The change [from a broad consensus supporting accommodation to dissensus and political polarization on this issue] has been sudden, remarkable, and unsettling."); *see also* Richard W. Garnett, *Religious Accommodations and—and Among—Civil Rights: Separation, Toleration, and Accommodation*, 88 S. CAL. L. REV. 493, 501 (2015) ("[R]eligious exemptions and accommodations are increasingly seen as departures from the rule of law, . . . as threats to the progress made in the cause of racial justice, or as disingenuous ploys by those hostile to abortion rights or legal recognition of same-sex marriage."); *see generally* Douglas Laycock, *Sex, Atheism, and the Free Exercise of Religion*, 88 U. DET. MERCY L. REV. 407, 407 (2011) ("For the first time in nearly 300 years, important forces in American society are questioning the free exercise of religion *in principle*—suggesting that free exercise of religion may be a bad idea, or at least, a right to be minimized.") (emphasis in original).

[32] *See* Conkle, *supra* note 27, at 1773–80.

TABLE OF CASES

INDEX

253